The People with No Name

✤

The People with No Name

IRELAND'S ULSTER SCOTS,
AMERICA'S SCOTS IRISH, AND
THE CREATION OF A
BRITISH ATLANTIC WORLD,
1689–1764

✣

PATRICK GRIFFIN

PRINCETON UNIVERSITY PRESS

PRINCETON AND OXFORD

Copyright © 2001 by Princeton University Press
Published by Princeton University Press, 41 William Street,
Princeton, New Jersey 08540
In the United Kingdom: Princeton University Press, 3 Market Place,
Woodstock, Oxfordshire OX20 1SY
All Rights Reserved

Library of Congress Cataloging-in-Publication Data

Griffin, Patrick, 1965–
The people with no name : Ireland's Ulster Scots, America's Scots Irish, and
the creation of a British Atlantic world, 1689–1764 / Patrick Griffin.
p.   cm.
Includes bibliographical references and index.
ISBN 0-691-07461-5 (cl : alk. paper—ISBN 0-691-07462-3 (pbk. : alk. paper)
1. Scots-Irish—United States—History—18th century. 2. Scots-Irish—
United States—History—17th century. 3. Scots—Ulster (Northern
Ireland and Ireland)—History. 4. Scots—Ulster
(Northern Ireland and Ireland)—Migrations—History.
5. Presbyterians—Ulster (Northern Ireland and Ireland)—History.
6. Ulster (Northern Ireland and Ireland)—Emigration and
immigration—History. 7. United States—Emigration and immigration—
History. 8. United States—History—Colonial period, ca. 1600–1775.
9. Great Britain—Colonies—America. I. Title.
E184.S4 G74 2001
973′.049163—dc21   2001021264

British Library Cataloging-in-Publication Data is available

This book has been composed in New Baskerville

Printed on acid-free paper. ∞

www.pup.princeton.edu

Printed in the United States of America

1   3   5   7   9   10   8   6   4   2

3   5   7   9   10   8   6   4   2

FOR MARY HOPE

✢

When there is no vision, the people perish.
Proverbs 29:18

❖ *Contents* ❖

❖ *Maps* ❖

✤ *Acknowledgments* ✤

It is a pleasure to thank the many people who supported me throughout this project.

I have received a number of grants that made the research and time devoted to writing this book possible. The English Speaking Union and Society for Colonial Wars in the state of Illinois underwrote trips to the archives in Belfast and Derry. Northwestern University provided funds for research in Pennsylvania as well as a dissertation year fellowship, which allowed me to devote all my energies to writing.

Archivists on both sides of the Atlantic provided great assistance along the way. I would like to thank the staffs of the Public Record Office of Northern Ireland, Presbyterian Historical Society of Ireland, Union Theological College, Magee College, and the Armagh Public Library. On the American side of the ocean, I received a warm welcome from the librarians at the Historical Society of Pennsylvania, Chester County Archives, Lancaster County Historical Society, Cumberland County Historical Society, York County Historical Society, Dauphin County Historical Society, the American Philosophical Society, and the Presbyterian Historical Society in Philadelphia. The Newberry Library, which graciously gave permission to reproduce the maps for this book, deserves special mention. For permission to reproduce and revise material which has appeared elsewhere in print, I would like to thank the editors of the *Journal of British Studies* and the *William and Mary Quarterly*.

On trips to these archives, I incurred a number of personal debts that shall be a pleasure to repay. In Ireland, the Bradleys of Donegal, Battersbys of Meath, Griffins, Heddermans, Bradys, and Lyons of Cork, and Richardsons of Limerick put me up—and put up with me—over long weekends. I am also grateful to John McCabe, who offered valuable tips for negotiating Belfast's archives, and to my neighbor Dan Lebryk, who helped me make sense of Pennsylvania warrant maps. Special thanks also to my in-laws, Joe and Dympna Doran, who took care of the kids on a number of occasions while I traipsed around the world.

A great many scholars have also lent me their valuable time. At Northwestern University, I was very fortunate to have the likes of Joe Barton, Bill Heyck, and the late Bob Wiebe around. Each unstintingly offered his take on my project, pointing me in directions I could not have imagined on my own. Northwestern's early American community—in particular, Chris Beneke, Seth Cotlar, Chris Front, Dave Gellman, Karen O'Brien, Andy Podolsky, Chernoh Sesay, and Brad Shraeger—offered support and critical readings of my work. Jim Merrell deserves special mention for his close reading of two drafts of the book, for steering me toward wonderful sources for the American side, and for his patience and good humor. I would also like to thank David Armitage, Bernard Bailyn, Patricia Bonomi, Nicholas Canny, James Horn, Ned Landsman, Ian McBride, Phil Morgan, John Morrill, A. G. Roeber, Jim Smyth, Ian Steele, and Marilyn Westerkamp, each of whom commented upon earlier drafts of the manuscript.

My editor, Thomas LeBien, and the staff of Princeton University Press have been wonderful throughout. Thomas in particular made what might have been a difficult process enjoyable and engaging. I would also like to thank Jenn Backer, who did wonderful and exacting work as copy editor for the book as well as Alison Zaintz, who was the book's production editor.

Of course, this book would not have been possible without Tim Breen. Tim not only advised me throughout my graduate career, taught me how to write, and showed me how the academic world works, but continually challenged me to make the most of my abilities. I would like to thank him for all those times he cracked the whip, as well as for those moments he should have but relented. As trite as it sounds, I could not have asked for a mentor and friend more generous with his time and energy. In many ways, this book is as much a product of Tim's dedication to the craft as it is mine.

Last but certainly not least, I would like to thank my family. My father and mother, Michael and Johanna Griffin, and sister, Joan Jacobs, looked after Michael while I commuted to Philadelphia and stayed in Ireland. I hope this book in some way serves to thank them for their advice, encouragement, and support throughout the years. My sons, Michael and Liam, bore the brunt of extended research trips and made the best of a father punch drunk from a lack of sleep and distracted by the next chapter. Fortunately, their antics provided the perfect tonic for hours cramped behind a keyboard. Although Maggie arrived only a short while before I finished the project, she offered me hours of delightful companionship at night while she adjusted to a western hemisphere sleeping schedule. And of course my wife, Mary Hope, sacrificed more than anyone to see this project through. Since words cannot convey my thanks and esteem for her, let the dedication suffice.

The People with No Name

Identity in an Atlantic World

Between 1718 and 1775, more than 100,000 men and women journeyed from the Irish province of Ulster to the American colonies. Their migration represented the single largest movement of any group from the British Isles to British North America during the eighteenth century. In a first wave beginning in 1718 and cresting in 1729, these people outnumbered all others sailing across the Atlantic, with the notable exception of those bound to the New World in slave ships. By sheer force of numbers, this earliest generation of migrants had a profound influence on the great transformations of the age. Even before they left Ulster, they contributed to the triumph of the Protestant cause in Ireland, paving the way for an unprecedented extension of English power into the kingdom. They also figured prominently in the British transatlantic trading system by producing linen, one of the most important commodities exchanged throughout the empire. Sailing when they did, Ulster's Presbyterian migrants played a formative role in the transition from an English to a British Atlantic. Before their migration, Puritans and adventurers leaving England during the seventeenth century for the North American mainland and the Caribbean dominated the transatlantic world. After men and women from Ulster boarded ships for America, the cultural parameters of the Atlantic broadened, as they and thousands of land-hungry voyagers from the labor-rich peripheries of the British Isles sought their fortunes in a vast, underpopulated New World. In America, Ulster's men and women again had a hand in a number of defining developments of the period, including the displacement of the continent's indigenous peoples, the extension of the frontier, the growth of ethnic diversity, and the outbreak of religious revivals. In the abstract, therefore, the group contributed to the forces and processes that dwarfed the individual but yoked together disparate regions into a broad Atlantic system.[1]

The group's participation in these seminal transformations, however, escaped the notice of contemporaries. Indeed, colonists in America consigned these men and women to irrelevancy. While the scale of Ulster Presbyterian migration impressed American colonists, the behavior of individuals from Ulster did not. Settling on the frontier far from the east, the "so called" Scotch-Irish seemed "audacious," leading a Pennsylvania official to declare, "The settlement of five families" from Ulster "gives me more trouble than fifty of any other people."[2] The famous "American Farmer," Hector St. John de Crevecoeur, doubted that they could become "Pennsylvanian" or American. Distinguishing Ulster's migrants from the more industrious and sober Scots, Crevecoeur argued, "The Irish do not prosper so well." In particular, he found that "they love to drink and to quarrel; they are litigious and soon take to the gun, which is the ruin of everything; they seem beside to labour under a greater degree of ignorance in husbandry than the others."[3] Far from significant contributors to the epic developments of the age, the men and women who sailed from Ulster seemed to their contemporaries the period's sordid refuse.

Although Ulster's earliest migrants tried in vain to convince Pennsylvanians that they were "not quite as bad as we are represented,"[4] they particularly bristled at the titles their neighbors bestowed upon them. Although contemporaries used the term "Scotch-Irish," migrants did not. A Presbyterian minister who traveled to Pennsylvania during the first wave of migration despised such "ill natured titles" as "Scotch Irish" and protested any comparison of his people to the "Irish."[5] Referring to themselves simply as "frontier inhabitants," Ulster's Presbyterian migrants had a better idea of what they were not than what they were.[6] Their confusion is understandable. The group's Irish background offers few clues in finding a fitting name. These Protestant men and women rejected any suggestion that they were "mere"—or Catholic—Irish. Similarly, although they had reconstructed the institutions of Scotland's Presbyterian kirk in Ulster, during the eighteenth century they did not regard themselves as "Scotch," which at this time in Ireland connoted radicalism. In most cases, Ulster Presbyterians called themselves "northern dissenters" in recognition of their status within Irish society as well as their geographic concentration in Ulster. However, in Pennsylvania, a colony an ocean away

2

from Ulster and one in which religious toleration prevailed, such a name became meaningless.[7]

For the eighteenth century, therefore, the Presbyterian men and women who left Ulster for Pennsylvania proved an elusive people to pin down. In both Ireland and America, they inhabited the cultural margins of a dynamic Atlantic world centered in London. They tended to move from place to place, leaving a scant paper trail in their wake. Although these men and women embraced Scottish traditions, their experiences in Ireland diverged from those of their coreligionists within the kirk. In Scotland, Presbyterians enjoyed established status; in Ireland, they did not. Though not Irish, they considered Ireland their kingdom and, consequently, along with other inhabitants had to contend with Ireland's political and economic subordination to English imperial interests. But they did not enjoy the same political power and religious rights that those Protestants who received communion within the established Church of Ireland did. By law they could not participate in official government institutions, and they tended to rent, rather than own, arable land. Finally, after sailing to America, they bypassed eastern cosmopolitan towns and cities to settle on the frontier. Poor and mobile, they scratched a precarious existence out of the woods beyond the reach of the law and polite society. The people with no name did—and still do—elude easy classification.

The indefinable nature of the migrants from Ulster seems at odds with the experience of other groups who moved throughout Britain's Atlantic world during the eighteenth century. Far from blurring, most ethnic and national identities were coming into sharp focus at this time. In the Old World, subjects from England, Scotland, Ireland, and Wales were busy fashioning themselves into Britons. As the formation of the early modern British state reached a point of completion with the Glorious Revolution, politically powerful provincials, as well as the English, coalesced around a concept of Britishness rooted in prescriptive notions of individual rights, the consent of the governed, the ancient constitution, and Protestantism.[8] Under this veneer of emerging nationalism also lay a unifying ethnic identity emerging from a shared belief in the origins of mankind and the unique place of Britons within the world. Although championed by a group of intellectual elites within the Atlantic archipelago, this ethnic theology bound to-

3

gether men and women living in England with those who settled the Celtic peripheries of Ireland and Scotland.[9] In the early modern period, therefore, a common set of political institutions premised on the sovereignty of the King-in-Parliament and a mutual belief in the distinct place of Britons in God's plan allowed people throughout the British Isles to invent a sense of themselves as a people.

In the New World, especially in the Middle Colonies, identities also became more coherent over the course of the eighteenth century. Within a region of great diversity, migrants from Europe created ethnic, religious, or, as some would argue, ethnoreligious identities to carve out meaningful cultural space in a plural world.[10] Each group of migrants to the New World overcame the religious and regional divisions of their place of origin to invent markers of membership that bound the group together. Only in America, therefore, did men and women who left Scotland become Scots, or migrants from German-speaking regions of Europe discover a semblance of German unity. This process of invention called on these migrants to resurrect Old World ways, often religious traditions and practices, and infuse them with new meaning. So, for example, on reaching America, migrants from far-flung regions of Scotland united around the vital piety of the Scottish Calvinist tradition and in the process redefined themselves as Scots. To embrace evangelical Protestantism in the Middle Colonies was to assert a Scottish, as opposed to an English, identity.[11]

No less than the New World's Scots or Germans, Ulster's Presbyterians were caught up in this dynamic of redefinition on both sides of the ocean. Indeed, by some accounts, at one time or another the group embodied, if not embraced, a number of emerging forms of identity. At times they defined themselves as Britons, sometimes joining with Ireland's established churchmen to repel the threat of Catholicism; at other times their interests diverged from those of the established church as they invoked their rights as loyal Protestants to enjoy a full measure of religious and political liberties.[12] In America, they acquired an ethnic identity by rooting their shared sense of self in traditions imported from Ireland or retained from Scotland. How we view the origins of, for example, vital piety determines whether Ulster's Presbyterians became Scots, Scots Irish, or Irish in the New World. If evangelical fervor arose from Scottish traditions, Ulster's migrants merged with Scots in America; if in Ireland, they invented some semblance of Irishness.[13]

The Ulster Presbyterian experience illustrates how slippery terms like "identity" prove. Often employed but rarely defined, "identity" most often connotes a group's "sense" of itself, suggesting that individuals from the same region with a common past gravitate toward ethnic, religious, or British markers of identification. Assumed more than dissected, identity implies equilibrium, stability, and coherence. The group gropes for a unifying principle, it is argued, and finds one at the end of the day. Therefore, although the content of identity may differ from group to group, the proffered story line usually appears the same. To define the identity of groups within Britain entails charting the acceptance of a bundle of traits, ideas, or practices—recognized as British—by peoples inhabiting the British Isles. In America, the task involves tracing the evolution of traditions carried from Europe and resurrected in America, and then recounting how this act of transmission allowed each group to lay out distinguishing cultural boundaries.[14]

This approach, however, does not work for the elusive Presbyterians of Ulster. Any search for the group's Britishness—or its participation in an archipelagic process of state formation—must take into account the fact that these people did not comprise the political nation, those few who held the reins of political power.[15] For the New World side, by overemphasizing the group's Scottish origins we risk rendering these men and women invisible, losing them amid the Scots who peopled the Middle Colonies. Similarly, focusing on their experience in Ireland underestimates the Scottish roots of their traditions. In short, failure to take these people on their own terms, as men and women without easily identifiable identities, is to distort the group's experience. Since mapping a genealogy of traditions raises significant concerns, uncovering how Ulster's migrants understood themselves and their world entails exploring the circumstances they encountered. To do so involves reconstructing in detail the world migrants left and the one they peopled.

Ulster's earliest migrants lived during momentous times. Even if thousands had not elected to journey to America, the period on the eve of migration would have been of crucial importance for Ulster's

Presbyterians. These years witnessed the Glorious Revolution, the enactment of penal laws, and the rise of a political Ascendancy. In the period preceding mass migration, Ireland also drew closer to Britain through increased trade, as well through a redefinition of the political relationship among the three kingdoms of England, Scotland, and Ireland. Upon arrival in the American colonies, migrants encountered societies also caught in the throes of profound change. This period saw the development of provincial political institutions and a frontier economy, the growth of transatlantic trade, and the Seven Years' War. As migrants arrived, the colonies were also evolving from societies dominated by the descendants of Englishmen and women into ethnic and racial mosaics. They left an Old World and settled a New World, therefore, during a critical moment for Britain, Ireland, the American colonies, and the empire.

Although living on the empire's margins, Ulster's Presbyterians had to come to terms with each of these developments. They did so in three ways in both Ireland and America. First and foremost, Ulster's Presbyterians moved. Thousands, of course, ventured across the ocean. In America, many Ulster settlers did not sit still, instead striking out for new frontier regions. Second, religious traditions sustained the group during times of often profound change. Ulster's men and women drew on many aspects of a Reformed Protestant heritage, demonstrating a great capacity for reshaping older traditions to address their immediate needs. Third, at moments when the group confronted threats to life, liberty, and property, Ulster's Presbyterians asserted their rights as freeborn Britons to full participation in the state and empire, even as others sought to curtail them.

In such a world of flux and motion with a number of adaptable traditions to employ, no single concept of the group emerged. In fact, by reconstructing the Ulster Presbyterian response to a broader social reality, a much different picture of identity formation emerges. In both the Old and New Worlds, any attempt to fashion a single vision for the group generated ambivalence, struggle, and in some cases indifference. For Ireland's migrants, identity, as it has been used, proved ephemeral, disappearing and reappearing in a different guise, and changing in response to conditions they encountered and traditions they employed. Amid periods of change men and women defined and redefined their understandings of themselves and the world around them. The messiness of the Ulster Presbyterian response to a larger world, therefore, underscores the limitations of identity. The term obscures the richness and detail of experience, underestimates contingency, and mutes dissonant voices.

For the men and women who left Ulster, identity resembled less an ideology, vision, or static set of traits than a dynamic process through which individuals struggled to come to terms with and acted upon the world around them. Only as men and women confronted the challenges and possibilities of everyday life, familiar and unfamiliar material conditions, as well as the extraordinary, did they reinvent traditions to give these developments meaning. Identity, then, for these people did not amount to the group's acceptance of unifying cultural markers—quite the contrary. Ulster's Presbyterians continually remade themselves as they struggled to make sense of experience in rapidly changing contexts by giving a useable past a number of different and often contradictory meanings.[16] Because they moved between cultural margins in the Atlantic archipelago and America, Ulster's migrants negotiated this dynamic in two settings in short order. Ultimately, the shared experience of this two-step process—one in Ireland, the other in Pennsylvania—defined the complex ways Ulster's Presbyterians understood themselves and their world.

Exploring this process of identity formation on both sides of the ocean offers a closer glimpse of the larger transatlantic community Ulster's Presbyterians inhabited. By most accounts, the eighteenth-century British Atlantic world resembled a structure, system, or place—much like a map on a wall—with England at its center, and Ireland and America on its peripheries. Sketched on a broad canvas, the contours of the Atlantic world were defined by lines of trade fashioned by a merchant elite, channels of institutional authority created by governing officials, and the perpetual motion of migrant groups. The Atlantic was, of course, all this.[17] But it was much more. Ulster's Presbyterians, and people like them, animated this world. They suffered the dislocation of migration and produced and consumed the goods that filled the hulls of ships. They flocked to hear itinerant preachers, withstood sieges and Indian raids in imperial wars, and cleared land on the frontier. Little came easy in such a world. Eighteenth-century Ireland and America presented distinct challenges to Ulster's migrants, each requiring a different set of responses from the same font of tradition. Although the process of identity formation for Ulster's men and women would bear striking similarities on both sides of the ocean, the ways in which individuals struggled to reinvent traditions reflected the cultural imperatives of each society. Movement, Reformed Protestantism, and rights discourse—the tools migrants used in the face of broad change—took on profoundly different meanings in each context. The group's participation in the developments that defined the eighteenth-century Atlantic and the ways they negotiated these, therefore, reveal a grittier, more properly proportioned world, made up of a complex composite of similar yet distinct societies.

The Ulster Presbyterian transatlantic experience underscored a story of men and women on the cultural margins controlling their destinies as best they could in the face of profound transformations beyond their immediate control. Migrants did not make sense of sweeping change by deploying simplistic formulas as defensive measures; rather, on both sides of the ocean they displayed creativity and resourcefulness in giving meaning to a larger social reality. As each chapter of their experience unfolded, they groped for, fought over, and employed the cultural materials and practices the world had to offer to comprehend and manage the transatlantic forces that threatened to overwhelm. To be sure, in doing so they had to reinvent themselves. But in the process they also created their world.[18]

The Transformation of Ulster Society
in the Wake of the
Glorious Revolution

IN THE SUMMER of 1689, war came to the northern Irish port town of Derry. A few months earlier, thousands of Protestants from the surrounding countryside began fleeing into the walled city on the River Foyle after Derry's inhabitants refused to allow the quartering of a regiment of Irish Catholics and Scottish Highlanders in their midst, and as the army of the deposed English king, James II, attempted to subdue the countryside. The troubles had their origins in England the previous year. Fearing that James planned to reestablish "popery" in a Protestant kingdom, members of England's Parliament had urged William of Orange, protector of the United Provinces of the Low Countries and husband of James's daughter Mary, to invade the country. James fled England for the Continent before William's invasion force. He then arrived in Ireland on March 12, 1689, at the behest of his French ally Louis XIV. Both believed that if the Catholic James gained control of Ireland, he could retake the crown of England from his Protestant son-in-law, who had assumed the throne with Mary. As James approached the walls of Derry, one of only two fortified towns in Protestant hands, the inhabitants met him with musket fire and shouts of Protestant Ireland's allegiance to William and Mary. Undeterred, his French and Irish Catholic commanders blockaded the town, ran a boom across the Foyle, and initiated a siege campaign. If the townspeople would not surrender, James's army would starve them into submission.[1]

The refusal of the people to submit stemmed less from the international significance of the war of the two kings than from their fears of a victory by James. Over the course of the seventeenth century, England's government had sponsored a policy of conquest by colonization in Ireland, hoping to displace the kingdom's native Catholic pop-

The Province of Ulster Surveyed By Sʳ William Petty,
Divided into its Counties and the Counties into their severall Barronies, Wherein are distinguished the
Archbishopricks, Bishopricks, Cityᵴ, Places that return Parliament Men, also the Roads and Bridges.

Sir William Petty's Map of Ulster (1680), courtesy of the Edward E. Ayer Collection of the Newberry Library.

ulation with loyal Protestants from England and Scotland. The plan hinged on entrusting those settlers who had been members of the established church in England with control of Ireland's political institutions and its official church, the Church of Ireland, to the exclusion of other groups. Through a policy combining coercion, co-optation, and conquest, these "churchmen," as they were called, confiscated the richest lands in Ireland, proclaimed theirs the established church of the kingdom, and assumed privileged positions in the Dublin parliament. Dissenters, those Protestants who refused to conform to the rites and episcopal edicts of an established church they judged tainted by Catholic vestiges, also peopled the kingdom during the seventeenth century. Most settled in Ulster, favored an unadorned form of worship and a Presbyterian church government free of bishops, and because of their nonconformity did not enjoy the full spectrum of legal and political liberties churchmen did. But while divided along confessional lines, Protestants shared a common fear and hatred of Catholicism. In 1641, Papists rose in the kingdom, killing thousands in Ulster and nearly overturning the Protestant settlement of the kingdom. In the face of a renewed Catholic threat, Ireland's Protestants again found common ground.[2]

Indeed, the problems for Ulster's Protestants began as soon as James assumed the throne in 1685. In that year, James elected a Catholic, Richard Talbot, to the Irish peerage under the title of earl of Tyrconnell and placed him in charge of the Irish army. True to Protestant fears, Tyrconnell purged Protestants from the ranks and the officer corps. He then pushed to have Catholics admitted to local corporations that controlled local and national political affairs, gave them seats in the Irish Privy Council, and established them as judges. In 1687, when Tyrconnell assumed the lord lieutenancy for the kingdom, many Protestants believed he would use his power to overturn Ireland's land settlement by dispossessing Protestants of lands. Many feared, therefore, that a counterrevolution was afoot, one that could undo the privileged place of Protestants in the kingdom.[3]

Ulster's Protestants paid a dear price for contesting the counterrevolution. The 30,000 refugees and 7,500 officers and men besieged in Derry suffered terribly. By one witness's count, 587 bombs fell on the city. During the day, most inhabitants had time to avoid falling mortars. At night, many had no such luck. People dug holes in the floors of houses and huddled with their families. Few slept. A Presbyterian minister caught in Derry, John Mackenzie, testified to the "Sickness and Famine" that felled the besieged. George Walker, a clergyman of the established Church of Ireland and one of the governors of the besieged town, wrote that the people were "in great want of Provision in the Town, and are so crouded, that they are very noisom and full of Vermine." Common ailments included "Bloody-Flux, Small-Pox, Feavers, and Agues." Men, women, and children scrounged for whatever food they could find, increasingly without success. Derry's people "were forc'd to feed upon Horse flesh, Dogs, Cats, Rats and Mice, Greaves of a year old, Tallow, and Starch . . . [and] also salted and dried Hides." Despite these hardships, however, "they unanimously resolv'd to eat the Irish, and then one another, rather than surrender to any but their own King William and Queen Mary." After 105 days during which thousands starved, William's forces finally broke through the boom on the river and relieved the city.[4]

Although the siege had ended, the war carried on. Over forty thousand troops marched through Ulster that summer, causing mayhem wherever they went. Devastation was meted out by both sides. James's army met defeat at Enniskillen in Fermanagh, where Protestant defenders repulsed his troops trying to lay siege. William's troops reduced the coastal town of Carrickfergus to rubble. "The continual plying of the Bombs for Five Days together," one eyewitness reported, had turned the town into "a dismal heap of ruine."[5] James's Irish armies terrorized the Protestant population by burning churches and meetinghouses, plundering homes and farms. The "sufferings of Ministers, and people by the Irish army," Presbyterians from Antrim believed, demonstrated "many evidences of God's wrath against us." For these people, the "Glorious Revolution" in Ireland was anything but glorious. Ulster's Presbyterians referred to the period as a time of "confusions" and "sad troubles," a day-to-day struggle over "great danger" and "abounding privation."[6]

The war in Ireland came to an end in 1690, but not the hardship. William defeated James in a decisive battle in Leinster at the Boyne, pursuing the Irish army through the south of the kingdom until James fled Ireland for France and his army capitulated at Limerick. The land, as one contemporary put it, had "been laid wast." For a long period, travel proved dangerous because of "Rapparies on the Road," remnants of James's defeated army roaming the countryside. Derry retained its image of a besieged town. Almost ten years after the event, William Molyneux, a member of the Irish Parliament, noted that "the old houses have suffered much by the siege of it, as well as the inhabitants by the Famine caused there."[7] Derry's newly installed bishop of the Church of Ireland, William King, found his see "almost desolate" with "country houses and dwellings burnt." King testified to the wholesale devastation of the area. "Great tracts of land," he wrote, "were burnt up so that the same fire spread eighteen miles and ran over almost all the neighbouring regions."[8]

But if the devastation proved general, the unity of Ireland's Protestants did not, fading even as James's cause foundered. George Walker and John Mackenzie agreed on the significance of Protestant stands at Derry and Enniskillen and the privations suffered, but little else. In London, Walker published his recollection of the siege, replete with descriptions of the valor and loyalty of his coreligionists from the Church of Ireland. From the earliest moments of the Derry affair, he hoped to persuade readers, members of the established church had demonstrated their loyalty to William and Mary. Mackenzie believed Walker's account underestimated the role of dissenters, the majority of the besieged. He countered by discussing the steadfastness of Derry's Presbyterians, their role in closing the gates to the town, their contempt for James, their many martyrs, as well as the vacillation of churchmen. With the end of any Catholic threat for the foreseeable future, both hoped that Derry's importance in the war would win special recognition for those who had made the greatest sacrifices.[9]

Although in the years after the revolution Ulster's Presbyterians struggled to secure a reward commensurate with the suffering they had endured, they did not see their hopes fulfilled. While in England and Scotland dissenters bettered their lot after the Glorious Revolution, the Williamite Settlement changed little in Ireland. Members of the established Church of Ireland continued to control the land and political institutions of the kingdom, and William's defeat of James reinforced Ireland's status as a second-class kingdom. The revolution, however, heightened expectations for all groups. Both churchmen and Ulster nonconformists struggled to secure conflicting visions of the revolution in line with Britain's. While Anglicans hoped to empower their Parliament in Dublin and buttress the confessional state, northern dissenters placed their hopes on openly practicing their religion. In this atmosphere of contested expectations, fear and suspicion of the aims of dissenters and of their tight-knit ecclesiastical structure led elites in Ireland to enact measures that effectively barred Presbyterians from the kingdom's political life.

The period, however, also heralded unforeseen opportunities. The reassertion of England's preeminence in Ireland transformed Ulster's economic life. English policymakers continued to subordinate Irish economic concerns to those of England—and later also Scotland—but they did allow Irish merchants to export linen duty free to Britain and the American colonies. In Ulster, where money was scarce and rents hard to come by, landlords encouraged the manufacture of linen. As the production of linen invigorated a stagnant economy, what began as a means to supplement income from farming became by the 1730s a widespread means of survival. The growing trade transformed the Ulster countryside in the years after the Williamite war and drew men and women into a burgeoning world of trade that stretched across the Atlantic to the British North American colonies.

With the economic and political changes, Ulster Presbyterian society also underwent a transformation. The rise of linen affected regions unevenly; some individuals fared better than others. Tied to the trade and manufacture of linen, a new group of leaders among Ulster's dissenters emerged, and the Presbyterian church adapted to meet their needs. Afraid of the lure of conformity, ministers began tailoring their messages to this weaving and trading elite and granted them power and prestige within congregations. For those on the fringes of the linen-producing regions, economic change still brought opportunity. But the fallout of the period also left them susceptible to market downturns and relegated them to marginal roles within the church.

THE period in the wake of the Glorious Revolution was a defining moment for the British Isles, during which relationships among kingdoms and between groups were fundamentally altered.[10] The drive to impose English institutions and an English notion of sovereignty on a multiple state, which began with the Tudors in the sixteenth century, reached a point of completion. William's accession to the throne laid the foundations for the modern British fiscal-military state and the groundwork for the construction of British nationalism, both of which transformed the constituent societies of the Atlantic archipelago. In the years after the revolution, England came to dominate the peripheries, leading in 1707 to union with Scotland and later to a declaratory act for Ireland subordinating its Parliament to Britain's. The Glorious Revolution required all inhabitants of the British Isles, including Ulster's Presbyterians, to reevaluate their place in a burgeoning empire.[11]

Certainly for dissenters in other kingdoms, the Williamite revolution heralded substantive change. When James II issued his Declaration of Indulgence in 1687, raising the possibility of official toleration for both Papists and nonconformists and an alliance between the disgruntled groups, England's churchmen reevaluated their views of dissent. Because nonconformists were a small minority—they made up little more that 5 percent of the English population, and a much smaller percentage of the gentry and aristocracy—and because they played important roles in a developing mercantilist economy, the benefits of toleration outweighed the costs. Toleration, it seemed, was a small price to pay for political stability. Legislation still barred nonconformists from unfettered access to political power; only occasional conformity offered dissenters a direct voice in government. Moreover, toleration in principle proved limited in practice, a far cry, for example, from comprehension—or absorption—within the established church upon which some Presbyterians pinned their hopes. Nonetheless, after 1689, churchmen could no longer recreate the confessional state.[12]

Scottish dissenters fared even better. Although like their coreligionists to the south in England Scotland's Episcopalians held much of the land and had enjoyed established status before the revolution, Presbyterians gained control of the church and state in Scotland after the revolution. Undoubtedly, the unwavering support of Presbyterians for William's cause and the numerical superiority of Presbyterians among lowlanders encouraged the government to turn a blind eye as they purged Episcopalians from a Convention Parliament charged with reorganizing Scottish society in line with the revolution. The fear of Jacobitism, or continued support for the exiled king, however, determined the direction of the political and ecclesiastical settlement in Scotland. Ultimately the government's need to obtain a supply to maintain a standing army because of the threat posed by Jacobitism and the Jacobite sympathies of the Episcopalian clergy allowed Presbyterians to claim established status.[13]

When comparing their situation to that of dissenters in Britain, Ulster's nonconformists believed they merited toleration. With William's victory, Ulster's Presbyterians hoped that the persecution they had endured during the period of the Restoration was coming to an end.[14] "Without the prospect of any other particular Advantage to themselves," recalled a minister, Ulster's Presbyterians "did not barely *roar* and *foam* against Popery, but effectively *stemm'd the Torrent of it.*"[15] Indeed, they believed their claim for toleration was especially powerful by virtue of their unequivocal opposition to Catholicism, "their loyalty to King William and their zeal for the Revolution."[16] For their part, all they sought was "Liberty to worship God . . . without being prosecuted for it, a Liberty not denied to Dissenters in other parts of the Kingdom."[17] Therefore, repealing disabling laws, in their eyes, would repay "a Debt . . . *for the Expence of their Blood and Fortune.*"[18]

The same pressures, however, that allowed dissenters in England to gain toleration and Presbyterians in Scotland to claim supremacy could not be brought to bear on either the Irish or English government to grant toleration. Few British leaders feared that Presbyterians in Ulster would form an alliance with the Catholics of Ireland. In Ireland, where Catholics made up three-quarters of the population, few Protestants saw common cause with Popery. Northern dissenters also lacked political leverage in a kingdom where land and religious profession determined access to power. "The body of our dissenters," a government official noted, "consist of the middling and meaner sort of people, chiefly in the north, and in the north there are not many of them estated men when compared with those of the Established Church."[19] Moreover, although by the time of the revolution Presbyterians could claim as many congregants as members of the established church in Ulster, churchmen outnumbered them throughout the whole island. Finally, as opposed to the Scottish example, established churchmen in Ireland counted few Jacobites in their number. All Protestants supported William.[20]

Indeed, on all fronts the Revolution Settlement reinforced the old order. English policymakers had the same concerns with stability and revenue in Ireland as they had in England and Scotland. Maintaining a large standing army and bringing solvency to the treasury, however, entailed giving churchmen a free hand in organizing Irish society. In the years after the revolution, members of the Church of Ireland increased their share of the land at the expense of Catholics, who saw their holdings dwindle from almost 25 percent during the period of the Restoration to 14 percent by 1704.[21] The Glorious Revolution, in fact, is better conceived as counterrevolution defeated.[22] With the collapse of James's cause in Ireland and the flight or suppression of leading Catholics, churchmen could reassert the power they had been exercising in the kingdom for more than thirty years, assuming a position of "Ascendancy."[23]

Ireland's constitutional relationship with England also failed to change in any substantive way. To be sure, the enactment of penal laws, designed to destroy the power of Catholics, necessitated an unprecedented expansion of state authority into Ireland on several fronts. As more Englishmen took over the administration of government and church in Ireland, it became clear that public patronage would be based on English political considerations. England's Parliament also asserted its power by limiting Ireland's legislative independence and restricting its trade. In 1691 it had insisted that the Irish Parliament present it with outlines of bills, and it soon seized control of Ireland's budget and revenue collection. The upper house also asserted its prerogative, snatching ultimate appellate jurisdiction from the Irish House of Lords. Moreover, beginning in 1696, Parliament curtailed Irish trade with the North American colonies and a year later attempted to suppress the burgeoning Irish woolen industry. The government of George I officially sanctioned these ad hoc measures by passing the Declaratory Act, which confirmed the kingdom's full legal subordination to the Parliament in London.[24] Although these measures proved a bitter pill to swallow for Ireland's Ascendancy, they were not without precedent. England's Parliament had already legislated on a number of occasions for Ireland

and restricted its trade, most notably with the Navigation and Cattle Acts. The moves merely cemented the relationship between the two kingdoms.[25]

In this context, the only revolutionary changes in the years of the Settlement involved Protestant expectations. This dynamic determined the form the Revolution Settlement took in Ireland and forced everyone involved to redefine relationships. On the constitutional front, members of the Ascendancy, reevaluating the issue of parliamentary subordination, looked enviously at the example of Scotland. They responded in two ways. First, some hoped an invitation to union would also be extended to Ireland.[26] Second, because union amounted to, in the words of the Irish Parliamentarian William Molyneux, "an happiness we can hardly hope for," many embraced a patriotic discourse, clamoring for Ireland's political autonomy and a sovereign Irish Parliament. As early as 1698, Molyneux challenged the right of English statesmen to dictate for Ireland. Drawing from the Whiggish rhetoric of the Revolution Settlement, Molyneux argued that "to tax me without Consent is little better, if at all, than down-right Robbing me." The dean of Saint Patrick's Cathedral in Dublin, Jonathan Swift, assumed Molyneux's mantle in the 1720s in the wake of Ireland's Declaratory Act. In his "Drapier's Letters" Swift summed up Ireland's reward for loyalty to Britain as "the Privilege of being governed by laws to which we do not consent."[27]

In this context, the growing northern Presbyterian menace appeared as one more threat to the Ascendancy's control of the kingdom, already imperiled by the continued loss of political power to the English Parliament. In particular, members of the Ascendancy feared the group's tight-knit ecclesiastical system and its links to coreligionists in Scotland. During the first half of the seventeenth century, nearly 100,000 lowland Scots left their homeland for Ulster. The earliest migrants ventured to Counties Down and Antrim across the Irish Sea from Scotland. By 1610, Scottish tenant farmers from the overpopulated southeastern regions of Ayrshire, Wigtonshire, and Galloway peopled six Ulster counties set aside by the English government for plantation by Protestants from Britain. Settlers established themselves in the ecsheated counties of Donegal, Fermanagh, Tyrone, Armagh, Cavan, and Coleraine—later renamed "Londonderry"—where English, Scottish, and, in a few cases, Irish Protestant worthies received huge tracts of land surrendered or taken from rebellious Catholics.[28]

As migrants continued streaming into the province during the period of the Cromwellian protectorate, settlers initiated a "Presbyterian revolution" by establishing a tight-knit church organization akin to the one they had left in Scotland. In 1642, when a Scottish army arrived in Ulster to quash the Irish Catholic rebellion, chaplains and officers encountered Scottish migrants with few Presbyterian institutions. To be sure, settlers had assembled themselves into congregations by erecting meetinghouses at convenient sites throughout the countryside, as they had created sessions in which lay elders resolved disputes within the community, scrutinized church attendance, and dispensed charity and justice. But they had little else. Newly arrived Scottish troops introduced the rudiments of the Presbyterian system by establishing a presbytery in Carrickfergus to coordinate congregational affairs, adjudicate disputes, ensure that ministers fulfilled their responsibilities, and admonish congregations to pay ministerial stipends. Over the next twenty years, Scottish migrants erected five more presbyteries, located at Antrim, Down, Route, Laggan, and Tyrone. By 1690, after the creation of the Synod of Ulster, the northern Presbyterian system comprised nine presbyteries, three sub-synods, and 120 congregations serving a population of 150,000 Scottish migrants and their descendants.[29]

Settlers from Scotland retained close ties to their homeland. At the time of the Glorious Revolution, Ulster congregations from time to time requested the services of Scottish ministers as pastors. Indeed, during the troubles, many ministers fled back "to their respective charges in Scotland" to enjoy again their "native air."[30] After the war, most young men from Ulster who aspired to the ministry received their theological training at Scottish universities in Edinburgh or Glasgow, and in some cases answered calls to minister to congregations in "North Britain."[31] Connections extended beyond the ministry. Irish sessions expected lay migrants to carry "testimonials" detailing their behavior within Scottish parishes before gaining admission into Ulster Presbyterian congregations.[32] In some cases, ministers from the Scottish kirk even informed the Ulster synod if disreputable people with false testimonials were abroad. In one such instance, the congregation at Connor learned that four women who had "fled from church censure" in Scotland and four others whom the kirk had excommunicated had reached Ireland. Upon orders from the Presbytery of Down, the Connor session requested its congregants to "enquire in the parish that non of them be harboured."[33]

Settlers from Scotland also adopted Scottish ecclesiastical practices, in particular subscription to the Westminster Confession of Faith. Calvinists had conceived and adopted the Westminster Confession of Faith over the years as an expression of their vision of a visible church and as a viable alternative to the Thirty-nine Articles of the Episcopal Church. Drawn up by English and Scottish Calvinists in 1643 as "the most perfectly written expression of the Christian faith," the Westminster Confession of Faith served as a statement legitimating ecclesiastical structure unfettered by episcopal oversight and laying out orthodox belief. The Confession restated the basic elements of Reformed Protestantism. The Scriptures, it posited, "were given by divine inspiration, and . . . are a perfect rule of Christian faith and practice." It also maintained that Father, Son, and Holy Ghost "are one God, the same in substance, equal in power and glory," and supported "all doctrines common to the Protestant churches at home and abroad."[34] In 1690, when the Scottish Parliament disestablished the Episcopal in favor of the Presbyterian Church, Scots confirmed their allegiance to the Confession. Following what one Belfast minister called "the laudable Example of the Church of Scotland," in 1698 the Synod of Ulster recommended "that Young Men, when licens'd to preach, be obliged to Subscribe the Confession of Faith, in all the Articles thereof, as the Confession of their Faith."[35]

Migrants also introduced Scottish-style communion services, which further served to integrate the community. Most congregations held these services once or twice a year. A week before, elders were dispatched throughout the bounds of the congregation to "bring a list of the names of the communicants . . . that they may be considered," and to inquire into any scandals.[36] The session then called miscreants who had "offended God and his people" to remove the scandal.[37] Elders took up collections for widows and orphans, as did those from the parish of Aghadowey who paid stipends to at least ten indigent congregants a month.[38] Portions of the money also went to help Presbyterians outside of the congregation, as, for example, in Antrim in 1687 when congregants contributed to "a collection for James Watson, now a captive with the Turks, for his relief."[39] Usually, however, the synod or local presbyteries requested congregational funds for more mundane concerns. Within two months, for instance, Aghadowey's parishioners contributed to collections for a man who lost his house in a fire and for a widow whose husband had perished at sea.[40] Members of other congregations attended, and neighboring ministers assisted and delivered sermons. At one communion service at Belfast, Presbyterians from around the area heard nine sermons in four days, beginning on Friday the Fast Day and culminating with three sermons on the Sabbath.[41] The numbers of dissenters at these services impressed—and alarmed—Anglican authorities. One churchman noted that Ulster's Presbyterians "gather together many parishes to make a great shew at their sacraments to which people come sometimes forty miles and 3 or 4000 at a time."[42]

While Church of Ireland clerics struggled to raise money and hold together small congregations, Presbyterianism in the north flourished. The strong position of Presbyterians in Ulster was further consolidated by a large influx of Scots into the region in the 1690s. One alarmed churchman declared, "The number of People is wonderfully increased in *Ireland* since the Battel of the *Boyne*, in the Year 1690." By his reckoning "above Four score Thousand Families of them have since that time, transported themselves from *Scotland* into that Kingdom; and they are possessed not only of almost the whole Province of *Ulster*, but are in great numbers, in many Parts of the other Provinces."[43] By more conservative contemporary estimates, as many as 50,000 men and women migrated, initiating a new period of growth.[44] In 1689 Ireland had 86 Presbyterian ministers, most of whom lived in Ulster. By 1702, the number of ministers had grown to 130.[45] Described by Queen Mary at the time of the revolution as "the worst in Christendom," the established church by 1728 could only support 600 beneficed clergymen and 200 curates throughout the whole kingdom, many of whom ministered to a number of parishes.[46] About this time, nearly 140 Presbyterian ministers worked in Ulster alone.[47] Comparing the record of the two churches, it was not unreasonable to claim, as one churchman did, that if unchecked, the highly organized Presbyterian system would "extend to Dublin, and cross the kingdom to Galway . . . [and] soon stretch to Cork and Kerry."[48]

Fear and suspicion, therefore, defined the ways in which Ireland's Ascendancy viewed northern Presbyterianism. The Presbyterian disregard for ecclesiastical courts and the fact that the kirk had supplanted Anglicanism as the established church in Scotland led the Ascendancy to view Ulster's dissenters as dangerous rivals for supremacy in the kingdom. More alarming still, the Calvinist William III doubled the royal grant or regium donum to Ulster Presbyterians, members of a technically illegal church.[49] To members of the established church, this customary gift to loyal dissenting Protestants amounted to a "Fund to plant and propagate their Schism in places where the numbers and Wealth of the Dissenters have not been sufficient to form a Conventicle or support a Teacher."[50] On a visitation to the north in 1700, one churchman reported to Bishop William King how "the dissenters increase . . . in the north by new accession of people from Scotland, that they have settled many of their ministers where none were before the troubles," adding that "they make it their business to obstruct and destroy the discipline of our church."[51]

Churchmen scoffed at arguments about supposed Presbyterian "loyalty." According to William Tisdall, vicar of Belfast, Ulster's dissenters saw their church "Superiour to, and independent of all Authority of the Civil Magistrate." In Tisdall's estimation, northern dissent was a "Grand Political Machine that subverted the Constitution."[52] In particular, as the bishop of Down complained, "they proceed to exercise jurisdiction openly and with a high hand over those in their possession." They not only placed themselves outside the jurisdiction of ecclesiastical courts, but also outside the bounds of the political and ecclesiastical status quo.[53] Far from loyal, they posed a threat. As one churchman put it, "When their Power and Numbers are increased, they will employ their Utmost Strength, and most Vigorous Endeavors to Overturn (now their hand is in) this Truly Apostolical Government of the Established Church."[54]

In response, authorities attempted to check the growth of the Presbyterian Church and its presumption to regulate the everyday lives of its adherents. With a Tory administration in power in Britain, the reign of Queen Anne witnessed the high point of Ascendancy antipathy toward the Ulster Presbyterian system. Suspicious of any group that threatened the position of the established church, Tories had little sympathy for the concerns of dissenters; indeed, some Tories, who continued to support the cause of the exiled James, favored Catholics over nonconformists. In these years, "the High Church," a minister recounted, was "rampant and flaming."[55] Churchmen harkened back to the Restoration by enforcing old laws on the books. Local bishops declared rites such as marriages and funerals performed by dissenting ministers null and void, an ignominy not even applied to Catholics; indeed, by law Ulster churchmen were not recognized as Christian clerics. Established churchmen, an Ulster Presbyterian lamented, "are violent to a degree beyond what they were formerly, and are pursuing people as fornicators who are married by us."[56] Gilbert Kennedy of Tullylish declared that Church of Ireland bishops "are violent where I live. Four of my flock have been lately delivered to Satan for being married by me."[57] Such prosecutions had worldly ramifications. One minister recounted how "some officials in this part of the kingdom . . . pursu[ed] both ministers and people in their Courts for their non-conformity to the rites and ceremonies of the Church." He added that voiding marriages had the effect of making "their children incapable of succeeding to their estates and of divers other privileges as being bastards."[58] The established church by "rigorous methods" also collected tithes from northern nonconformists, a group which, according to Archbishop Hugh Boulter, "it may easily be supposed do not pay tithes with great cheerfulness."[59]

On another front, Irish Tories lobbied their allies in England to enact discriminatory legislation. Although, it remains unclear how it transpired, in 1704 Tories in Britain inserted a sacramental test clause into an Irish "popery bill," a move a Scottish minister called "the ordinary blind for persecution of Protestant Dissenters."[60] The resulting legislation, which required all civil and military officials to receive communion in the Church of Ireland, effectively barred dissenters from office under the Crown and drove them out of municipal corporations, which controlled most parliamentary elections. Although dissenters still held the right by law to vote and sit in Parliament, the Test

Act served as a de facto exclusion from public life.[61] As Archbishop of Cashel Theophilus Bolton explained in 1730, "the government here is entirely by the constitution in the hands of the members of the established [church]" and "among the Lords there is not one dissenter, nor much more than one in 100 among the Commoners."[62] In 1714, Tories in Britain also pushed to extend the Schism Act to Ireland, in an effort to place all educational establishments under the control of the Church of Ireland, and in the same year suspended the regium donum. Far from the experience of Presbyterians in England and Scotland, the fallout of the Revolution Settlement left Ulster Scots without toleration and with a Test Act.[63]

Parliament's hostility toward northern dissent during the later years of Queen Anne's reign proved exceptional. When Whigs controlled Britain's Parliament, as they did under William and Mary and later under George I, Ulster's Presbyterians received a sympathetic hearing. In both 1692 and 1695, northern ministers solicited the English government for help in gaining toleration. They also asked Scottish Presbyterians for advice in approaching potential sympathizers. Similarly, in 1708 English dissenters contributed funds to a new campaign for repealing the Test Act. In each of these cases, the British government tried to persuade the Irish Parliament to undo disabling legislation. These attempts, however, met with overwhelming opposition from Ireland's Lords and Commons, Whig and Tory alike. In the face of such intransigence, Britain's government backed down. With a Whig administration in power under George I, the British government again favored the cause of dissenters in Britain and Ireland, instructing the lord lieutenant to pursue a repeal of the Test Act in the Irish Parliament.[64] In 1719, the Irish government finally relented, passing a Toleration Act allowing dissenters to practice their religion openly. Although the measure drew support from Irish Whigs who argued that dissenters could "with great safety be confided in" and viewed disabling legislation as "cruel as well as unjust,"[65] in fact, the act was little more than a preemptive measure supported by the established clergy to forestall any substantive reform. As one Ulster minister explained, by this time the High Church enemies of Presbyterians had "their horns cut" and appeared "muzzled," but conceded that "these bears, being robbed of their whelps, are much enraged."[66] Northern dissenters remained subject to ecclesiastical courts and still had to pay tithes. And, of course, the sacramental test stood unchanged.[67]

ALTHOUGH in the years after the revolution Ulster's dissenters faced the prospect of religious and political persecution, the severest challenges the group experienced in the wake of the Williamite war stemmed from the unsteady economy. The devastation of the war threw the province into disarray. Even five years after hostilities in Ulster had ceased farmland remained sparsely tenanted.[68] Most tenants eventually returned, but to a province reeling from economic dislocations and caught in the grips of depression. Prices for land and food remained low in the years after the fighting ended; but few could afford much of either. Trade was at a standstill. To be sure, some profited from the war. A Presbyterian merchant community, which had emerged in the 1650s, did develop further during the years of the Williamite war; indeed, some claimed Presbyterians had fared too well amid the widespread destruction. Those that "used before the late War to beat upon the Hoof after a Pony laden with Pedlars Goods to the Fairs and Markets of the Kingdom, are now Masters of Ships at Sea, and Warehouses crammed with Merchants goods at home."[69] These few merchants, however, proved the exception. Money, or the lack of it, proved the most vexing issue. A member of the established church in the north, Henry Conyngham, complained that "I cannot raise a farthing, so great is the scarcity of money."[70] During the first decade of the eighteenth century, little money entered the kingdom, and what little there was tended to flow to England. English policy either devalued Irish coinage, which encouraged the flow of money outward, or increased its value at times when England was short of specie.[71]

The scarcity of specie, in turn, placed men such as Conyngham in a further bind. If they could raise little money, neither could their tenants. "If this kingdom continue in the miserable degree of poverty it now labours under," he argued, "nobody can expect rents in money, and what is worse, all commodities are at so very low rate that, even in commodities, tenants will not be able to discharge half the rents." Paying rents in work and in kind in the years after the revolution, therefore, offered little hope to cash-strapped landlords.[72] For more than ten years after the siege of Derry ended, Presbyterians could not even raise enough money to support their church. Church records from the period illustrate the problems presbyteries encountered pressuring congregants to pay ministerial stipends. In one such instance, a congregation could not even put a roof over a minister's head. The Presbytery of Route chastised the people of Aghadowey because their minister, Mr. McGreggor, had "no certain lodging in the parish," asserting it was "not consistent with the credit of the Gospel, for a minister to go from house to house." His congregants found him a home, but could not come up with his stipend and the "ground rent for the meeting-house."[73]

In these circumstances, landlords had little alternative but to offer leniency. Some landlords, of course, attempted to squeeze their tenants. Others, however, argued for more favorable terms for tenants. Officials of the Goldsmiths' Company, one of a number of London concerns holding land in and around Derry, ordered their collectors to go easy. "The company's tenants," a directive read, "(in consideration of the sum of £200 part of arrears due to this company, and of the great sufferings and calamities they underwent in the late war, and also of the good service they performed at the late siege of that city), have an abatement of two years' rent, and three years for the payment of £600 in arrears." The company had cause to be magnanimous: its plantation in Derry amounted to only one of its concerns, and prospects of collecting overdue rents appeared dim. Officials, therefore, had the ability to preach patience. Other landlords, more reliant on the money coming in from rents, had no such luxury, trying all they could to entice settlers to their undermanned estates. In areas such as Armagh, which relied on the butter and livestock trade for specie, landowners reduced their "entry fines," a sum of money due the landlord on signing the lease usually equal to one year's rent. Arthur Brownlow of Lurgan, for example, reduced the total entrance fines on his estate from £112 in the years 1680 to 1689 to £35 for the ten years following the war. The fine per taking fell more than 600 percent from £8.65 to £1.44.[74]

Linen rescued landlords from their plight. Ulster settlers had a long tradition of weaving linen for household consumption. As early as 1660, dissenters spun and wove linen in the Lagan Valley. Moreover, the migration of skilled French Huguenots and northern English craftsmen added increased expertise to local linen manufacture.[75] But it was the ongoing warfare with France in the late seventeenth century that transformed Ulster's cottage industry. English merchants had difficulty importing linen from the Netherlands or Saxony and, therefore, could not meet the rising demand for cheap cloth in the English market. Because little linen could be expected from English and Scottish producers, the government turned to Ireland, a kingdom where low prices for food and rent ensured an affordable product. Over opposition from English merchants with an interest in the German linen trade, Parliament passed an act in 1696 allowing Irish linen producers to export certain cuts duty free to England and Scotland. As one Irish official put it, "since it [the linen trade] can be of no prejudice to Great Britain and . . . is in a manner all that is left to Ireland and ought therefore to be encouraged as much as possible." Even though Presbyterians would benefit, landlords realized linen could bring specie back into the kingdom, thus alleviating their money problems. With the linen trade, therefore, English concerns converged with Irish interests.[76]

Landlord interest in the industry was strong. In 1711 a number of Ulster churchmen established the Linen Board in Dublin, an organization composed of seventy-two trustees who had great influence in both Parliaments. The board subsidized the industry, providing cottiers with flaxseed and spinning and weaving equipment at a discount, procuring funds to establish bleachgreens, and awarding prizes for innovation and quality.[77] Landlords then encouraged their tenants to spin and weave linen. "The better sort of people," a contemporary explained, "introduced the sowing of flax seed and made the tenants' wives spin the produce, which they had woven into coarse linens." According to one landowner, the revenue from the trade ended a cash crunch. "The flax seed, wheels and reels given on public account [by the Board]," he believed, "enabled them to pay the advanced rent of their farms, and in some measure to keep their ground." The wife of a County Down landlord, Sophia Hamilton, went so far as to propose the erection of a school to train youngsters in the arts of manufacture.[78]

In no time, the trade took off. If international war accounted for the creation of a viable linen industry in the north, peace brought unexpected returns. "It was the Peace establish'd throughout *Europe* after a long and expensive War," the Irish writer Arthur Dobbs observed, "that made the Markets quick and high every where in 1714 and 1715. There seem'd to be a new Force given to the Circulation of Trade, after so long a Stagnation."[79] Whereas in 1700 Ulster Scots produced little more than 12,000 yards of linen for the English market, within twenty years this trade accounted for one half of all of Ireland's exports. Ulster producers sent 700,000 yards of linen to England in 1704, 1.5 million by 1710, and 6.4 million in 1740. A Bristol merchant argued that "The people in the north of Ireland make good cloth, sell it at reasonable rates and would every year make much more, had they a vent for it." Although the vitality of the regional economy ebbed and flowed through the first decades of the 1700s, so successful was the linen market at the time that many contemporaries complained that Ulster had done unfairly well.[80] As one Irishman put it, "for reilly the Linnen Manufactory is become the best branch of traid this Kingdom has."[81]

Within a few decades, linen had transformed the landscape of northeast Ulster. Landlords and local merchants sponsored fairs devoted to the buying and selling of linen. A little more than ten years after the war, the town of Lurgan was by one contemporary's account "one of the most thriving and flourishing villages and a most considerable market town in the province of Ulster."[82] Change was even more striking in Newry. During the war, the town had been "burned down by the Duke of *Berwick.*" Every home was "in Flames" except for "a square Castle or two, and five or six Houses only escaping, which the *Irish* had not time to destroy." Within thirty years, Newry was "in a thriving condition; being the largest and most trading town in the County [Down]; to which Increase the Linnen Manufacture hath much contributed." The townspeople had constructed stone bridges connecting Newry to Dublin and Armagh, which served to transport linen woven in the region.[83]

Trading networks emerged. At fairs, locals sold their wares to merchants for goods, credit, and flaxseed. Factors from Dublin attended regional fairs, as did yarn jobbers and weavers eager to buy yarn at one fair and sell it for a profit at the next. Location again played an important role in determining which villages sprang up as local markets. The village of Rathfryland in County Down, for instance, developed into "one of the greatest Marts for Linnen in the County" because of its proximity to "the High Road from Newry to Downpatrick."[84] As trade increased, linen drapers concentrated on towns with more established linen markets. Local producers then sold their wares to middlemen who then resold the product at regional towns. Weavers mainly marketed unbleached or brown cloth. Linen drapers whitened the linen before reselling it to factors from Dublin who transported the goods to Dublin's white linen hall for shipment to Britain.[85]

Port towns tied this growing network into a larger world. The passage of the 1696 act curtailing Irish trade with Britain's colonies hurt Belfast merchants who relied on the provisions trade with the West Indies, and the reexportation of American tobacco. Increasingly, however, Belfast became an important center for linen shipping. Although ships from Dublin took most of the linen out of the province, by 1698 Belfast's merchants shipped ten times the amount of linen they had only six years before. In the north, most roads led to Belfast. From a small town of 1,000 in the 1660s, Belfast developed into what William Molyneux called in 1708 "a very handsome thriving well peopled town, a great many new houses and good shops in it. The folks seemed all very busy and employed in Trade." By the middle of the eighteenth century, Belfast boasted over 8,000 inhabitants employed in a number of occupations.[86] The Rosemary Street Presbyterian Church in the 1720s included a number of weavers and merchants, and many involved in ancillary trades, such as carpenters, shoemakers, hucksters, coopers, tailors, tanners, maltsters, and snuff makers.[87] By 1729, according to Arthur Dobbs, Belfast had grown into Ireland's third largest port, behind only Dublin and Cork, and the greatest shipping concern in the north. By Dobbs's estimation, the port serviced 370 ships totaling over 9,000 tons.[88] Derry, once devastated by war, also experienced great growth. Though lagging behind Belfast, Derry ships had a combined tonnage in excess of 2,000, making it the second largest port in the north.[89]

By the 1720s, the production of linen was displacing agriculture as the mainstay of the economy in the northeast. As more tenants embraced the market economy, they began to view the land as a commodity to be mortgaged or sold for capital. Moreover, time and money took on new meanings as people worked looms and wheels late into the night and purchased more goods from merchants.[90] Increasingly, locals in the region who excelled at weaving devoted most of their time to the craft. "This People's Manufacture," a churchman argued, "doth generally, if not altogether, consist in Linnen-Cloth, with which they do not only furnish *Ireland*, but do frequently send great Quantities of it into several Parts of *England*." Most of them, he continued, "are so intent upon this kind of Manufacture, that the very Husbandmen and their Servants, when they return from their Labours abroad, such as Plowing, Sowing, Fencing, etc. do imploy themselves by their Fire-sides in this kind of Work." While the men "sit reeling of Linnen-Yarn," the women "are busy in Spinning; and by this Constancy and Diligence, that Country produces great Quantities of good Linnen yearly."[91]

The potential profits to be derived from linen production in a cash-tight economy along with changing demography explained the frenzy for linen in the northeast. A weaver could realize profits of 300 percent if he grew the flax, his wife spun the yarn, and he bleached the cloth. If he sold the unfinished cloth to a bleacher, the weaver could still realize a 200 percent profit. As long as families lived close to market towns, men and women could expect to make a 100 percent profit for spinning alone. Such margins encouraged many to lease smaller plots of land and to devote more time to spinning and weaving and less to farming. Weavers relied on proximity to local markets and a small plot of land to grow flax for women to spin and on which to grow potatoes and oatmeal. The food produced on a few acres of land allowed weavers to hold their linen until it could fetch a fair price, or to see them through when prices for food were too high at the local market.[92] By the 1730s in the "linen triangle" of the towns of Dungannon, Lisburn, and Newry, where weavers were prepared to pay a high rent for proximity to a number of local markets, linen manufacture became "the dominant element in the popular economy."[93]

These changes had lasting effects for landlord-tenant relations. The advance of linen manufacture enabled some who had previously been unable to pay their rents, which was the landlord's primary concern, now to do so. On the Rawdon estate near Moira, for example, only one-tenth of tenants were considered poor in 1716 by contemporary standards.[94] By the 1730s, an observer noted, linen, the "Staple Commodity" of the "Commonality" of County Down, "freed [them] from much of that Poverty and Wretchedness, which are too visible among the lower in other Parts of the Kingdom."[95] By the same token, however, renting land in the northeast became more competitive, leading to the further subdivision of holdings and increased rents. In some cases, landlords lost control over who resided on their land. Since the industry developed without the benefit of technological advances, the growth in trade depended upon more families in the northeast becoming involved in manufacture. Some farmers took advantage of the rage for linen by leasing parcels of their land to weavers. By the 1730s, this class of middlemen, who acted as intermediaries between the landlord and the families relying on spinning and weaving to meet their rents, expanded in the linen region.[96]

Even though linen transformed Ulster and enriched some, most tenants still led a tenuous existence. Without the aid of landlords enthusiastic for improvements or supportive of the moral economy, hardships would have continued. "I presume you are now soun to destrebute the King's flaxseed to the cunterey," wrote a Dubliner to a friend in Antrim, "for it is the chief thing they have hereabouts to live by." No doubt, Ulster's tenants were better-off than those in other parts of Ireland. Nevertheless, with less land devoted to tillage, the linen trade took on a much greater significance; indeed, reliance on linen defined the lives of many. "The undertenants are all very poor," wrote a landholder in Armagh. "They are so far from selling corn that they can hardly get bread," he explained. "They pay their rent with linen cloth having no other way."[97]

As the northeast pulsed with new economic life, other regions also experienced growth. Spinning and the production of lower-quality, or coarse, cuts of linen were spreading to the west and south of Ulster, in Counties Derry and Tyrone. While men and women in Donegal did not participate in the weaving industry, many in this area and in western Derry spun yarn for the textile industry in northwest England.[98] In the south of the province farmers raised livestock and reclaimed wasteland for tillage to feed the growing towns of the northeast.[99] Even men and women on the rugged Antrim coast had a hand in the linen market. Tenants on Rathlain Island, for example, paid their rents with the proceeds from burning seaweed. Charred kelp was one ingredient used in potash, a bleaching agent.[100] The production of linen had become so profitable by 1730 that the tenants in places that specialized in producing food for growing towns also began manufacturing cloth.[101] Soon these regions too grew more susceptible to the economy's reliance on linen. Those in the east had forsaken farming for weaving, and although inhabitants of the west wove less, they too had a stake in the linen market. If weavers failed to sell their wares to merchants, spinners and those who supported the burgeoning linen regions with foodstuffs also stood to suffer. Yet the south and west of Ulster, while part of the growing economy, had lower population densities than the northeast. Subdivision of land was rarer, as tenants were harder to come by. Therefore, although susceptible to downturns in the linen trade, farmers in these regions negotiated from a position of strength if times grew tough. If rents went unpaid, landlords had little leverage.[102]

The linen economy also transformed Ulster Presbyterian society. Within the church, the rise of families who earned their bread not from the land but through trade and manufacture challenged the preeminent place of Presbyterians landholders and in the process disrupted relations within congregations.[103] Dissenting members of the gentry had grown accustomed to assuming positions of leadership within parishes, often by serving as elders or renting land to the congregation for the meetinghouse. Indeed, the few landed Presbyterians represented the most reliable patrons the church had. Now they confronted a group of men who wore their newfound wealth conspicuously. The young men in Down, noted an observer, dressed in an "immeasurably lavish" manner and were "never thought sufficiently fine or fashionable unless they send abroad for [their clothes]."[104]

Upstarts soon clamored for more status befitting their newfound wealth. In 1707, people from the congregation of Knock in County Down began a long-standing feud over the arrangements of seats in the meetinghouse. Elders and ministers placed their most influential congregants in the front of the meetinghouse, but as more men and women established themselves as weavers and merchants who paid a larger percentage of the ministerial stipend, this arrangement began to change. A person's position in the meetinghouse and the number of servants he could accommodate in his seating section reflected his position and rank in society. At one Sabbath meeting "in the time of singing of Psalms, before sermon in the forenoon," a fight broke out over seats. "Some of Hugh Montgomery's servants," the minutes of the presbytery read, "sitting in a half seat placed before David Williamson's seat" set off the tussle. "The said David Williamson did with his cane push the aforesaid servants, and then rose up . . . over-throw[ing] the seat, tumbling off the persons that sate upon it." More than a year later, the case remained unresolved. The Presbytery of Down found that "several members are so troublesome and obstinate in the matter of their seats in the meeting house that they threaten all such with the civil law who shall possess their seats that formerly belonged to them."[105]

Nearly every presbytery dealt with congregational seating disputes. Two years after the Montgomery/Williamson incident, the Presbytery of Down once again tried to adjudicate a confrontation over seating. In this case, one congregant, Mr. Nivin, "was fully satisfied with the seat he now enjoys, provided he may have leave to settle a form four feet in length for the accommodation of his servants." Envy gripped the congregation. Two other wealthy members, Mr. Cample and Mr. James Hamilton, agreed not to quarrel with Nivin "provided they have leave to settle seats four feet in length."[106] With seating at a premium, those without ample funds often lost their choice positions in the meetinghouse. John McKay of Ardstraw refused to accept new seating assignments and engaged in "disorderly practices in being disobedient unto his Rev'd Pastor." McKay stood accused of "keeping a seat in the meeting house contrary to the order both of the Presbytery and Session, and for casting several undeserved reflections on his Rev'd and aged Pastor."[107] In Donegal, when one congregant lost his seat to Alexander Ewing, who was better able to pay the ministerial stipend, the wronged "took a hold of him, viz: Alex Ewing by the neck and pull[ed] him out of the seat, and the sd. Alex pushed him off with his staff." In the same congregation one member of the church called his minister a "lyor," declared that he would "oppose the minister in the pulpit," and slashed a rival in the hand with a sword after he lost his seat.[108]

At first, members of the General Synod decried the new signs of wealth in Ulster. In 1700, elders and ministers chastised those "too gaudy and vain in their apparel and . . . too sordid," beseeching all to "avail Powderings, vain Cravats, Half shirts and the like."[109] Officials of the cash-strapped Presbyterian Church, however, learned to accommodate their new prospective patrons. In September 1709, the Presbytery of Down, which had heard the Montgomery/Williamson dispute, declared that ministers, not elders, "have power to cast out the seats of the deficient [in paying stipends]." Congregants who could pay were responsible "for the whole seat, and all that sits in it."[110] Those without such funds had "to quit the ground whereon the table before the pulpit stands," the best area in the meetinghouse.[111] In 1718, the congregation of Broadisland faced the same problem that the Presbytery of Down had struggled with. The session ran into great difficulties because those supporting the minister did not have seats in the meetinghouse. Members with ample cash promised "paying down immediately, or giving security, for paying their proportion of the remaining arrears" to obtain seats in the meetinghouse that reflected their status in the community.[112]

Sermons reflected the growing importance of these members within congregations. In particular, ministers devised new justifications to account for the growing wealth of some and tenuous poverty of many. James Orr, an Antrim minister, proclaimed that "the soul of the diligent shall be made fat." For the men and women who wove and spun linen, this message had a special appeal. For "the Lord," as Orr reminded his congregants, "approves of such are industrious in their callings."[113] James Duchal argued that wealth in itself did not lead to happiness, but a soul in tune with God could bring riches. "We cannot live with our riches, health or reputation," he reminded his charges, without "a mind that's full of God, and so is full from itself." If men and women followed this logic, "God will provide for and bestow a competence on us." Duchal admonished all, rich and poor, "not [to] be slothful in Business, but diligent and frugal, from a sense of duty to himself, to his relations and dependents, and to the public."[114]

Religious metaphors took on a commercial cast. John Kennedy believed good Christians had to "inhabituate trade in truth and become purchasers of truth." He encouraged his followers to "buy the truth and sell it not[,] buy it at any rate sell it at none." The wealthy had a special obligation to "be liberall to the poor [and] spend it much for God," and "Neither under nor overvalue riches," but "be rich in grace, to abound in wealth." Kennedy's sermons proclaimed a new message of what he called "spirituall prosperity." By attuning the church's message to the changing secular world, he could encourage those making money in the linen trade to forsake the choice of many of the dissenting gentry in receiving communion in the established church. The Presbyterian Church would be a welcoming place. "Put much of your stock in God's hand," he advised, "it will be the surest pay for you."[115]

For those with little "stock," however, such sermons gave little solace. No doubt, those living a tenuous existence understood the gist of Kennedy's message; they, too, lived in a world defined by the market. Moreover, even if the poor would not attain the wealth of some of their neighbors, they could, according to the new commercial message of sermons, grow rich in faith. In 1716, a minister from Killinchy implored his congregants "under poverty and straits as to worldly things" to look toward the Lord. "Your diet and other provisions and accommodations," he reminded them, "are very scanty, mean and uncomfortable. Are you, at the same time rich in Faith, rich towards God?"[116] Ministers, then, preached the value of patience and acceptance of one's lot in life during a period in which wealthier neighbors challenged their betters.

IMMERSION in a larger world, to be sure, did not herald a golden age that some prophesied in the wake of the Presbyterian defense of Derry and Enniskillen. Religious and political disabilities illustrated just how far and to whom "Britishness" extended. The economic revolution in the north, however, placed a group of dissenters on the cultural margins within an empire of trade, transforming the landscape, redefining relationships to the land and landlords, bringing the possibility of wealth, and linking local towns, entrepots, and port towns to Britain and the broader world. But the meteoric rise of the linen industry in the period after the Williamite revolution placed Ulster dissenters in a perilous position. If rents and food prices increased, or if the linen trade fell on hard times, many stood to suffer, especially the poorer members of the community. The period, therefore, brought high but dashed expectations and new but troubling opportunities. And as a newfound means of wealth created divisions within the dissenting community, a fearful Ascendancy enacted laws forcing the group to retreat into a well-organized Presbyterian system.

"Satan's Sieve"

CRISIS AND COMMUNITY
IN ULSTER

The transformation of Ulster in the years after the Glorious Revolution presented the province's Presbyterians with a paradox. During the years when the tight-knit church came under pressure from the Ascendancy, Ulster became the preeminent linen-producing region in the British Isles. At the very moment dissenters encountered new economic possibilities within a broader Irish society, the policies of the Ascendancy pressed men and women to rely more heavily on church structures set apart from the institutional life of the kingdom to order their lives. Ulster's Presbyterians tried to make sense of such contradictions by taking stock of the state of their church and of their place in Irish society and a larger world. Their attempt to do so, however, did not lead to consensus but to conflict. Indeed, in these years Ulster's men and women articulated two incompatible programs for responding to change. And these distinct visions reflected the socioeconomic divisions the group was already experiencing.

For many, the position of the group within Irish society and the broadening possibilities of the period caused little concern. A number of men and women took advantage of the opportunities their new world offered. Most lay people and ministers attended fairs and markets. But some strayed further, showing little hesitation to ignore the discipline of the church, instead taking their disputes to the kingdom's official courts. None of this, of course, was new. Ulster's dissenters had a long history of challenging their pastors and embracing life beyond the bounds of the meetinghouse. Nonetheless, as linen was becoming a mainstay of the northern economy and while Presbyterians struggled with the disabilities of the Test Act, ministers decried the falling away, alleging that each blow to the integrity of the Presbyterian system weakened the position of dissenters in the kingdom. The perception of declension, then, emerged from the group's troubling experience within the Irish confessional state.

To negotiate their transformed world and a sense of declining holiness, some northern dissenters attempted to buttress their most viable institution, the Presbyterian Church. These Ulster Presbyterians invested the vision of a consolidating church with greater meaning. To remedy the many ills befalling the group as a whole, a number of ministers and laity called on the people to turn their backs on the kingdom's official institutions and instead support the church structures and practices that an earlier generation of migrants had imported from Scotland. While these "Old Lights" did not decry economic prosperity, they condemned the changes that they believed it entailed, particularly the disregard for the disciplinary power of the church. They met theological and political innovations with hostility. Moreover, they continued to argue that the Presbyterian Church was divinely ordained. And as such, they hoped to achieve some form of established status for the Presbyterian Church in the north, thus putting it on more equal footing with the Church of Ireland. Doing so, they argued, would allow Ulster's men and women to maintain a safe distance from the civil institutions of the kingdom. In short, Old Lights alarmed by the intrusion of a troubling world sought to strengthen community on old terms.[1]

A second group embraced their new world. Younger and coming from wealthier areas of the north, "New Lights" advocated innovative theological and political ideas that they believed better spoke to a society of increased opportunities. Although they drew from the common font of the Reformed tradition, New Lights championed a British notion of rights and offered innovative ideas of community based on the equality of all individuals. Ulster's New Lights, like their Old Light brethren, found the disabilities they suffered as dissenters odious; however, New Lights did not seek to create an established Presbyterian Church for Ulster. They contended that the very notion of an establishment, compelling individuals to act against the dictates of conscience, contradicted the liberating rhetoric of the Glorious Revolution. Finally, they drew their supporters from those who had profited most from the new economy.[2]

The two visions could not coexist within the church. Conflict erupted within Ulster Presbyterian society in 1719 when Old and New Lights began to struggle over the merits of subscription to the Westminster Confession of Faith as the basis of ministerial communion. While one party implored all to declare their assent to the classic formula of British Calvinist theology to check heresy and buoy the dissenting church in a confessional state, another denounced the measure as an infringement of individual rights. In 1722, Alexander McCracken, a minister from Lisburn, warned "we are in the sieve and Satan is helping to sift us out." The devil, it turned out, wore a familiar face; McCracken believed Ulster Presbyterian society was "like to be run down, not by persecutors, or open enemies or strangers, but by our bosom friends."[3] By 1726, the church split. Old Lights drove their New Light brethren and their followers out of the Synod of Ulster.

Out of the crucible of contention, however, Ulster's Presbyterians—Old and New Lights alike—tried to invent a sustaining vision for the group. Although the ministry and laity could not control the forces tearing the church in two, through the subscription debate Ulster's Presbyterians discovered a language with which to contest their second-class status in the kingdom. Taking a cue from Ireland's churchmen, who used a patriotic discourse to challenge a British Parliament's presumption to legislate for Ireland, Ulster's dissenters adapted New Light arguments to champion their rights as British Protestants. They would use a British rhetoric to come to terms with the group's place in the Irish confessional state and the challenges stemming from immersion in a larger British world. Ironically, only by splitting the church did adversaries discover common ground, some basis for uniting the group.

As LINEN remade the province's countryside, it also captured the imagination of Ulster's Presbyterians. In Benburb, County Tyrone, Reverend John Kennedy kept a diary of his daily comings and goings. While baptizing infants, ministering to the sick, comforting the dying, and composing sermons took up most of his time, he also traveled to the fairs in and around Benburb, and throughout Tyrone and Armagh. At these, he became a linen trader of sorts. In 1724, he visited more than ten fairs, traveling as far afield as Lisburn. On one occasion in Dungannon, he purchased "8 score cloths," some of which he sold a short time later at Stewartstown. Kennedy did not weave linen, but he organized his life much like the weavers who lived around him. He planted potatoes on his small holding, grew some flax, and purchased most of his goods at local markets, including coats, oatmeal, livestock, and a horse. Kennedy made a habit of attending fairs at places where he had official and unofficial church business. The breaks during presbytery and sub-synod meetings found him at local fairs haggling with weavers, jobbers, and merchants. Indeed, he even attended the market at Armagh when he visited the cathedral to pay his tithes.[4] In Ulster, linen became a prized article, one that bequeathed status and economic security, so much so that owners went to great, often unusual lengths to retrieve it if stolen. In 1706, for example, William Patterson and John McClellan, congregants from a parish in Donegal, traveled to Derry to consult Anne Newal, a fortune-teller, about the theft of their linen. Newel "did cast figures" and told the men that "a man with straight black hare and his daughter with a mole on her breast were those who did take a web out of the loom and dews out of the work-house."[5]

The rise of linen and the creation of structures and institutions necessary to market and ship the fabric also allowed many Ulster Presbyterians to move into a wider imaginative world, stretching beyond the confines of local community. Although the production of linen relegated women to spinning wheels, a year-round chore, wives and daughters accompanied fathers and husbands to sell their wares.[6] At fairs and markets, where linen was bought and sold, women rubbed shoulders with men from other walks of life, including merchants, soldiers, and administrators, Papists and churchmen. Women showed little reluctance passing their time with "stranger[s] from this place,"[7] men from outside the Presbyterian community. Sessions complained of women attending fairs at "unseasonable hours,"[8] and for "staying out all night . . . at the fair and drinking with idle persons." Some were accused of catching the "french pox" on fair day and of consorting with "wool comber[s] and strollers through the country" or "yearn merchants."[9] While these sites epitomized the growth of a larger world of trade, they also stood outside the controlling view of the session, the congregation's disciplinary body. In 1705, for instance, Agnes McMihan of Connor confessed to "uncleanliness" with a stranger, "but whether [it] is the sin of fornication or adultery she knoweth not." McMihan claimed that "as she was going to Antrim market she met a man coming from the town who was clothed in reid plush," who, she alleged, seduced her.[10] At these events, some young women also relied on Anglican curates and "Popish priests" to witness marriages. On one such occasion in 1704, Anaple Kissok went so far as to marry a British soldier "upon Shane castle fare day the back of a hedge with a priest."[11]

Frustrated by the biases of the session and realizing as their world expanded that they had alternatives, some women also looked to the kingdom's official courts for justice. In fornication cases, if the man claimed he was innocent, as William Ogilvie did in 1728, the woman could pressure him to change his testimony if "she had made oath of the same (viz.) that he was the father of her child before a magistrate."[12] In one especially bitter dispute in 1723, a Larne woman who accused another of theft faced the countercharge that she "had born two bastards before marriage." Neither woman would "subject [themselves] to the Determination of the Committee," instead having "evidence sworn before a Justice of the Peace and law."[13] Those who did appeal to the session to adjudicate disputes within a Presbyterian community found at times that their cases went unheard. When, for instance, Elizabeth Morton of Carmoney "obtained a warrant to apprehend" William Johnston, who then "went to the consistorial Court . . . and then satisfyed that Court," the session "could not safely proceed." Two years later, the case still unresolved, Morton again approached the elders and minister at Carmoney for justice. The session refused to open an inquiry, declaring that "we are not willingly to tamper in a matter which may occasion clashing with any of their courts."[14]

In a society with an elaborate civil and ecclesiastical justice system, congregants could shun the session for redress, appealing to the civil magistrate or Bishop's Court to clear themselves of charges of libel, adultery, and theft, issues over which the session claimed jurisdiction. Most congregants who appealed to ecclesiastical and civil courts apparently did so as an alternative to the stern discipline of the session. Some preferred these courts because, as one man explained in 1713, attending the session "would prejudice him in his worldly interest."[15] At courts run by Church of Ireland clerics and justices of the peace, men and women had an opportunity to purge themselves by oath without facing the witnesses the session called or declaring guilt before the entire congregation. If the session wished to pursue a matter, men and women could trump its authority by going "forthwith to swear before the magistrate."[16] James McIlroy of Templepatrick, for example, "refused to make public confession (for his sin of fornication) before the session and saith he can gett more easie off" from another court.[17]

Appealing to civil or ecclesiastical courts provided individuals with a venue to clear themselves or press their cases beyond the reach of Ulster Presbyterian society. Sessions were reluctant to question the rulings of civil or ecclesiastical courts. For example, just as women sought redress in civil courts to pressure men to admit illicit sexual relations, men understood that they could use the same courts in a preemptive manner to assert their innocence. In 1725, although John Houston "cleared himself in the Ecc. Court by compurgation," Margaret Gilbert still declared "he was guilty with her." The session, however, was reluctant to touch the case, nor would it "allow her to own the same in publick Least the law take hould fit by reason he hath purged himself as aforesd."[18] Marie Ferguson learned the same stern lesson in 1715 when she charged that William Rabbe fathered her child. Rabbe "denyes the same and is about to purge himself at the officiall Court," the session reported. Because of Rabbe's decision, the session had to "delay . . . any further appoyntment."[19] In another memorable instance, Richard Berry approached a justice of the peace over slander. Berry claimed a fellow congregant wronged him by accusing Berry of saying "he needed not [a mistress] for he had milked himself over the bed-stock by taking his yeard in his hand or between his fingers and thumb." In such an embarrassing situation for the congregation, the session beseeched Berry "to stand to the determination of the session and not to go to the law." The threat of "the law" not only ensured Berry would not meet with the full force of the session's disapproval, but also placed the session in a bind. Both courts claimed jurisdiction over moral offenses such as onanism.[20]

At times congregants, therefore, ignored the session. In 1715 one congregant from Down believed his minister "more like a Mountebank than a minister" who neither could "read the word of God, study, nor know it."[21] Three years later a parishioner from Lisburn claimed the session was made up of "kneaves, roogs and liars," and another said "he will be shot before he will stand publickly before the congregation."[22] Some Ulster Presbyterians refused to remain silent if they did not receive a fair hearing, arguing, as one man from Burt did in 1709, that the "session [was] unjust in their proceedings with him more than heathens and pagans and the conclave of Rome."[23] And some, such as Abraham Miller of Carmoney, declaimed the church's authority in public, leading his session to denounce him for "schismatical traffiquings."[24] Women at times also treated the session with disdain. Barbara Miller of Donegal "cohabited with a man for several years as her husband and acknowledge[d] she was not formally married." Yet, as the meeting found, she was "not . . . convinced of sin" nor would she "submitt to order."[25] In another case, after Mary Cran refused "to submitte to the session," the elders and minister declared her "a person of no good fame being ignorant, foolish, and wicked in her conversation" and ordered that other congregants avoid her.[26]

In one case, even a minister showed little reluctance to place the session in a compromising position. In 1710, Robert Darroch, a Presbyterian minister from the town of Monaghan, refused to allow the presbytery to visit his parish. With the members of the presbytery assembling in Monaghan, Darroch issued a statement "declin[ing] the above alledged appointment, all subjection or submission to it, . . . [and] do also protest against all and every intermeddling, inquiring, tryall, examination of persons cited, . . . visitation keeping in this Congregation of Monaghan or sentence passing in any thing relating to me or my people." As a justification for his behavior, he claimed what "he had done was according to his light and reason." Darroch, in fact, tried to preempt the interrogation of his congregants, who accused him of "brawling, quarrelling, and drunkenness in public." In particular, members of the congregation recounted how Darroch challenged one man to a duel, attacked another with a pitchfork, and was in the habit of "vomitting from drink." To add further insult to the stunned elders and ministers of the presbytery, Darroch ordered the doors of the meetinghouse "fast locked," effectively putting an end to the visitation.[27]

To retain his charge, Darroch presented his protest to the civil authorities, during which he "read a declaration of his faith with remonstrance and reasons," renouncing the presbytery's claim on him and his people. "I declared myself," he thundered to the presbytery, "no member with you . . . nor under you or the synod of Monaghan's jurisdiction in any respect," adding, "And do hereby protest against you exercizing any Jurisdiction over me; or intermeddling with me without my own consent." In effect, Darroch called into question the legitimacy of dissenting church judicatories holding their people accountable for offenses under the purview of civil authorities. By seeking the protection of a civil court in a confessional state, Darroch had a right, as he put it, to "resolve upon suffering in so far as our Gracious Queen and other inferior Magistrates shall not see fitt . . . to Grant me the benefit of that Clemency and Connivance extended to other Dissenters," as well as "their protection against any party of Dissenters extending their power and jurisdiction."

Churchmen saw that Darroch's refusal to acquiesce to the church's authority revealed weaknesses in the Presbyterian system. They, therefore, encouraged Darroch. Alexander Montgomery, a churchman from the area, wrote officials in Dublin about the case, arguing that the presbytery of Monaghan proceeded against Darroch with "so great [a] deal of formality and solemnity as much as if they had a thousand Acts of Parliament to support them." Before "one thousand spectators," Montgomery asked the assembled ministers and elders "by what authority" did they presume to try Darroch. The members of the presbytery responded that "they had none but her Majesty's Connivinces," which permitted "the exercise of their Religion, reached to allow them some little Rules, and power over such of their own persuasion as voluntarily submitted." Such trials, they suggested, "preserv[ed] order amongst them." Montgomery had little appreciation for such arguments, especially in the case of a dissenter seeking the protection of the church as by law established. "It would never be hoped by them," he declared, that the queen "could tolerate in them such impudent bare faced acting's against Law."[28]

Despite the churchman's protests, the trial went on. Congregants from Monaghan brought witnesses who demonstrated the shakiness of Darroch's newfound principles. One alleged that Darroch had advocated "getting pardon for Shane Bannock the Tory." Darroch, the witness charged, argued that the Jacobite rapparie "would do the country service." His identification with the Revolution Settlement tarnished, Darroch faced stiffer charges for his views of the established church. A second witness claimed that Darroch considered the clergy of the Church of Ireland "to be idle, only reading a few prayers and two penny sermons." Yet another congregant heard Darroch claim that "the Presbyterians were the only Loyal subjects to the Queen." Beaten at his own game, Robert Darroch could not find refuge with the authorities. In 1712, he remained quiet as the synod divested him of his charge.

Of course, ignoring the session, as Darroch had, was nothing new. As early as 1694, a Letterkenny man, Joseph Semple, accused his minister of "causing poor people to stand publickly for scandale . . . [and] caused some of meaner capacity in the world to give publick satticefaction, while others of greater substance, he took pryvate satticefaction of."[29] Two years later, Mary Frisall of Donegal approached the civil court to censure Robert Allen, a married man, for committing adultery with her. She chose this route because the session was reluctant to press the matter against Allen.[30] But after the turn of the century, such cases came at a crucial time for the church, bringing to the surface tensions that underscored the peculiar plight of dissenters in a confessional state. The church's presumption to stand outside the purview of established civil and ecclesiastical structures of the kingdom rested on its ability to muster support from all within the Ulster Presbyterian community. Moreover, at the end of the day, neither session, presbytery, nor synod had the power—with the exception of excommunication—to restrain congregants from placing one set of courts over another. Each episode in which church judicatories used heavy-handed tactics to restrain their congregants played into the hands of churchmen eager to enforce more rigorously laws disabling dissenters. Indeed, the allure of conformity, encouraged by appeals to alternative jurisdictions, had a greater effect on northern Presbyterianism than did the disabilities of the Test Act.[31]

ALTHOUGH in all likelihood the number of men and women ignoring the session did not increase in the years they encountered a wider world, the clergy believed otherwise. While ministers such as John Kennedy greeted the transformation of Ulster's economy with enthusiasm, they also decried the byproducts of change and their consequences for the church. The session at Carmoney lamented "the distrest state of the Ch: of God as also the sad circumstances of this Congregation," which amounted to "a visible decay among the Godly."[32] "The land is polluted," ran one jeremiad, "Rioting and drunkenness, chambering and wantonness, strife and envying . . . are too common with us." The cry of declension cataloged a "Decay of Religion" in a "degenerate" and "licentious" age, a general decline likely to call down the wrath of an angry God.[33] By the time of the Darroch case, however, ministers chastised congregants for refusing to show due respect for the officials and institutions of the church. As early as 1709, the Monaghan presbytery complained of "so much trouble with congregational affairs."[34]

Such challenges to church judicatories had consequences for the political fortunes of dissenters in the confessional state. These misdeeds, church officials believed, affected not only the integrity of the Presbyterian system, but its stand against episcopacy. The presbytery of Strabane argued that some men and women failed to show "obed[ience] to the Discipline of the church" and were "very negligent in attending sessions and days annointed for prayers."[35] To combat the "remarkable decay of practical godliness," the Sub-Synod of Derry similarly pointed to the importance of church institutions, warning the people to "guard against having any fellowship with popish priests in their marriages . . . and against such principles and practices as have a tendency to break down our hedge of government." Ministers reminded their congregants that "you have a special call, to obey them that have the rule over you" and that "the Synod, Presbyteries, and church sessions, are Judicatories of Jesus Christ." To the evident chagrin of ministers and elders, the laity and even some clergymen had realized they had choices, which they were prepared to exercise.[36]

To negotiate a changing world, as well as the perceived backsliding, some harkened back to the period of consolidation, and from it, invented a vision for the group. Drawing from a tradition of Scottish Calvinism rooted in an ambivalent Reformed tradition, some Presbyterians tended to emphasize the tenets of predestination and submission to authority. From this perspective, individuals played a negligible role in securing salvation; only God's grace saved. Predestinarian churchmen also held to a traditional notion of church government, seeking to maintain the integrity of the ecclesiastical body by steering the church along an established course.[37] "Our Lord," wrote one Ulster minister in 1689, "will have his people under bands, they must not walke at randome as Libertines without any thing to bound them but their own will, they must be under his yoke [and] give obedience to all his commands." The church represented the mortar holding individuals together: "This love that is betwixt Christ and his people flows from them being ingrafted into him and . . . he is the head of believers and believers the members that are united by a holy faith unto this head." By the 1720s many still had the same faith in unity. Individuals cut off from community lost all sense of direction because, as one cleric claimed in 1721, "divine truth . . . [and] divine mystery cannot be fully expressed nor conceived by mortals."[38]

A large number of Ulster dissenters increasingly came to conceive subscription to the Westminster Confession of Faith as the cornerstone of Presbyterian community in Ulster. Although at first few attached much importance to the 1698 overture calling for ministerial subscription, members of the synod who held predestinarian views began insisting that presbyteries enforce the measure. In 1705, the synod mandated written subscription to the Confession before candidates to the ministry would be licensed as a response to the case of a Dublin dissenting minister, Thomas Emlyn, brought up on charges of espousing antitrinitarian doctrines. In the following years, similar controversies over rising latitudinarian—or heterodox—opinion, erupted throughout the three kingdoms. In 1717, the Church of Scotland initiated a three-year inquiry into the teachings of a professor of divinity at Glasgow, John Simson, accusing him of espousing Arminian doctrines. A Glasgow instructor elevating reason over saving grace proved especially troubling to the Synod of Ulster, whose candidates for the ministry trained in Scotland. No sooner had the Simson trial ended than the Bangorian Controversy in the Church of England and the Salter's Hall debate among English dissenters broke out. In the former, Bishop Benjamin Hoadly of Bangor called the confessional state into question, arguing that individual conscience, not ecclesiastical prerogatives, should determine matters of faith. In the latter, dissenters tied to no ecclesiastical structure debated the merits of subscribing a creed to ferret out those who contested the doctrine of the trinity. The pro-subscribers lost.[39]

The Westminster Confession of Faith, some came to believe, provided a formula to avert these problems. As the only dissenting institution of its kind in the British Isles, the Synod of Ulster was susceptible to both issues raised by the English controversies. If appeals to individual conscience could imperil the established church, they could also undermine the highly institutionalized ecclesiastical structure of Ulster Presbyterians. On the other hand, the Salter's Hall controversy made clear the need to strengthen church judicatories as a means to keep heresy in check. No formula, many northern dissenters contended, could better serve as a guard against heterodoxy than the Confession. "This is so full, and plain a Declaration of the Divinity of our Lord," one minister declared, "that no Arian, Socinian, or Clarkist, can Subscribe to it."[40]

Ministerial subscription also promised to ease the disabilities the group suffered. After failing to secure the repeal of the Test Act or to gain toleration during the reign of Queen Anne, members of the synod hoped for better treatment from King George I. With his accession to the British throne, many Ulster dissenters believed that universal subscription to the Westminster Confession of Faith would demonstrate the doctrinal orthodoxy of their church, strengthening their case for official toleration. At the General Synod of Ulster of 1716, "It was agreed by us all unanimously as a preliminary to all ensuing debates . . . that all the propositions contained in the above formula are divine truths." The synod proposed "the Confession of Faith as the terms of a toleration," adding that "the tolerating of us upon our subscription to it would give the public sanction of authority to our standing by and preaching up all our known principles contained in the Confession of Faith."[41]

This sentiment stemmed from a belief that Presbyterianism as practiced by Ulster nonconformists represented the true expression of a Christian church. Subscribers professed to "believe the Government of the Presbyterian Church in Ireland, to be agreeable to the word of God."[42] Many argued that northern dissenters, by virtue of their numerical superiority in Ulster and the divine ordination of their church, deserved to be established in the region. Although they decried the discrimination they faced from churchmen, they did not scruple the notion of an Ascendancy premised on some type of union of church and state, only its present manifestation in Ireland. "The Yoke of Common Prayer, of Kneeling, of the Sign of the Cross, of the Surplice," Alexander McCracken of Lisburn declared, "is the Devil's Yoke and they that bear it are in the way to Hell."[43] Indeed, McCracken argued that Ulster's dissenters should establish "a scheme of government for ourselves in this country," based on the "Synod by delegation." McCracken, a champion of subscription, claimed that legislation that handicapped individuals for their allegiance to a true church could force dissenters "to maintain the present establishment of England, both in Church and in State, as they are established by law . . . and fully conform to the Church of England." This, he added, northern nonconformists "resolve not to do."[44] As members of a divinely ordained church, Presbyterians had an obligation not only to resist the Ascendancy but also to obey the institutions and practices of the church, including the Confession, which proponents judged inspired by the "holy Spirit."[45]

The push for subscription, therefore, emerged from a distinct vision of the northern Presbyterian Church in Irish society. As Belfast minister Robert McBride explained, only with subscription could "Peace and Order . . . be secur'd" amid the changes brought about by immersion in a wider world of trade and ideas. Similarly, members of the Sub-Synod of Derry proclaimed the Confession the best means for "preserving the purity and Unity of the church." The concepts were not unrelated. As their experience as nonconformists who had created an elaborate ecclesiastical and social system had taught them, peace, order, purity, and unity worked in conjunction with one another. Without one, the others faltered. Only without "breaches," the sub-synod argued, could the "hands of protestants be strengthen'd," ensuring that individuals "wou'd not be as clouds carried about with the wind." While orthodoxy preserved the group's integrity, unanimity closed the door to heresy. As the "Truth of God," the Confession captured this dynamic for a divinely ordained church.[46]

ALL, however, did not agree with this interpretation. A group of ministers—"New Lights," as they came to be known—challenged the rationale behind subscription, arguing that manmade creeds represented an infringement on religious liberty and the God-given prerogative of Protestants to determine their own minds or, as it was called, the right to private judgment.[47] After the revolution, Ulster Presbyterians encountered new secular ideas that complemented certain aspects of the Reformed tradition. All Reformed Protestants championed the unmediated relationship between God and individual. By the early eighteenth century, some began to fuse such Reformation concepts as scriptural authority and the sanctity of conscience with natural rights theory and latitudinarian ideas to challenge the constraints of predestinarian interpretations of Calvinist doctrine. Many northern ministers encountered ideas such as these in Scotland. Several Ulster clergymen, most notably Francis Hutcheson, studied under the innovative Gershom Carmichael, Glasgow's first professor of moral philosophy. Carmichael, credited with the introduction of the natural law tradition into his subject, was the first instructor to use Locke's *Two Treatises* in any British university, and he often lectured on the works of Whig political theorists. Here many also studied under the controversial divinity professor John Simson.[48]

New Lights introduced such ideas to the church in Ulster. In 1705 John Abernethy and James Kirkpatrick founded the Belfast Society. Kirkpatrick cited the "improvement of Christian Knowledge" as the reason for the organization's existence. But he added that many "have Wrote and Publish'd Elaborate Discourses upon, the Rights of Conscience, the Rights of Private Judgement, Christian Liberty," as well as "the Essential Principles of Protestantism, and the Scriptural terms of Christian Concord and Unity."[49] Ulster's New Lights were not strangers to the new currents of thought so many feared. They maintained, according to a contemporary, "a free and friendly correspondence with some of the schismatics on the other side of the water." Both Abernethy and Kirkpatrick studied in Scotland with Simson. Moreover, one of their allies, Samuel Haliday, attended the debate at Salter's Hall.[50]

In 1719, John Abernethy set off a firestorm within the synod with his publication of a pamphlet citing his reasons for refusing to subscribe to the Westminster Confession of Faith. "Let every man," Abernethy declared, "enjoy the Freedom of following the Light of his Conscience," a privilege consistent with "the General design and Terms of Christian Revelation."[51] He argued that "*God is to be obeyed rather than Man*," adding that "the Right of private judgement [is] *sacred* and *inviolable* . . . [and] no Encroachment must be made upon it." No church government had the power to circumvent conscience which, according to Abernethy, "is not Accountable to, nor can be restrain'd in so judging, by any Power on Earth." The decisions of church authorities could only "bind the Conscience as far as men are Convinc'd, and no farther."[52] Like Hoadly, he suggested that "Enlighten'd Judgement" always trumped church prerogatives.[53]

New Lights argued that they, not their Old Light brethren, represented the truest heirs of the reformed enterprise. "By the Laws of Christ," Samuel Haliday declared, "Christians are obliged *to search* the *Scriptures* . . . and to judge for themselves concerning the Sense of the divine Oracles." Nowhere in the Bible did he find a mention of subscription. "If it had been in the Mind of God," he argued, "that with Respect to religious Actions, Christians should submit their Conscience to any Human Authority, He would have conveyed that Authority in the clearest, in the most express and strongest Terms." If Christ granted no power, it did not exist. Haliday asserted, "I do not find, that the Reverend Synod in *Ulster*, nor, indeed, that any Assembly, Synod, or Council whosoever, have received Authority for Christ, to make new Laws binding his Subjects, which he never made."[54] Subscription, not the refusal to subscribe, was an unprecedented departure from the Reformed tradition. "We have got a NEW FUNDAMENTAL into our Religion," James Kirkpatrick argued, "which was no Fundamental for fifteen Hundred Years and more after the Christian Faith was fully Revealed and Recorded in the Sacred Writings." The Confession, Kirkpatrick continued, "was never found out amongst us in the North of *Ireland* until the Year 1705, nor in *Scotland* before the Year 1690, or thereabouts, nor in any other Church in the World that I know of either before or since."[55]

The New Light critique of church government also drew its strength from emerging secular discourses challenging the prerogatives of the state. Invoking such concepts as the consent of the governed and the inviolability of individual rights, nonsubscribers asserted that because "Freedom is the Birth-right of Mankind," each person "has a Right to judge for himself in matters of Religion." Enforced subscription, therefore, was "contrary to the essential Rights of natural Equity, Eversive of Christian Discipline, a Snare of Conscience, [and] destructive of the Liberties of Christians."[56] New Lights also asserted that the practice of excluding from church privileges those who objected to the Confession violated "the Rights, which Jesus Christ has expressly granted to his Subjects," most notably conviction of private judgment. " 'Tis the essential and unalienable Right of every Man and Christian," proclaimed Haliday, "to profess and act agreeably to the Conviction of his own Conscience . . . Nay it is every Man's indispensable Duty to make use of this Right."[57]

Like Scottish "patriots" who emulated a metropolitan patriotic language to make sense of their society in the wake of the Union of 1707, and their Irish counterparts, such as William Molyneux and Jonathan Swift, who fashioned a rights-based discourse to challenge an English Parliament's presumption to legislate for Ireland, Ulster Presbyterians like Abernethy used similar rhetoric to contest subscription.[58] But the New Light patriotic discourse had a distinct ring. Nonsubscribers saw no contradiction in the belief that enforced subscription was "contrary to the Rights which the King of the Christian Church has granted to private Christians."[59] Nor were they resorting to hyperbole when they intoned that church prerogatives often "Disenfranchise[d] the *Free-Born* Subjects of Christ."[60]

New Lights offered an alternative vision of community. "If every one," Abernethy asked, "may do what is good in his own eyes, how shal order be preserv'd in the World or in the Church?" In answer, he argued that conscience could also serve as the foundation for community: "The same principle of Conscience *equally* obliges us to dutys wherein No Humane power do's Interpose, as in the relation of Equals and to acts of Charity." For charity, "in some Cases might direct them to wave their Privilege, and Comply with their weak Brethren for avoiding Offence."[61] As Kirkpatrick argued, "it is the Duty of Christians to *forbear one another in Love.*"[62] New Lights did not advocate a breach within the church, but they did argue that the individual's conscience trumped the prerogatives of church society. "Let none be shock'd in their Charity towards others, or in hopes of their own acceptance on that account," Abernethy declared. "No Christians," he argued, could "carry their Zeal for agreement so far, as to break in upon the Essential Condition of our Title to God's Favour, which is acting sincerely according to the Inward Conviction of our Minds."[63] By this reasoning, enforced subscription was more liable to occasion schism. "Those Tests," Haliday contended, "might become the Fatal Engines of tearing into Pieces the mystical Body of our Redeemer."[64]

Moderates sought to reconcile the factions. Old Light and New Light ministers were refusing, as one minister explained, to "keep up the former harmony . . . in preaching and communion at the Lord's Supper."[65] In 1720, the synod passed a series of "Pacifick Acts," which conceded that "if any person call'd upon to subscribe shall scruple any phrase or phrases in the Confession, he shall have leave to use his own expressions," provided the presbytery "judge such a person sound in the faith." In this spirit, a few ministers published pamphlets calling for moderation, imploring partisans from both camps to maintain communion with one another despite differences.[66] John Elder from Aghadowey, for example, made a plea for "maintaining Christian Liberty, and at the same time, exercising Moderation." Although Elder considered himself a "moderate subscriber," he chastised hard-line Old Lights—"high fliers," as he called them—for attempting to split the church. "The Testimony of my Conscience," Elder wrote, urged "maintain[ing] Religious Communion with all my Reverend Fathers and Brethren in the Ministry."[67]

But these attempts failed. A full-blown crisis erupted in 1721 over the selection of a minister for one of Belfast's two congregations. The candidate, Samuel Haliday, had come under suspicion for holding heterodox views when a fellow minister claimed Haliday had rejected a trinitarian theology and "joyn'd the Arian party." A number of Ulster's ministers protested Haliday's installation, objecting to his association with English radicals. Alexander McCracken, for example, believed that with Haliday's arrival "riseth a jealousy amongst the people that there are some amongst us that are unsound and are falling in with the non-subscribers in England and our confession is now to be laid aside," and with the admission of such ministers "our Confession is struck at in doctrine, worship, discipline, and government." The synod cleared Haliday of the charges of heresy. Subscription proved to be another matter.[68] Before the General Synod of 1721 the majority of ministers asked Haliday to subscribe to the Confession of Faith. Haliday refused, arguing that he did not "*disbelieve any of the important Articles of the Christian Doctrine contained in that Book,*" but because "my Scruples, are concerning THE LAWFULLNESS OF SUBMITTING TO HUMAN TESTS OF DIVINE TRUTHS."[69]

With Haliday's refusal, Old Lights stepped up their rhetorical attacks. Matthew Clerk, who established his reputation as a champion for subscription in 1723 with his "Answer" to *A Letter from the Belfast Society,* argued that the logic of nonsubscription undermined church institutions and, therefore, the immutability of truth. "It cannot be supposed," he believed, "that God hath given Authority to any of Mankind, to make his private Judgement his rule in any Case." Instead, God invested such institutions as synod and presbytery to "take care that true Religion be kept up, and supported, and commanded People to obey them." According to Clerk, nonsubscribers could not faithfully adhere to the Scriptures because their beliefs tended toward error and spurious notions of cultural and religious relativism. A person's "Essential Unalienable Right of Judging for himself," for instance, did not lead the individual to the truth: "It is a Prop will bear all Religions and Opinions equally; there being as many *Heathans* in the World as *Mahometans,* as many *Mahometans* as *Christians,* as many *Papists* as *Protestants,* with a great many *Jews* . . . and all of them Judging themselves in the Right."[70]

Some Old Lights argued that the New Light represented nothing less than an open door to heresy. "There is a general laxness of principles," a Scottish minister complained, "among too many of the new intrants to the ministry, even in the north of Ireland."[71] New Light theology, with its emphasis on the role of the individual in effecting salvation, proved troubling to a church that had not encountered such ideas. When a young Francis Hutcheson, for example, was installed in an Ulster parish, one congregant complained how Hutcheson "fashed a' the congregation with his idle cackle, for he has been bab- bling' this 'our about a good and benevolent God and that the souls of the heathan themselves will gang tae heaven if the follow the licht o' their aen consciences." He added, "Not a word does the daft boy ken, nor say about the gude auld comfortable doctrines of election, reprobation, original sin, and faith."[72] A minister similarly alleged "that Mr. Kirkpatrick uses to kneel in time of public prayer in the Church," only one of a number of "novelties" that seemed to "be on the growing hand, and spreading among others."[73] Bridling at any innovation, some accused nonsubscribers of preaching messages dis- rupting Britain's churches, particularly "Arian and Arminian doc- trines . . . [that] have got footing in England and their books are scat- tered among us." Fearing the growth of latitudinarian tendencies in the church, especially those questioning the integrity of the Trinity, one minister wrote, "How far the nonsubscribers are here in concert with these of their minds abroad . . . whether *Arians, Socinians, Clarkists, Freethinkers, Enthusiasts, Personal Perswasionists, and Libertines,* is best known to themselves." Only the Confession could thwart the advance of such worldly individuals.[74]

Finally, Old Lights suggested that the New Lights, by premising their logic on the prerogative of the individual, imperiled the "rights of societies."[75] Old Lights harkened back to the past, to the era of consolidation, to ask, "Have particular *Persons* a Right to Defeat the *Decisions,* that are *Profitable* and *Expedient* to the *Community* to whom they belong, by their *private Judgement?*"[76] Charles Mastertown con- tended that through the Scriptures, "Pastors of every Reformed Church, have a good Warrant for their Uniting in some Publick Col- lection of Gospel Truths, and for making the due Profession of Adher- ence to a competent Number of these Truths." After men and women entered into such a "Solemn Agreement . . . in Opposition to Danger- ous Errors," any violation "needs affect the Publick Communion of such a Church to great Disadvantage."[77] In such an instance, as Robert

McBride argued, "He is not worthy of being continued a member of an associated body who declines duty merely because it is injoined him by the Society, with whom he desires to be incorporated."[78]

Indeed, by Old Light reckoning, the New Light agenda appeared to be a manifestation of larger changes gripping Ulster Presbyterian society. In 1724, the Sub-Synod of Derry issued a "seasonable warning" to its people, enjoining "every minr: within our bounds to read it publickly in his congregation the first Lords day after it comes in hand." The document observed that "the present state of religion" was defined by a "remarkable decay of practical godliness the abounding of vice, profaneness and Immorality: as also errors destructive of real religion, spread and maintain'd, the sacred oracles of God wrested, the necessary means of grace too much despised, and some even denying the very Lord that brought 'em." The ministers and elders of the sub-synod argued that "ought we not then to bewail it, that in our day, so many are ready to be toss'd to and fro with every wind of doctrine." The members exhorted their people to pay due respect to the church's judicatories, arguing that the sessions in particular were found "well express'd in our Westminster Confession of faith," and that "they who lessen the Authority of these Judicatories, and weaken our hands in discipline open a door to error and Immorality."[79]

To thwart the attempts of those "endeavoring to unsettle Christians as to articles of their faith,"[80] Old Lights began insisting that the laity also declare their assent to the Confession. In Charles Mastertown's Connor parish, for example, before gaining admittance to the Lord's table, younger communicants had to "sollemnly profess our hearty desyre to believe in God the Father, the Son and the Holy Ghost according to the severrall articles of the Christian Faith as they are . . . summed up in our Confession of faith and shorter and longer Catechisms."[81] Similarly, some required that parents "profess the Westminster Confession, as the Confession of their Faith" before baptizing their children, even though, as Abernethy alleged, " 'Tis certain the much greater part of them can't do it with Understanding."[82] Finally, one-hundred-fifty congregants of Alexander McCracken's parish affixed their signatures to a declaration lambasting "the many unhappy mischiefs that have followed upon some Ministers among us refusing to subscribe the Westminster Confession of Faith." The Lisburn people declared themselves "fully satisfied with the great truth of the severall doctrines therein contained," resolving "to adhere to and maintaine it in opposition to all heresy's unsound doctrines that are eversive of it, and those that Promote them and their abettors."[83]

As a minister observed, "the Diversity of Sentiments among Ministers had taken Air among the People."[84] Congregants refused to support ministers or to adhere to the rules of presbyteries not of "their persuasion."[85] Most lay people backed the Old Light cause. Abernethy complained that "it is a matter of great Trouble to us to hear, that some Congregations in the North (or at least some part of them) . . . give great Uneasiness and Disturbance to their worthy Pastors." He found that "The generality of the Laity concur in laying the Blame of their Dissentions upon the Ministers; they seem to think that their [the Minister's] Disagreement among themselves, justifies the utmost License the People take in despising, reflecting upon, nay and deserting their Ministers."[86] In 1721, a Scottish minister reported that "the people of Belfast are withdrawing from him [Haliday], and building another Meeting-house."[87] By 1722, the synod had received eighteen petitions urging all ministers to subscribe. Two years later, the people of Connor locked their meetinghouse door to a nonsubscribing preacher.[88] Although Abernethy admitted that ministers of his persuasion were being "deserted by their People," he still contended that "when the Prejudices of the People are against Principles both True and Important, they ought not to [be] silently indulged, but rather oppos'd in the openest manner." He conceded, however, that "In the present Case the Prejudice seems to be against the Fallibility of Human Composures, and the necessity of Examining all Decisions of Men by the Scriptures."[89]

Many, however, found the New Light message appealing. At the parish of Urney, several people would not "Subject 'emselves to the Ministry of the Rev. William Holmes," a hard-line subscriber, instead attending a nearby congregation headed by a nonsubscriber. Congregants from the parish of Creggan asked for a demission from the Old Light presbytery of Armagh in favor of the presbytery of Killyleagh, home to a number of nonsubscribing ministers. A minister from Downpatrick, whose congregants before 1726 had "stuck pretty close to him," deserted him after that point for a nonsubscribing presbytery. Even McCracken's Lisburn congregants, despite issuing a scathing attack on the New Light, also divided over the issue of subscription.[90] Abernethy correctly pointed out that both Old and New Lights were having problems. The laity, he observed, were "reproaching or deserting Ministers, meerly on the score of Subscribing or nonSubscribing."[91] In short, nearly all Ulster congregations, no matter their ideological bent, experienced "unhappy divisions" during the 1720s.[92]

The divisions within the church over subscription approximated those experienced by congregations with the advance of the linen trade and the transformation of the economy. James Kirkpatrick suggested that, as a rule, rural folk tended to support subscription. "Nothing is more Common amongst poor Country-People, and amongst all who are Ignorant of the State of the Controversy," he argued, "than to vent their Jealousies against the *nonSubscribers*, and to say plainly, that *there must be something at the bottom of their nonSubscribing more than what has yet come to light*."[93] In 1727, the nonsubscriber Michael Bruce of Hollywood "made all his people forsake him; so that now he hath about ten or twelve familys hearing him." With little income, Bruce traveled to Belfast every two weeks to lecture "for which he hath twenty pound settled on him."[94] Conversely, a Scot observer noted that "being in toun, and in a collegiat life" Kirkpatrick and Haliday did not experience many desertions but had "the best congregations of any of them." He also added that they drew their support from the "gentry and rich people," who in general were "favourable to their principles." As Charles Mastertown claimed, the nonsubscribers controlled the "chief men" of Ulster.[95]

New Light principles, in fact, appealed to large numbers of urban Ulster Presbyterians. Charles Mastertown reported in 1723 that two of three congregations in Belfast found the Old Light message "odious." Indeed, men such as Kirkpatrick enjoyed a substantial following in the port town. During one summer evening in 1723, Kirkpatrick spoke before "a vast audience in this town." Implying that Old Lights were planning to evict nonsubscribers from the church, he kept the crowd enthralled "with little interruption for nine or ten hours."[96]

Kirkpatrick even had enough pull with some in Belfast's building trades to stop the construction of a new meetinghouse for Old Lights in the town. "Mr. Kirkpatrick," a contemporary wrote, "put the people of Belfast, who were building the third Meeting-house for Mr. Mastertown, to a vast deal of trouble." After Mastertown and the elders had agreed on the price for materials, Kirkpatrick "got the ouner to stop all, and refuse to let them have them."[97]

Yet if congregants did not desert their pastors, even in more marginal areas, New Light ideas had a great effect within congregations. In Charles Mastertown's parish in Connor, younger congregants echoed New Light scruples over the Confession of Faith, objecting to "publick censures because . . . if it were not allowed by Scriptures it wod not be put in practice." Thomas Buys, a parishioner from the small west Ulster town of Aghadowey, even questioned the divinity of Jesus on the same grounds, "saying it was not Christ's prerogative to forgive sins, adding that if it was his prerogative why did he not say it." The issue of conscience also stymied ministers. Isabel Fulton, for example, refused to heed a decree of the elders and ministers of the Killyleagh presbytery demanding she not divulge the father of her child because "she could not do [so] with a good conscience." And, Daniel Kinley of Lisburn refused to stand before McCracken's session, claiming "he could no do anything that was not agreeable to his conscience."[98]

New Light ideas also had a greater hold on the imagination of the ministry than the number of ministers subscribing would suggest. On a visit to the north, Francis Hutcheson noticed "a perfect Hoadly mania among our younger ministers."[99] Similarly, William Livingston, an Old Light minister, wrote a colleague in Scotland in 1720 that there were "only about 14 or 15 subscribers of the younger brethren who by their behavior on all occasions gave too much reason to suspect them at bottom to be nonsubscribers." Livingston found at the moment of truth, however, "their courage failed them and they voted with the majority."[100] As Charles Mastertown conceded, "the number of those in the Synod who are for a strict adherence to our confession as a term of communion seems to be but small," adding that "a vast number are so carried off that they could make greater concessions to the nonsubscribers than some of us with peace yield unto."[101]

The church had become, by one contemporary's estimation, a "wasp's nest."[102] The synod in 1725 bowed to the inevitable by agreeing to a separation, segregating New Lights and some of the moderates such as Elder in the presbytery of Antrim, and a year later excluded the presbytery of Antrim altogether from ecclesiastical communion. Nonsubscribers controlled two presbyteries within Ulster, and subscribers held the synod. The church had divided along fault lines that defined two distinct visions of the group. In a society transformed by the growth of the British state, the influence of British ideas, and immersion in a British Atlantic trading world, no single notion of identity, particularly one rooted in the era of Ulster Presbyterian consolidation, offered a panacea for negotiating change. The subscription controversy illustrated, as Abernethy surmised, that "Contending Parties" harbored "differences in the View of the World."[103]

ALTHOUGH Old Lights captured the synod, it appeared that Ulster's Presbyterians would come to terms with their position in Irish society along New Light lines. Ultimately, the New Light critique of the place of dissenters in the Irish confessional state proved more attuned to the reigning political discourses within Britain than an Old Light vision premised on the divinely ordained church. Nonsubscribers believed the best means to improve their position as dissenters in a confessional state lay not in lionizing the structure or truth of their church but in clamoring for rights as British Protestants. They, therefore, adapted the rhetoric they used to contest church mandates to challenge government prerogatives. "Every Man," Abernethy believed, "has a right to judge for himself in Matters of Religion, and that this right ought not to be restrain'd by Acts of Parliament, by Temporal Rewards and Punishments, . . . annexing worldly Emoluments to some Opinions and usages, and a deprivation of Civil Privileges to others."[104]

As British Protestants, Ulster's dissenters, regardless of the supposed orthodoxy of their church, were entitled to rights. "Magistrates," declared John Abernethy, "have no more Authority than any of the rest of Mankind . . . in the Matter of Conscience." Just as the church could not impel subscription, authorities could not coerce dissenters through laws. Thus, Haliday argued, "I cannot obey those Laws, out of Conscience without betraying true Liberty of Conscience," adding "that to require of me an absolute blind Obedience to such Commandments is to destroy Liberty of Conscience, and Reason also."[105] Moreover, even if individuals were so inclined, they did not possess the right to abrogate conscience. Another clergyman argued that "nothing can be more evident that this liberty is one of the most essential unalienable rights of human nature, which no man, nor body of men have authority to deprive us of, . . . nor are we our selves at liberty to make a surrender of it."[106]

The New Light approach to the Irish confessional state relied on an understanding that although rights rested in the individual, in Ulster they drew their strength from the persecution of the community. Just as God gave individuals a conscience that no one could dominate, they believed, He also endowed societies with a right to consent to their rulers. Embracing this logic, Abernethy had argued that "As the *Consent of the People* is the only *Just Foundation* of Government; the Right of the Person Governing must be deriv'd from the same Spring," a liberty he claimed was "the Undoubted Right of the People."[107] While nonsubscribers contended that the synod's push for subscription imperiled individual conscience, they argued that because "the Interests of the Church and State are inseparably interwoven," the government ensured that "*Dissenters* should be oppress'd and depriv'd of the *Common Rights* of Subjects."[108] In this way, New Lights advocated a message that could appeal to both subscribers and nonsubscribers.

Armed with this reasoning, Ulster's nonconformists launched an attack on the foundations on which their provincial status rested, the privileged position of the Ascendancy. Like churchmen who viewed Scotland's constitutional settlement with envy, New Lights continued to compare the position of Ulster Presbyterian society to the status of nonconformists in Britain. "The Northern Dissenters," claimed a government official, "were not at all satisfied with such a toleration as the Dissenters in England enjoy, but insisted on and expected the same allowance of the exercize of their religion and ministry as those of the Episcopal communion enjoy in North Britain."[109] In 1730, the synod asked all ministers "to offer the best expedients they can think of for supporting and strengthening our common interest without the least regard to parties or any unhappy debates that have been among us." This invitation extended to the presbytery of Antrim, which furnished funds—and talent—for a coordinated campaign to repeal the Test Act.[110] A year later, northern dissenters sent a delegate to London to initiate a campaign that was to last two years. In this effort, Ulster's Presbyterians spoke with one voice. "It is said," Jonathan Swift maintained, "that £30,000 have been returned from England, and £20,000 raised here from servants, labourers, farmers, squires, whigs, etc. to promote the good work," a sum that he believed was "sufficient among us to abolish Christianity itself."[111]

To be sure, Presbyterians still employed arguments focusing on just rewards for service rendered. But increasingly, ministers of a New Light persuasion on behalf of the synod petitioned the king and Parliaments of Great Britain and Ireland, and lobbied the lord lieutenant by relying on patriotic discourse. New Lights sought to overturn the Test Act—a "Brand of Infamy," as Abernethy called it—because it "oppress'd and depriv'd" Ulster's men and women of "the full Possession of their Civil Rights in common with their fellow Subjects."[112] Abernethy led the effort to overturn the Test Act by publishing a series of pamphlets. In his appeal, he stressed the issues of individual conscience and consent by claiming that the Test Act represented "a manifest infringement on Natural Rights and Liberty."[113] But in his *Nature and Consequences of the Sacramental Test*, Abernethy also contended that no government possessed the prerogative to abridge the "people's" rights "by Acts of Parliament, by Temporal Rewards and Punishments, and in Matters purely of Religion and Conscience," arguing that the group labored under "Grievances and Incapacities which are inconsistent with the *common Rights of Subjects*."[114] Inevitably, Ulster dissenters called the basis of the Irish confessional state into question. As Samuel Haliday suggested, Ulster Scots would never rest easy as long as "the Established Church can be said to *impose* her *Liturgy* and *Ceremonies* . . . [and] the Civil Magistrate will arm the Imposers with a coercive Power."[115]

To the Ascendancy mind, such arguments did not bode well for the established church; indeed, forthright appeals such as these for dismantling the Test Act ipso facto bespoke treason. One churchman recounted how during the time "the Dissenters sent up agents from the north to solicit . . . the members of parliament." Their appeal "soon occasioned a great ferment both in the two houses and out of them, and brought a greater number of members to town than is usual."[116] Again, dissenters encountered an unsympathetic audience in the Irish capital. "These very schismatics," Swift wrote, "are now again expecting, soliciting and demanding (not without insinuated threats, according to their custom) that the Parliament should fix them upon an equal foot with the established church." Such pleas to repeal the test struck at the heart of the Irish confessional state in which religious denomination determined access to political power. For Swift, the issue boiled down to "Whether those people, who in all their actions, preachings, and writings, have openly declared themselves against regal power, are to be safely placed in an equal degree of favour and trust."[117] Their notion of conscience, he believed, would destroy the rights of all. "As to the Presbyterians allowing liberty of conscience to those episcopal principles," he argued, "when their own kirk shall be predominant . . . I believe no reasonable churchman (who must then be a dissenter) will expect it."[118]

Swift had little choice but to appeal to old Ascendancy fears; in fact, northern dissenter rhetoric left him with little room to maneuver. Much as churchmen had emulated metropolitan discourse to challenge a British Parliament's intrusion in Irish affairs, men such as Abernethy used the language of the Williamite Settlement to attack the privileged position of the Ascendancy. Like other British groups, Ulster's Presbyterians too identified with a Glorious Revolution that celebrated liberty and individual rights, sought to control the prerogatives of unfettered power, and mandated consent as the basis of government. Dissenters at times also voiced discontent with British intrusion into Irish affairs. Presbyterians in Derry, for example, protested the minting of Irish coins by an Englishman, the so-called Wood's Halfpence, with such vehemence that Bishop William Nicolson feared a "a general conflagration" in that city. Some even hesitated to petition the Parliament of Great Britain to repeal disabling legislation because, as the Presbytery of Monaghan explained, "by making application to have things done with them that properly and de primo lye before our own Parliament . . . [we] so expose ourselves to that charge of betraying the Privileges of our Native Country."[119] Indeed, the Ulster

Presbyterian experience in some ways paralleled that of the Ascendancy, which over the course of the eighteenth century came to view the link to Britain with increasing ambivalence.

The "badge of slavery" the sacramental test represented, however, precluded widespread empathy with the Ascendancy. Inhabiting a land where religious persuasion represented a means to power or a justification for the exclusion from it destined Ulster's Presbyterians to second-class status in a second-class kingdom. The structure of the Irish political and ecclesiastical settlement, premised on the confessional state, also determined the religious form that appeals for rights took. It is not surprising that ministers led the charge against the test using arguments of religious toleration. Although they used a language that formed the foundation of the eighteenth-century British state, they tailored it to their position in the kingdom. This response to the Revolution Settlement, therefore, reflected, challenged—and in some ways, reinforced—the confessional nature of the Irish state.

The campaign to undo the Test Act, however, failed. No bill to repeal the measure reached the floor of Ireland's House of Commons. As the rights-based attack on the Ascendancy's position petered out, Ulster's dissenters finally learned the practical limitations of "Britishness." Therefore, the last, and potentially most unifying, of the various attempts to make sense of a period of profound change came to naught. The factions within the church, despite pulling together for the campaign, drifted further apart. Moreover, a number of men and women, despite pleas from ministers and elders, continued to contest the consolidating vision by looking for meaning away from the session and meetinghouse. At the end of the day, the members of the group shared little except a common set of experiences as dissenters concentrated in the north.

"On the Wing for America"

ULSTER PRESBYTERIAN MIGRATION,

1718–1729

In 1729, as Ulster's Presbyterians prepared for another assault on a Test Act that denied them a full measure of God-given rights, the British government noticed a troubling trend at work in Ireland. Lord Carteret, lord lieutenant of Ireland, wrote a number of Irish officials that he "Regret[ed] to hear that such great numbers of Protestants have left the North of Ireland." From 1718 to 1719, thousands of men and women from Ulster sailed for America. At first, the movement drew little attention from either the Irish or British government. When another wave crested by the late 1720s, however, administrators in both kingdoms grew alarmed at the growing scale of migration, fearing that as northern Presbyterians sailed to the New World, the Protestant cause in Ireland would suffer. Carteret instructed the Lords Justices of the kingdom, those officials chosen to oversee Irish affairs during the viceroy's absence, "to enquire further in to that matter and to report on the cause of it, and if any method can prevent this growing evil." He explained that "It is represented that the greatest part of the people who have gone away, as well as those who propose to go are Protestant Dissenters." The flight of Presbyterians from Ulster, Carteret suggested, made migration an imperial concern.[1]

Those who reported back to Carteret disagreed on the specific reasons for migration. Landlords blamed the clergy of the Church of Ireland for the exodus, implying that tithes were driving families from Ireland and leaving tenants with less disposable income to pay rents. Clerics of the established church struck back that rack-renting landlords were responsible. Those who sympathized with the Protestant nationalist cause argued that the fault lay with policies that subordinated Irish to British interests. For their part, Ulster's Presbyterians saw the moment as an opportunity to strengthen their campaign for the repeal of the Test Act, alleging that migration stemmed from the disabilities dissenters suffered in the north. Aware they were speaking to a captive audience, most used the fears aroused by migration as an opportunity to air their grievances and to campaign for their own vision of Ireland.

All, therefore, viewed migration through the prism of their experiences since the Williamite war. No doubt, the earliest movement coincided with a startling combination of economic problems, including poor harvests, slumping linen sales, and rising rents and tithes. Yet, also during this time Ulster's Presbyterians dealt with their second-class status, unprecedented opportunity, and the subscription controversy. That migration began in these years is no coincidence. Both the struggle to redefine the identity of the group in line with British liberties and the process of migration stemmed from a moment of cultural ferment, when Ulster's Presbyterians began to come to terms with the meaning and effects of the wider world of commerce and ideas they had embraced. To be sure, economic hardship triggered the impulse to flee Ulster for a better life in America. Yet, the ways in which the group understood the imperative to sail to the colonies underscored both their plight as market-producing dissenters in a kingdom divided along confessional lines and the grip a larger British world, embracing the Atlantic, had on their lives.

The same forces that led to a crisis for Ulster Presbyterian society also provided the means of escape. The Ulster Presbyterians' larger world embraced America. Although migrants often had an unrealistic picture of the colonies, colored by unscrupulous shipping agents, they traveled along the commercial and religious links they had established to the colonies in the years after the Glorious Revolution. Migrants determined which areas of North America they peopled by the viability of these preexisting ties, eventually settling on Pennsylvania. While the migrant trade developed as an extension of the linen and flax trades, making the imaginative leap to the New World possible, Pennsylvania appeared to men and women of the north as a perfect Ulster, one where opportunity coexisted with religious freedom. In these years, therefore, as they looked inward to make sense of profound change, they also looked outward to reconstruct their vision of Ulster.

By 1729, the year the scope of the "strange humour" alarmed the British government, migration had become a self-perpetuating mechanism. Stories of the American colonies reached those struggling with a prolonged cultural crisis, leading to unprecedented numbers seeking passage to Pennsylvania. The frenzy to leave in 1729 demonstrated in a tangible way that their larger imaginative world—British and Protestant, linked together by trade, religion, and ideas—was connected rather than separated by the Atlantic Ocean. Seen in this light, the responses of contemporaries to Ulster Presbyterian migration reveal that movement to America represented not only one symptom of a period of crisis and opportunity from the group's immersion in a larger world, but also one aspect of a single sequence of experience beginning in 1688 with the Glorious Revolution.[2]

WE DO NOT know, nor can we know, much about the specifics of early Ulster migration. We have a rough idea of its numbers and extent. Beginning in 1718 and culminating in 1729, thousands of Ulster Presbyterians sailed to the New World, the first wave of a movement that would see more than 100,000 land in America by 1775.[3] For the early period, no shipping lists exist, nor are all the crossings accounted for. Although Irish and American newspapers recorded the comings and goings of ships plying the Atlantic from time to time, these are far from comprehensive. Moreover, we lack a precise idea of where migrants came from. By some accounts, they seemed to have left almost every corner of Ulster.[4] The migrants themselves left few records behind, detailing their motives for sailing or their stations in life. Therefore, we must rely on contemporary accounts of the exodus to understand the reasons for and extent of migration.

This much is clear. In the 1710s and 1720s, a series of misfortunes conspired to stall Ulster's economic ascent. Problems began in the years 1717 to 1719 when harvests failed. Archbishop Hugh Boulter, the Lord Primate of Ireland, argued that Ireland experienced "little less than a famine every other year."[5] During this time, he was not far off the mark. Crop failures struck in the late 1710s, leading the bishop of Derry, William Nicolson, to lament he had "never beheld even in Picardy, Westphalia, or Scotland such dismal marks of hunger and want as appeared in the countenance of the poor creatures that I meet with on the road." Hardship continued into the early 1720s. In 1721, Nicolson explained that "the miseries of this kingdom are truly deplorable. The number of starving beggars daily increase in proportion to the general want of money wherewith to relieve or employ them." That year a "hard winter killed most of the cattle."[6] The following year conditions did not improve. "The wather is and has been soe extreim bad," an agent informed his Ulster landlord, "that we cane nather gate turf nor hay maid for violent rains and floods wch has dun us verry great daimage."[7]

Dearth coincided with a fall in the linen trade. From 1717 to 1718, the linen exported to Britain dropped from 2,400,000 yards to 2,200,000.[8] In the west of the province near Derry, where families focused on spinning yarn for the weavers in the east and in Britain, conditions proved worse. Over the same period, yarn exports declined by nearly 25 percent. This does not take into account the slumping demand from local manufacturers, proportionally greater than that traded to northern English manufacturers.[9] Bishop Nicolson reported that when the linen trade suffered, "Our trade of all kinds is at a standstill, inasmuch as that our most eminent merchants who used to pay bills of £1000 at sight are hardly able to raise £100 in so many days." In Derry, where the production of yarn buoyed the cottier economy, the effects of the slump were particularly evident. "Spindles of yarn, our daily bread," Nicolson informed a friend in England, "are fallen from half-a-crown to 15 d and everything else in proportion." He continued that "Our best beef, as good as ever I ate in England, is sold under three farthings a pound. And all this not from any extraordinary plenty of commodities but from a perfect dearth of money."[10]

In periods such as this, the structural problems of Ireland's underdeveloped economy proved costly. More often than not, Ireland's trade suffered from "irregular startings and flutterings."[11] Poor and uncertain international demand, an immature domestic market, consistently low prices, and a tight imperial money supply meant hardship for producers who relied on ready money from the sale of linen and yarn to buy food. Twice during the 1720s, British demand slumped for Irish linen products. In 1721, a Derry man reported that "The demands lately made from abroad, from Manchester chiefly, for our yarn and by others for our linen cloth is at a full stop."[12] In 1717, discrepancies between the English and Irish exchange rate raised the price of Irish goods, stalling Irish exports and drawing currency from the kingdom.[13] As Arthur Dobbs observed, Ireland's fragile economy relied too heavily on the international and imperial economy for its own good. "The succeeding Disturbances by the Rebellion in *Great Britain*," he wrote, "the Confusions in *France* on calling in a new coining their Money, and raising their Coin, the *Mississipi* Bubble in *France*, and *South Sea* in *England*, were plainly the Reasons of the considerable fall in our Exports to 1722."[14]

Finally, tenants paid dearly in these years for the leases they entered on the cheap in the wake of the Williamite war. In the 1690s when proprietors were anxious to secure tenants, landlords maintained rents at a level well below market value. At their expiration, however, they hoped to increase their rent rolls, especially since some regions of the province had flourished, not by farming, but from increased trade.[15] Recalling the state of affairs in 1696, for example, William Molyneaux, an agent for lands in County Armagh, wrote his employer that "all the leases except some few were renew'd with abatements of the rent for some certaine time till the poor people could put themselves in a condition of living and paying their land lord." He resolved that "if ever I renew them againe, I hope to raise them yet much higher."[16] After the turn of the century, some already were beginning to increase fines for new tenants. Arthur Brownlow, for example, increased the fine per taking on his estate near Lurgan to more than £10 from a postwar level of £1.[17]

Beginning in 1717, leases granted for twenty-one years expired. One agent, who made his money from rents, wasted little time. Henry Maxwell of Carrickfergus north of Belfast informed his undertenants that "there leases is now not good, and that they must pay more rent from this Alsants [All Saints Day] or leave the land."[18] Maxwell was not alone. In some areas held by the Merchant Taylors' Company near Coleraine, the rents of one middleman, a Captain Jackson, rose from a total of £310 to £582. Total rentals throughout the kingdom increased from £1.2 million in 1687 to between £1.6 and £2 million during the 1720s.[19] With the growing population, competition was increasing. The low price for lands that had drawn thousands of Scots to Ulster in the years after the Glorious Revolution was a thing of the past. In particular, land in the east, where linen was becoming the economic mainstay, rose in value, as more families tried to establish themselves on smaller farms close to substantial local markets. In these regions, therefore, landlords, as an agent explained, "need not feer tenants."[20] The scarcity of prospective leaseholders in the 1690s had grown into a deluge of those seeking land near markets. Meanwhile, with low prices and no substantive increases in agricultural productivity or efficiency of linen production, rising rents meant decreasing standards of living.[21]

By the end of the decade, circumstances took a turn for the worse. Another series of crises pushed the province to the verge of famine. In 1732, an Irish pamphleteer reflected on the causes of the "Ill Situation of the Affairs of Ireland" in the preceding years. Although he laid the economic troubles at England's doorsteps, he saw that hardship stemmed from a number of factors. "We are daily running in Debt," he explained, "our Publick Funds prove deficient; our little Trade is diminished." To these he added that "our Farmers are in a breaking Condition; the Value of Land is lessened; Money is scarce to a degree; and consequently our Credit sinking." These conditions, he argued, "form[ed] Combinations, to themselves hurtful, to the Nation destructive."[22]

In these years, Jonathan Swift crafted his "Modest Proposal," a scathing satire written in the midst of depression. Because the kingdom seemed never able to overcome periodic bouts with famine and hardship, Swift proposed a novel way to take care of Ireland's problems. "I have been assured," he submitted, "by a very knowing American of my acquaintance in London, that a young healthy child well nursed is at a year old a most delicious, nourishing, and wholesome food, whether stewed, roasted, baked or boiled," adding that "I make no doubt that it will equally serve in a fricassee or a ragout." Swift blamed both the landlords who "as they have already most of the parents, seem to have the best title to the children" and the British government. His new scheme, he boasted, would ensure that "the money will circulate among ourselves, the goods being entirely of our own growth and manufacture."[23]

Swift's modest proposal played against the backdrop of harvest failures in 1726, 1727, and 1728. Archbishop Boulter informed an English colleague in 1727 of a "terrible scarcity next to a famine that a great part of the kingdom now labours under by the corn not yielding well last year."[24] Ulster was especially hard hit. Oatmeal, the "bread of the north," was in short supply, and "sold for twice or thrice the usual price."[25] One Ulster minister, William Livingston, laid out the reasons for "the miserable condition of this poor country at the present time." In the months before the 1729 harvest, he had witnessed "such a dearth and scarcity of victual was never heard of in these parts. . . . Almost the whole product of the last harvest is already spent, there is not seed enough to sow the ground." In particular, he complained that "there is none or very little money amongst the inhabitants to purchase what is bought by sea from foreign parts."[26] Although famine did not strike the province, even American newspapers took note. The *Pennsylvania Gazette* reported in 1729 that riots were breaking out in the kingdom, stressing the "miserable Condition of the Poor in the North of Ireland, for want of Corn" and "the Death of great Numbers of black Cattle and Horses . . . by the Backwardness of the Spring."[27]

Although by 1728 Ulster's linen production had rebounded, the return to prosperity was short-lived. "The Linnen Manufacture," Arthur Dobbs argued, "has generally speaking an increasing Export." While, he continued, "in some years it abated a little . . . generally in the succeeding Years, it increased with double Force."[28] Dobbs was not far off the mark. From the low years of the late 1710s, producers in 1728 exported more than 4,500,000 yards to Britain. Two years later, however, that amount dropped to 3,800,000 yards, as Britain's revenue commissioners restricted Irish linen to combat a glut in the market. To make matters worse, the price per yard remained the same, or decreased, as more households manufactured the product and as demand plummeted. The drop, though less than the famous depression in the trade in the 1770s, was proportionally just as great.[29] Likewise, those in the peripheral areas of Ulster who raised livestock and crops or spun yarn for the eastern linen regions suffered throughout this period. Although with poor harvests the price for foodstuffs rose, farmers were in little condition to sell any on the market. Yarn exports again fell more than 10 percent.[30] In 1729, the lord lieutenant explained that in Ireland "for this year past, the rate of linen yarn has fallen to about half what it formerly sold for."[31]

In an eerie replay of the previous decade, while money became more tight, demands on tenants grew. Beginning in 1727, a new batch of leases—those granted for thirty-one years—expired, and as had happened ten years earlier, some landlords lost little time increasing rents. On an estate near Downpatrick, estate revenues increased from £1,244 in 1713 to £2,254 by 1731. On the Hertford estate near Lisburn, a linen-producing region, the landlord rented thirty-four farms for £90. By 1728, the same properties rented for £222.[32] And with landlords at long last clamoring for their fair share of the spoils of the new economy, the established clergy increased the amount they expected from tithes. Archbishop Boulter in these years argued that while "gentlemen" continued to raise their rents, they believed "that the clergy should still receive their old payments for their tythe." Boulter explained that churchmen contested this idea. "If a clergy-man," he declared, "saw a farm raised in its rent *e.g. from 10 to 20 l. per ann.* He might be sure his tythe was certainly worth double what he formerly took for it." Church of Ireland clerics, therefore, "made a proportionable advancement in their composition for their tythes."[33] Clergymen "farmed" the amounts due to collectors who stood to realize a percentage of money brought in. The system, especially in areas that had grown prosperous through trade, proved harsh, lead-ing an observer in County Derry to declare the tithes collected in "so vigorous manner as is not known and scarce would be believed in England."[34]

In trying to stay afloat after successive waves of misfortune, the sav-ings of even the moderately prosperous were eaten away. Endemically low prices meant that few were prepared to weather financial crises. Rising prices for scarcer food meant that most had little money for other expenditures.[35] After the lean years of 1717–19, for example, a number of families had problems coping with the South Sea Bubble crisis. The English financial fiasco of 1721 "has surely made us misera-ble to the highest degree, if starving be a misery," argued Archbishop of Dublin William King. "I lately had a Petition from 300 families con-cern'd in the Linnen, Silk and Woolen Trade," he wrote the arch-bishop of Canterbury, "Thirteen Hundred, beside Wives and Chil-dren, who are all out of employment and starving, having sold everything to get them bread," adding, "The Merchants have no

Trade, Shop Keepers need Charity; and the cry of the whole People is loud for Bread." Swift believed the problems lay mainly in the south of the country. "The whole country," he declared in 1726, "except for the Scotch plantation in the north, is a scene of misery and desolation hardly to be matched on this side Lapland."[36] Yet a land agent in County Down, in the heart of the region of "Scotch plantation," testified to the dismal economic performance during the time Swift wrote. "The tenants," he claimed, "are not worth a groate except what little graine they have . . . for there is no such thing as money." Agents might as well have tried squeezing blood from a stone. "The tenants," a Down agent reported in 1727, "have not paid any rent yet, which occasioned my goeing yesterday among them and pressed for money as much as I could, but they could not get any." Undaunted, he "therefore seized their corne."[37] Currency shortage and low prices allowed few to save enough to tide them over through difficult times.[38]

Although the Lords Justices reported to the lord lieutenant that they found "many conjectural reasons, but none certain . . . for their desertion," most that responded to Carteret's plea saw the slumping economy as the reason Ulster's Presbyterians left.[39] One of the Lords Justices, Thomas Wyndham, wrote that indeed he had observed "the spreading of a humour (which has been growing for some late years) among the tenants of Ulster, of quitting their lands there and transporting themselves to America." Wyndham acknowledged a "scarcity of oats . . . which is there the bread of the common people," which, he argued, "is the natural effect of three bad harvests." He hoped the food shortage would be "remedied by the late Proclamation against exporting corn."[40]

Although he failed to note that Ireland still exported grain to Britain throughout these years, Wyndham did take a parting shot at British mercantile and fiscal policy. Hardship, he argued, stemmed from "a visible decrease of the silver coin in this kingdom" and "a considerable loss of trade in general."[41] In 1718, Archbishop King in a more insistent tone lectured a colleague in England that "your Parliament is destroying the little Trade that is left us. These and other Discouragements are driving away the few Protestants that are amongst us." To drive home the need to remedy the constitutional relationship between the kingdoms, King suggested that "No Papists stir," and "being already five or six to one, and a breeding People, you may imagine in what conditions we are like to be."[42] Boulter likewise emphasized the crippling consequences of British monetary policy for Ireland. Writing influential friends in England, Boulter saw the problem of migration as an effect of "obstruction in the linen-manufacture" and the "want of silver," which he believed would "prove a terrible blow to that manufacture, as there will not be money to pay the poor for their small parcels of yarn."[43]

For their part, landlords attributed the fever to migrate to the policies of the established clergy. One respondent argued that those who left did not do so because of high rents but to "take this opportunity to run away from their creditors." He found that the people in particular complained of the "farmers of tithes," agents sent by bishops to collect tithes for a percentage of the take.[44] Boulter saw the practice of holding the clergy responsible as reprehensible. "The gentlemen here," he thundered, "have . . . been putting it into the heads of their tenants, that it was not their rents, but the paying of tythes that made them find it hard to live on their farms." He argued that "it is easy to see that this was a notion that would readily take with *Scotch* Presbyterians."[45] Boulter saw the practice of laying blame on churchmen as pernicious. Therefore, he requested the bishop of London "to talk with the ministry on the subject . . . and endeavour to prevent their being prepossessed with any unjust opinion of the clergy," and asked for the bishop's help "if any attempt should be made from hence, to suffer us to be stript of our just rights."[46]

Even landlords had to admit that rising rents had a role to play in migration. Landholders argued that they "did not let lands so much from the consideration of the real value of them, as from the bidding and proposals of the tenants themselves." Leaseholders signed agreements when "the times and trading (especially the linnen trade) . . . [were] pretty good . . . and had been too forward in offering for their farms greater rents than they find they are now able to make out of them."[47] No doubt, another report read, "many Protestant families have been induced to transport themselves from their native country to settle in America . . . From the great advantages they expect by removing." The report cited, however, "supposed hardship and discouragements they find in this Kingdom." In particular, prospective migrants found that "For these three years last past the seasons and harvests have been so bad in the Northern Counties that corn has risen to an excessive price" while "the rate of linen yarn has fallen to about half what it formerly sold for." In such dire straits they "complain that several gentlemen have lately raised their rents above the value of the lands" and also that "many landlords turn them out of their farms and give them to Papists." Finally, the people bemoaned "the want of, or shortness of their leases."[48]

Others put the blame squarely on the shoulders of landlords. Boulter argued that three poor harvests placed tenants in a bind. "Our farmers here," he wrote, "are very poor, and obliged as soon as they have their corn, to sell it for ready money to pay their rents."[49] Boulter lambasted the avariciousness of landowners in devoting more acreage to pasture. "Many gentlemen," he charged, "(as their leases fall into their hands) tye up their tenants from tillage."[50] Like Boulter, King blamed "the covetousness of the landlords" for the impulse to go. He claimed that "the truth of the case is this; after the Revolution, most of the kingdom was waste, and abundance of people destroyed by war; the landlords therefore were glad to get tenants at any rate, and set their lands at very easy rents." But by the 1720s "their leases are expired, and they obliged not only to give what was paid before the Revolution, but in most cases double and in many places treble, so that it is impossible for people to live or subsist on their farms." He concluded that "the landlords set up their farms to be disposed by cant, and the Papists, who live in a miserable and sordid manner, will always outbid a Protestant." Playing on prevailing fears of Catholics, only four years after the Pretender's abortive invasion of England, proved powerful stuff.[51]

King's analysis, however, relied on half-truths. No doubt the peak periods of migration coincided with increases in rents across the region. And in the years between the increases of the late 1710s and late 1720s, few migrated.[52] But landlords, in fact, had little incentive to "cant" or lease their holdings to the highest bidder. Since their income depended on steady tenants, landholders had few reasons to drive off tenants who could pay rents and make improvements. Weaving of linen increased the value of land, as did allowing tenants to sublet to those pinning their hopes entirely on linen production.

Moreover, even if they wished, landlords had to fly in the face of custom to evict one tenant for another. "Tenant right," which allowed
holders to accept or refuse a new lease, precluded "canting." Although
middlemen were more apt to treat their tenants in a "racking" fashion,
few landlords did. Certainly, without tenants landlords had no hope
of an income.[53]

Indeed, in times of economic difficulty or personal hardship, some
landlords went easy on reliable tenants. During the 1720s, some landlords had little choice but to continue offering abatements. In 1723,
for example, George Conyngham, an agent for the Goldsmiths' Company in County Derry, explained that "The Company of Ironmongers
and the Company of Merchant Tailors have of late sold and set their
estates in this county at so high a price that no doubt the Goldsmiths'
Company will expect that their estate should yield something near the
value of the other proportions." He cautioned, however, "if they do so,
they will find themselves miserably disappointed."[54] Others realized
earlier that raising rents too high made little sense. One agent of
the Vinters' Proportion argued in 1718 that "I Believe if the Lands
were now out of lease the Proportion might be Raised about £100 per
Anno. at the Rack Rent as the Times have been for some few
years past." The economic difficulties of the period, however, were
not lost on him. "The undertenants," he continued, "having Generally
a long Term as the Immediate Tenant has, and Markets being uncertain in this Kingdom makes it very Doubtfull whether it may be raised
so much at the Expiration of the recent Lease, and most Thinking
Intelligent People are of Opinion that Lands here must fall soon."[55]
Even in areas where the rents increased, such as the Clothworkers'
Proportion, they did not do so as much as first proposed, and in
some cases not at all. Captain Jackson, a northern land agent, had
proposed steep increases for the farms he surveyed. But rents on some
holdings increased by only a pound or two in 1717. For the "houses
and tenements at the Water side of Killane," which Jackson argued
were "supposed to be worth £5: or £10 more" and on which linen
producers worked, rents did not go up at all, but remained at their
pre-1717 level.[56]

Moreover, evicting or driving renters off the land, even in the face
of increased demand in regions near linen markets, proved difficult

to accomplish in a moral economy tying landlord and tenant together. "I vewed all your lands in and about [Carrickfergus]," reported an agent to his landlord in 1722, "most of which is verry good and verry improveable." He did not find, though, "on[e] Tenant that would make a new agreement." In the populous east, reliable tenants were not a precious commodity. "If they doe not cume to a new agreement you need not feer tenants, but none untill they have left the land," the agent cautioned, "for our foolish people in this cunterey thincks it a great sin to tacke land while the other tenant is in posetione."[57] Ulster Scots considered even breaching the tenant right as "scandalous." In 1723, for example, John Strahan of Carmoney brought Joseph Black before the session, arguing that Black had wronged him "by saying he [Strahan] hath unjustly taken his land over his head." Strahan contended that "some time agoe the Land-Lords agent and others desired him to take the said Land which he absolutely refus'd till it did appear that Joseph Black did give up the Land."[58]

Finally, pressing tenants too severely placed lands out of landlord control. Even if tenants owed their rents to middlemen, who did not have the same stake landowners did in offering abatements, tenants not only could sell the "interest" in their holdings but also the tenant "right" to a family seeking cheaper rents. Disgruntled tenants also could leave without paying what they owed to landlords, such as a customary "fine" on first assuming a lease—a not insignificant amount often more than the yearly rent—or money they borrowed on the strength of the lease. One landlord who had gone hard on his tenants learned as much in 1718. Writing an official, he complained that "if they were hindered to goe [to America] . . . it wod make them the louder to goe." He asked his friend to "oblige these Rogues who goes of to pay their Just Debts before they Goe and then Let all goe when they pledge."[59] When tenants left, rent rolls dropped. The trend of "Protestants being almost everywhere on the wing for America," a land agent warned, "has already reduced the value of our lands and will do more if a stop is not put to it before next spring."[60] The extent of the exodus, another explained, "must of necessity Reduce the Rents very low in all the Northern Countys."[61] If a group of tenants from one small region decided to go to America, the effects on rent rolls could be substantial, as occurred on the Grocers' Manor in County Derry in

1718, where an agent reported that twenty families had left or were planning to migrate, as well as two freemen with substantial holdings.[62]

While high demand in the east strengthened the tenant's hand, in the far west and south of Ulster landlords had even less incentive to press tenants. As a merchant from Derry explained in the late 1720s, "Lands are every where fallen 20 or 30 percent. I have my self some Farm Lands but five Miles from this City, which were worth £45 per Annum, and now the Tenants say, they must be reduced to £24 so you may judge how it is like to be with Lands more remote from any large Town."[63] Western regions of Tyrone, Donegal, and Fermanagh contained far fewer men and women than Antrim, Down, and Derry. Raising rents to uncomfortable levels or following lease terms to the letter would have left lands untended and unimproved, and rents unpaid. Certainly, landlords were at a further disadvantage in the west of the province. Indeed, in areas that supplied northeast Ulster with foodstuffs, a far different trend was at work. As prices for beef fell with a lapse in foreign trade, wrote one landlord in 1728, graziers "let many of their farms, and threw up others. The villagers again returned, retook their farms at easier rents, and the manufacture of yarn spread."[64]

In all likelihood, therefore, most migrants left regions with higher population density.[65] The ability to raise capital from unexpired leases offered many the ready means to pay for passage. "The richer sort," one report argued, "say that if they stay in Ireland their children will be slaves and that it is better for them to make money of their leases while they are worth something to inable them to transport themselves and familys to America."[66] In the more developed areas of Ulster with a greater demand for land near markets and transportation, tenants could sell the "interest" or remaining part of the lease and the "right" of first refusal when the lease expired. Moreover, tenants could expect some compensation from the landlord for any improvement if they surrendered the lease.[67] One group of churchmen argued that "several are gone who were in no needy circumstances, and others who sold their farms for considerable sums of money."[68] Those with a few years to run on their lease, therefore, were most able to pay for their passage. William Caldwell from County Derry, for example, sold the interest in the remaining years of his lease for £7 before he left for the colonies, and a neighbor who paid £1.75 a year in rent obtained the same sum.[69]

Although after years of economic crisis very few considered themselves the "richer sort," in fact, 80 percent of all migrants in this period paid their way to America, most with their families.[70] Contemporaries were right to emphasize that those who wove linen or spun yarn made up a disproportionate number of migrants. Only in regions such as the linen triangle and areas surrounding the town of Derry, including parts of Donegal and Tyrone, where demand for land was greatest and population densities highest, could men and women expect to raise money from the sale of interest and right. As an American newspaper reported, most who arrived "are Protestants, and principally Dissenters, and such as are remarkable for their Knowledge in raising Flax, and all other Branches of Linnen Manufacture."[71] No doubt, most had suffered during the periods of dearth, but few from starvation. Food had become dearer, the returns from linen declined, and in some cases rents had risen, if not to unbearable levels, at least to uncomfortable ones, but a stake in the land in market-oriented regions allowed most to pay for passage to the colonies.

IF THE economic picture of the migration story appears more complex than we had imagined, so too does the issue of religious and political disabilities. Although reports differed as to what economic problems sustained migration, churchmen tried to dispel any notion that discrimination led to movement. A circuit judge claimed the fault lay not with the Ascendancy or the economy, but with "the Presbyterian Ministers." Echoing the prevailing prejudices of the day holding that dissent stood for treason, Ezekial Steward argued that the ministers "have taken their shear of pains to seduce their poor ignorant hearers by bellowing from their Pulpits against the landlords and the clargey, calling them rackers of rents, and servers of tythes, with other reflections of this nature." These appeals, Steward believed, were "pleasing to their people." Ministers also filled the heads of their congregants with stories of how "God had appoynted a country for them to dwell in . . . and desires them to depart thence, where they will be freed from the bondage of Egipt and go to the land of Cannan."[72]

To be sure, Ulster Presbyterians portrayed the strains of the period in a very different light than did churchmen. An anonymous Presbyterian apologist, styling himself a "Gentleman in the North of Ireland," agreed that migrants "are not the poorer sort" and that the "fatal humour goes on to the great prejudice of the kingdom, the dispeopleing of our country, and decay of trade," and found it "owing in a great measure the present ill state and condition of the north of *Ireland.*" That condition, the writer admitted, stemmed from "seeing our lands wasting round us, and the best of our tenants leaving us in the midst of swarms of papists." By his reckoning, migrants, no doubt, complained of "rack rents, and rigours of some landlords and their agents, high and excessive tythes, and the severe manner of collecting them." Landlords in particular "had been too forward in offering for their farms greater rents than they find they are able to make out of them."[73]

But Presbyterian writers also pointed to discouragements churchmen either dismissed or ignored. Some took issue with "prosecutions in the spiritual courts for tythes, marriages, schools, etc." The "better sort of them" in particular complained "that they and their ancestors ever since the first settlement in the kingdom, have given constant proof of their true allegiance to their sovereign Princes, and as often as the cause of their country required it, have ventur'd their lives and fortunes, in the defence . . . of it." The Test Act, however, undermined their loyalty.[74] Ministers claimed that religious disabilities fueled the impetus to leave. In an address to the king, three ministers argued that "It was not till the second year of Queen Ann that the Protestant Dissenters in Ireland were put under any legal incapacities." Because of "hardship and oppressions which the Protestant Dissenters laboured under . . . they have in great numbers transported themselves to the American Plantations" where they hoped to enjoy "that liberty and ease which they are denied in their native country." This trend, they believed, imperiled the Protestant interest in the kingdom because as dissenters left, "the Papists of Ireland are daily growing in strength and number."[75]

Contemporaries saw the Presbyterian explanations of migration, which focused on "supposed hardship and discouragements they find in this kingdom," as a rhetorical ploy to add leverage for a repeal of the Test Act.[76] "Some would insinuate," Archbishop King reasoned, "that this in some measure [is] due to the uneasiness dissenters have in the matter of religion, but this is plainly a mistake." Ulster's dissenters, he argued, "were never more easy as to that matter . . . yet they never thought of leaving the kingdom, till oppressed by excessive [rents]."[77] King considered himself no friend of Ulster Presbyterian interests. He led the House of Lords in thwarting any legislation for toleration or repeal of the Test Act. Moreover, he expressed his thoughts at the time Ireland's Parliament considered granting dissenters toleration. He, therefore, had good reason to downplay the role of religious and political discrimination in leading to Ulster Presbyterian migration, especially since British policymakers were beginning to take notice of the movement. Similarly, Hugh Boulter, though more sympathetic to the grievances of dissenters than King, could not understand the Presbyterian complaints of "the spiritual courts,"[78] nor for that matter the issue of marriages. Boulter argued that "for some they had not been molested about their marriages." They also made much noise over "the oppression of Justices of the Peace," of which again Boulter could make little sense.[79] Another respondent admitted that the Presbyterians murmured about the "oppression" of "Tyth mongers, some by the county courts, and a good number by Justices of the Peace." Yet, these "are only imaginary and which people clamour against in order to have some excuse for their goeing."[80] Any insinuation of dissenters migrating because of tithes, marriages, or courts, churchmen feared, could renew British pressure to grant dissenters a full share of their civil rights. Undermining such claims, therefore, denied dissenters political capital.

Of course, Presbyterians, in their attempt to undo the test, used migration as leverage. As a Scottish minister argued, the effort to repeal the Test Act in 1730 grew from the migration of the previous decade. After "shoals" of migrants "alarmed the Government," many believed it was "a very proper season to get somewhat done for the easing our brethren's grievances there, especially the scandalous abuse of our Lord's ordinance by the sacramental test, which was one considerable incitement to them to come to America."[81] John Abernethy also mentioned the movement to America as yet one more reason to grant Ulster's dissenters their civil liberties.[82] To overturn the Test Act, dissenters showed little reluctance to juxtapose migration and religious disabilities. As Francis Hutcheson argued, the Test Act "which hes been so heavy to the Dissenters of Ireland ... was the occasion of the vast run of many thousands to America."[83]

In fact, Ulster's Presbyterians understood the combination of rising rents, failed harvests, and poor returns for linen as a product of what was happening to their communities and certainly saw their problems in a more complex light than established churchmen would have had the British government believe. Ulster Scots did not compartmentalize political and economic concerns, but viewed them as one and the same. In eighteenth-century Ireland, economic problems took on a political significance. In 1717, for example, a riot broke out in Armagh, where rents were skyrocketing. Presbyterians attacked churchmen with clubs, screaming, "Scoure the Tories and Papists for they are much alike." Others shouted, "Damn the Church of England People for most of them are Jacobites." In an atmosphere of high expectations and sordid reality, the mob articulated its dissatisfaction with the Irish status quo. Marking a sense of hopelessness, one rioter shouting "Scoure the Whigs" knocked down and bit the finger of a justice of the peace, who had been "eating oysters and drinking a glass of wine peaceably."[84]

The problems that occasioned such outbursts, both economic and political, Presbyterians believed, had their roots in the religious state of the community. When, for instance, supporters of the exiled King James invaded Britain, the General Synod mandated that each congregation "search their wages that have been evil and have brought on the melancholy and threatening state of affairs at this juncture."[85] Two years later, Presbyterians dealt with a "threatened invasion from abroad and the great storms in food tyme" by bewailing "the abounding of sin and wickednesse whereby God is greatly provoked to anger to inflict his Judgements on us."[86] So linked had a "visible decay of religion" and hardship become to Ulster dissenters that the Sub-Synod of Derry suggested seeking help from the British government, arguing that "considering our present fears and dangers, it might be seasonable to address our sovereigne King George, and the Lord Lieutenant of Ireland."[87]

Similarly, Presbyterians did not distinguish between the hardships of 1717–29 and the problems they experienced in the church. Ulster dissenters believed the economic challenges they confronted had religious origins, that their "many sins . . . provoked a holy and Righteous God to visit us with scarcity of bread."[88] Presbyteries and congregations throughout the province struggled to make sense of declining economic prospects, tight money, failed harvests, and a fracturing Presbyterian Church with a familiar discourse. In early 1718, the session at Ballycarry called for "a Day of humiliation and fasting . . . to be kept in the cong. on Wed. following and same be intimate from the pulpit because of the abounding sins as also the extraordinary raines that threatened the displeasure of God." Juxtaposing the natural and supernatural, Ulster dissenters argued the hardship of rising rents had their origins in growing divisions within the church. "This day the session met for prayer," read the minutes of the Ballycarry congregation as the subscription controversy began, "and to bewail the abounding of sin in our days and particularly the sin of oppression whereby many families here and elsewhere are reduced to straits and know not where to settle."[89] "Oppression and hardship" went hand in hand.[90]

Ulster's Presbyterians, therefore, understood the difficulties they were facing as a culmination of pressures they experienced since the Glorious Revolution. During the 1720s, many began to believe that the misfortune some experienced stemmed from the breakup of the church over the issue of subscription. In 1723, Ballycarry's elders and minister again beseeched God to undo the suffering the people experienced, setting aside a fast day "on acct. of the extraordinary drought and melancholy divisions among us." By the time of the failed harvest of 1726 as the church split, the session again ordered a fast "to impose a blessing on the arms of his Majesty K. George and his allies in case there be a warr and on acct. of the abounding sin and the great decay of practical religion and the little success the Gospel hath for converting sinners." The decline of godliness explained the many serious issues the congregation faced. The session requested its people "to pray for a blessing on the harvest, and on acct. of our uncomfortable divisions and the unhappy effects of them."[91]

In fact, as Presbyterians alleged, the impetus in some cases to leave stemmed from and exacerbated issues with which the church was struggling. As one respondent alleged, "women are a great cause of many of our people leaving the kingdom." Testifying to their increased role in the economy and their attraction to the larger world of trade, women found "very agreeable" the stories of the New World they heard at fairs and markets. Women learned "that they are much more desirable there than the natives of the country because they are much better housewives and the like, and that the men there use their wives like gentlewomen." To women attuned to the market opportunities around them, the move to America heralded upward mobility. Women with daughters "prevailed" on their husbands to leave "in hopes of making them gentlewomen." Some of those without children aspired to "getting rid of their husbands and getting better ones." Although the report added a few hyperbolic flourishes, it did contain a grain of truth. Northern dissenting women by the 1720s had become "very proper engines to work on" and "very successful in carrying a point, where they themselves expected to be gainers by the bargain."[92]

Moreover, migration strained the Presbyterian system. After the lean year of 1717, church bodies began complaining of the increasing problems some congregations were experiencing paying their ministers. In some cases, the synod or presbytery could collect funds to pay ministerial stipends for the poorest parishes. But in January 1718, the Presbytery of Strabane reported that the number of parishes without sufficient funds was imperiling this arrangement, pointing out "the great necessity some brethren of this Presbytery are under, for want of their proportion."[93] The problem reached epidemic proportions. By the 1720s, the Presbytery of Strabane reported that nearly all of its congregations were in arrears. Congregants from Urney argued that "they're sinking in ability, and look on themselves as intirely uncapable to support a Gospel minister among 'em." So bad had circumstances become in Omagh in County Tyrone that the minister declared that "he can't live with that people for want of a necessary support" and "put in for a share of the publick fund."[94]

The public fund, however, ran dry. In 1720, the Sub-Synod of Derry reported on the "Deplorable Condition of many of their Brn on the publick fund, and that several Congregations in their Bounds are likely to be laid Desolate by reason of Non payment." It asked the General Synod "to make the said Fund more Effectual" to "take a Voluntary Subscription from Ministers and Gentlemen in behalf of those Congregations." The plan failed. A year later, the sub-synod remarked that its plea met with "little Success in their negotiations towards getting a voluntary Subscription from Ministers and people for the support of weak Congregations."[95] In these circumstances, presbyteries, which funneled charitable contributions from more prosperous to poorer congregations, were unable to sustain the arrangement. "To prevent many inconveniencys which happen by the frequent recommendations of poor people for charity," the sub-synod ordered, "every congregation shal maintain their own poor."[96]

Financial problems exacerbated tensions that sessions and presbyteries were already experiencing. Insolvency became yet another excuse to ignore the disciplinary arm of the Presbyterian Church. In Carmoney, Joseph Campbell failed to attend public ordinances because of "fears of being apprehended by some Creditors." A year later, another congregant, Thomas Berry, claimed the same misfortune. In Berry's case, an elder of the session learned of his indisposal "in a public house" in Belfast, where a merchant "had imply'd the Bailiff to apprehend said Berry for debt." The session could do nothing for him.[97] Financial difficulties also further widened the gap between rich and poor, leading to growing disaffection within some congregations. Even by 1718, the first year of a succession of poor harvests, many had difficulty raising funds. So pronounced had the problem become that many in some parishes could not afford seats. In Ballycarry, the session was willing to listen to "Proposalls for ending all differences in the cong[regation] . . . on accompt of many of them not having seats in the meeting house."[98]

Throughout the 1720s, the system never rebounded from the shocks of 1717–19. In Ballycarry, for example, to ensure the people paid their minister, the session resolved to "debarre . . . of church privileges, namely catechizing partaking of the sacrament of the Lds. Supper [and] having baptism administered to their children" those who could not come up with their agreed allotment.[99] Even by 1722, when harvests were good, parishes reported problems looking after the poor. Indeed, the plight of the poor grew worse during the early 1720s. Because their "necessity seems to encrease," the session of Templepatrick, a congregation in one of the more prosperous regions of Ulster, agreed to enlarge their pensions.[100] By the late 1720s, such measures met with little success. In Omagh, in the linen region of County

Tyrone, the session could find no means to encourage its people to pay the minister. The presbytery intervened in 1729, ordering that "they who refuse to give in their payment are to look'd on as non-solvent and be overlooked in the settlement [for seats]."[101] Hard-line tactics, in turn, no doubt contributed to the growing tensions within congregations.

Cash-flow problems explain why congregations failed to raise enough funds to pay ministers or care for the poor. In arguably one of the most prosperous congregations of the north, collections for the poor dropped off during the years of crisis. In the parish of Armagh, one of the principal seats of linen production and marketing, the congregation usually enjoyed a budget surplus with collections usually outpacing disbursements. The surplus could then be used for re-pairing the church or contributing to synod initiatives. In 1716, for instance, the session collected more than £45 and distributed £41 for orphans, widows, church maintenance, and other initiatives. A year later, the congregation took in even more money—£57—from which it doled out £51.[102] The following two years, however, when linen sales fell and the average rate per letting increased by 60 percent in the region, collections plummeted.[103] In 1718 and 1719, the session amassed £46 and £45. Disbursements also dropped as did the parish's cash surplus. In 1718, the session distributed £45 mainly to the poor. A year later, with hardship increasing, that amount fell to £43. No doubt Armagh contained far fewer poor than other regions such as the Strabane, but its congregants too felt the pinch.[104]

With congregations such as Armagh facing insolvency, the policy of fiscal devolution failed. By the late 1720s, affairs at Armagh worsened. In 1728, after the harvest failure, as a newspaper reported, "when the price of Corn and Meal was so very high . . . many of the Poor were in a starving condition."[105] A year later, one that witnessed a good har-vest after three bad, congregants still had a difficult time paying their minister. Contributions to the ministerial stipend in the months after the harvest was brought in fell off. In May through July 1729, the session took in nearly £10 from the congregation. In August and Sep-tember, it barely collected £5, and even less in November and Decem-ber.[106] By 1730, the synod had admitted defeat, recognizing that many congregations could not maintain their ministers and growing numbers of poor. To look out for "the comfort of souls who require to be assisted," the synod explored "an expedient to make . . . publick Charity more Effectual." As a first step, the synod admonished its presbyteries to contribute some of its collections to bolster the "melancholy deficiencies of the Genll: Synods fund." The Sub-Synod of Derry decided to earmark three halfpence of every shilling it collected on the Sabbath to bring the Presbyterian general fund to solvency.[107] The move proved too little too late.

Those who migrated also heightened the church's financial problems, leaving congregations with fewer people of means and, in some cases, fewer ministers. The Presbytery of Strabane reprimanded the congregation of Derg for "a very bad acct of Mr Donaldson's stipend." The Derg session argued that the congregants had little money to pay their minister "on the acct of the removal of many families into America and the poverty of others that remain."[108] Because of "the desertion of many of their people to *America*," a churchman noted, "contributions, particularly in the north, are very much fallen off." Ministers "who have had *50 l. per ann.* from their flock do not receive *15 l.*"[109] Departures for America brought new tenants within the parish, men and women often reluctant to pay ministerial stipends. One session, for instance, complained that arrears grew "because many in these bounds possesse farmes that others had formerly and yet do not pay stipends accordingly."[110]

In such circumstances, ministers sometimes resigned their "pastoral relations" with a congregation to look for a more solvent parish,[111] or as in the case of Isaac Taylor, to leave for America. In 1720, Taylor complained that his people refused to pay his stipend. The congregants responded that they did so "because of the report that is in the country that he is going to America." Taylor did indeed go, citing "his want of necessary support at Ardstraw." Although he returned two years later, his congregants did not forgive him, leading Taylor again to petition the presbytery for help collecting his stipend and the arrears they owed him. On this occasion, he left his congregation again, not for America, but for the established church.[112]

To the Presbyterian community, therefore, migration had become a function of the many issues it was grappling with at the time. The impulse to migrate, Ulster's dissenters made clear, stemmed from their plight in a kingdom transformed by the market economy, a church grappling with new ideas and a crisis of discipline, and a society gripped by confusion. Migration also exacerbated these problems, giving men and women a means of escape from economic hardship, while leaving those left behind with a more onerous burden to bear. However, sailing to America was not a foregone conclusion. In 1674, Ulster's Presbyterians had experienced economic problems similar to those of the second two decades of the eighteenth century. "The poor tenants of this country," a contemporary had written, "have not bread to eat. There is such a great scarcity of victuals that many give up their farms and that those that hold them are not able to pay the rent."[113] Yet no exodus followed.

Migration occurred fifty years later because by the 1720s the New World, although distant, was not altogether foreign to Ulster's Presbyterians. Indeed though an ocean apart, vital ties bound the two regions together.[114] Derry, for example, grew into the preeminent North American trading town in Ulster, largely through the importation of flaxseed from New England and Pennsylvania. In 1705, Irish Tories lobbied their allies in England to allow the exportation of linen to British North America. The Linen Act of 1705 did not harm British industry, but it did allow policymakers to ensure that an American linen industry would never emerge, thus deepening the dependence of the colonies on British manufactures, an important mercantilist policy.[115] Although the transatlantic trade was slow to grow at first—fewer than one hundred yards were shipped in 1700—a year after the passage of the Linen Act, yardage exported to the American colonies grew threefold to 60,000. By 1720, that figure doubled again. In 1741, merchants shipped nearly 400,000 yards to the colonies, the single greatest Irish export to British North America. A barter arrangement of linen for flaxseed between Derry's and American merchants accounted for a substantial proportion of the fiber to keep the Irish linen industry running.[116]

Northern dissenters, of course, had knowledge of North America outside of trading links. One minister had tried to lead his congregation of one hundred forty men and women to New England as early as 1636 on the ill-fated *Eagle Wing* expedition. After the ship almost foundered halfway to America, the crew turned back. Quakers from

County Armagh had left Ireland in 1682 for William Penn's new colony in the New World. And the Scottish promoters of a colony in East New Jersey employed an agent in Belfast for their plantation scheme.[117] Moreover, a small number of Ulster Presbyterians, no more than a few hundred, left for the American colonies in the years during and just after the Williamite war. From 1688 to 1703, at least twelve ships left Belfast for the Chesapeake colonies, carrying small numbers of indentured servants.[118]

Perhaps the most significant link between Ulster and the American colonies in the years around the Glorious Revolution involved Presbyterian missionaries. As early as the 1680s, Francis Makemie from Donegal left the Laggan Valley for the eastern shore of Maryland, ministering to small numbers of English, Welsh, and Scottish Presbyterians before founding America's first Presbyterian congregations and eventually the Presbytery of Philadelphia. Others from the same area left after this time for other colonies. William Holmes moved back and forth between New England and Ulster in the 1690s. Josias McKee headed to Virginia as a missionary.[119] By the first decade of the eighteenth century, the religious ties between the Old and New Worlds were well known and well established. In 1714, Mr. Jervis, a young licentiate, asked the Down Presbytery to ordain him for missionary work in Maryland, "in hopes of finding a door opened there for his being useful in the ministry." Jervis lodged such an "extraordinary and uncommon" request because "a vessel going to that place was speedily expected into the Lough of Belfast." The presbytery proved reluctant to ordain Jervis until a merchant from Belfast "was empower'd by one of the Governors in Carolina to take over a Chaplain to that place providing he be ordained." Some argued that "seeing God in his providence had opened a door for Mr Jervis they think it sho'd not be obstructed." In previous years, Jervis may have had his wish, but not by 1714. The presbytery, despite the call from Carolina, refused to ordain Jervis, arguing "there being a Presbytery in Pennsylvania, to which Mr. Jervis may apply for ordination, in case his gifts be acceptable in that country."[120] In the years after the Glorious Revolution, therefore, Ulster's Presbyterians were acquiring firsthand knowledge of America through trade, sporadic migration, and missionary activities.

Religious ties, sustained by the movement of Presbyterian ministers back and forth across the Atlantic, explain in part the chosen destination of about half of Ulster's migrants during the hard years of 1718 and 1719. In 1718, a group of Presbyterians wrote to Governor Samuel Shute of Massachusetts "to assure His Excellency of our sincere, and hearty Inclinations to Transport our selves to that very excellent and renowned Plantation on obtaining from his Excellency suitable incouragement."[121] Both clerics and officials responded, inviting the men and women from Ulster. Thomas Lechmere, a customs official in Boston, wrote John Winthrop of Connecticut that the Irish "are come over hither for no other reason but on Encouragement sent from hence on notice given them they should have so many acres of Land given them gratis."[122] Reverend Cotton Mather, the leading divine of New England, hoped that "Much may be done for the Kingdom of God in these Parts of the World by this Transportation."[123]

A substantial movement followed. James McGregor led a group of his people from the Bann Valley parish of Aghadowey to Boston, as he put it, "to avoid oppression and cruel bondage, to shun persecution and designed ruin . . . and to have an opportunity of worshipping God according to the dictates of conscience and the rules of His inspired Word."[124] James Woodside returned to New England at this time with some of his congregants, after he "moved that there may with the Leave of this Synod be Testimonials given him to goe to New-England."[125] A few others led parts of their congregations across during these years, occasioning a minister to declare, "There is like to be a great desolation in the northern parts of the kingdom by the removal of several of our brethren to the American plantations." He added, "No less than six ministers have demitted their congregations, and a great number of people go with them; so that we are alarmed with both ministers and people going off."[126] Over a two-year period, from 1718 to 1719, approximately 2,600 Ulster Scots headed to New England.[127]

At first, Mather welcomed the new arrivals, whom he viewed as "United Brethren," or members of a worldwide community of Calvinists who shared similar theological notions. "We are comforted with great numbers of our oppressed brethren coming over from the North of Ireland unto us," he wrote a friend in Scotland in 1718. "That which adds very much to our comfort," he continued, "is, that they find so very little difference in the management of our Churches from theirs and yours, as to count it next unto none at all." The migrants, he found, "sit down with us, and we embrace them as our most united brethren, and we are likely to be very happy in one another."[128]

But cordiality faded soon after the group's arrival. Lechmere, who hoped to entice the Irish "to settle our frontiers as a barrier against the Indians," complained that "these confounded Irish will eat us all up, provisions being most extravagantly dear, and scarce of all sorts."[129] Ulster's Calvinists, moreover, did not favor the congregational form of church governance of the New Englanders, and problems arose as they tried to set up congregations based on the Presbyterian model of government. Mather concluded that the migration of Ulster Presbyterians "has been a marvellous grief unto us . . . [and] that among our United Brethren who have lately come from Ireland unto us . . . there have been some who have most indecently and ingratefully given much disturbance to the peace of our churches."[130] Five years after they began arriving, Mather still pressed for "the Vindication of our churches from the *Scotch-Irish* calumnies."[131]

The movement of whole congregations led by their ministers to New England, however, proved exceptional. Half of those who left during the late 1710s, and more than two-thirds throughout the whole first wave, headed to Pennsylvania, in nearly all cases without their ministers. In 1717, Jonathan Dickinson, a Philadelphia merchant noted that "a small vessell from Leverpoole brought 135 . . . passengers from the North of Ireland," adding that "they say a Considerable Number will follow next summer."[132] The movement of the summer of 1717 amounted to a trickle. Over the next two years, the numbers would grow considerably. Throughout the summer of 1719, Dickinson counted "about twelve saile of ships Laden with Scotch-Irish."[133] Of the nearly five thousand men and women who left Ulster for the colonies in the late 1710s, fully one half headed to ports on the Delaware.[134]

No doubt, the religious toleration for which the colony was noted attracted Ulster's Presbyterians, as did the fact that America's only presbytery met in Philadelphia. And Ulster's migrants knew this. Some men and women carried testimonials to the colony. Congregations and presbyteries drafted these documents for congregants moving from place to place within Ulster and between the province and

Scotland. With a fledgling Presbyterian system in place in Pennsylvania, the practice extended there as well. On leaving their congregation of Ballymoney, for example, James and Mary Ralston secured testimonials for their trip with their three children. The certificate attested to the fact that they had "lived within the bounds of this Cong'on from their infancies and behaved themselves christianly, honestly, soberly, inoffensively and free of Scandal known to us now at their removal . . . to Pensilvania in America." The testimonial continued that they "may be received into any Christian Cong'on where Providence may determine their settlement or abode."[135]

Most, however, journeyed to the Delaware ports of Philadelphia and New Castle because most ships from Ulster headed there. Ulster linen was in high demand in Pennsylvania. Newspapers advertised the arrival of ships from Ireland carrying "White and Brown Sheetings, Shirting Cloth, Brown Linnen."[136] With few skilled weavers and a shortage of labor, Pennsylvanians looked to Ireland to procure linen. The transportation of people arose as an ancillary activity to this trade for linen and flax. Since much of the flax from America was grown in Pennsylvania, many Irish ships that headed to Ulster set sail from the Delaware laden with bulky flax and flaxseed. These returned with linen, which took up much less space than flax, leaving room for people and also guaranteeing that passage to Delaware ports, compared to other ports that did not have similar trading links to Ulster, remained inexpensive. Although the business of shipping people, because of the costs of provisioning, remained relatively unprofitable, the "trade in strangers" to Pennsylvania allowed shipmasters and shipowners to cover the expenses of the westward leg of the transatlantic journey.[137] In all, an average of one thousand passengers a year arrived in New Castle during the 1720s, peaking in the last few years of the decade. At least one thousand landed in Pennsylvania in 1727. That number more than tripled in the following year.[138]

From this arrangement, a network emerged tying prospective migrants to America. Large shipping concerns controlled much of the migrant trade, but smaller factors tied into the linen industry also participated. Ships' captains, their promoters, and agents traveled to market towns and fairs in an attempt to line up men and women for the journey. Agents, taking advantage of the market network established to support the linen industry, traveled far inland, offering passage in the 1720s for less than £7.[139] According to such men, their job amounted to "encuraging his Majesty's subjects as they were pleased to cale thire Indectment from on plantation to another."[140] Yet almost all, Anglican and Presbyterian alike, saw these men as playing a more pernicious role, blaming these agents who journeyed to the hinterland to round up passengers as a large reason for the large numbers that left. "Masters and owners of ships in the Kingdom," a contemporary reported, "who for the profit of extraordinary freights which they get on this occasion, send agents to markets and fairs and public advertisements through the country to assemble the people together."[141]

Because of the large number of ships that plied the sea between the Middle Colonies and Ulster, competition was stiff, driving down prices and encouraging promoters at times to exaggerate the appeal of Pennsylvania. "These persons," a contemporary noted, "represent the advantages to be gained in America in colours so alluring that it is almost impossible to resist their artifices."[142] Boulter reported that "some agents from the colonies in *America*, and several masters of ships . . . have gone about the country, and deluded the people with stories of great plenty and estates to be had . . . in those parts of the world." He found that "they have been the better able to seduce people, by reason of the necessities of the poor of late."[143] These men, a Presbyterian believed, "go about and send their factors and agents round the country, tempting and ensnaring" migrants, extolling the "fruitfulness and commodities of the country." Agents told migrants that "if they will but carry over a little money with them, they may for a small sum purchase considerable tracts of land, and that these will remain by firm tenure as a possession to them and their posterity for ever." Their tales of a "good and comfortable settlement" in the New World, he claimed, struck a chord.[144]

From these networks, the trade in servants also emerged. Although only one in five migrants bound themselves to a term of service in the colonies to obtain passage to America, a rudimentary system developed. Because the trade in servants paid better than the transportation of paying passengers, merchants sent special agents throughout the countryside to round up prospective servants. These agents again resorted to overinflated rhetoric.[145] They told "the poorer sort" that "great wages is given there to labouring men,"[146] sometimes "double or treble of what they can do here."[147] In most cases, the ship's captain transported those unable to pay with the expectation he would cover his expenses and turn a profit on selling the labor of servants to the highest bidder. In one such instance, Charles Alison raised the money for the passage of his family by binding out his son Samuel for "a Certain Term of years."[148] In other cases, Ulster merchants, such as Daniel Mussenden, contracted with shipmasters to underwrite the feeding and transportation of prospective servants in return for a significant profit. In 1729, Mussenden agreed to pay for the passage of thirty-two men, obliging the master of the *Bruerton*, John Fowler, to pay Mussenden £100 on his return. Any profit Fowler realized on the sale of the thirty-two on arrival he was free to keep. The contract obliged Fowler to "safely land the said servants in Philadelphia or Pennsylvania . . . and in no other place, the dangers of the seas excepted." If Fowler failed to do so, he was liable to Mussenden for £200.[149]

In 1729, the numbers that wanted to leave overburdened the developing migration system.[150] At the beginning of the year, the *Pennsylvania Gazette* learned that "Multitudes of People are preparing to transport themselves to America."[151] In August of that year, the *American Weekly Mercury*, a Philadelphia newspaper, reported that "there is arrived there [New Castle] this last week about Two Thousand Irish, and abundance more Daily expected."[152] Indeed, the numbers of Ulster Scots arriving in 1729 shocked Pennsylvanians. "There is gone and to go this Summer from this Port [Derry] Twenty-five Sail of Ships, who carry each, from One Hundred and Twenty, to One hundred and forty Passengers," the *Pennsylvania Gazette* recounted. The report continued that "there are many more going from Belfast, and the Ports near Colerain, besides great Numbers from Dublin, Newry, and round the Coast."[153] "The whole north," a contemporary noted, "is in a ferment at present, and people every day engaging one another to go next year" to America, adding, "The humour has spread like a contagious distemper, and the people will hardly hear any body that tries to cure them of their madness."[154] By 1729, Ulster witnessed the complete culmination of the forces drawing it into a market world. In that year, the harvest failed for a third consecutive time, the linen trade slumped, and the Presbyterian financial system neared collapse. In 1729 alone, between five and seven thousand men, women, and children—most from Ulster and most Presbyterian—headed for America, the vast majority to Pennsylvania.[155]

With so many clamoring to go, for the first time the trip became especially dangerous. Of course, even during normal years, the crossing often proved trying. In 1720, for example, the *Essex* was taken by pirates, who "abused several women," by the Banks off Newfoundland. A similar fate befell the passengers of the *Sizargh*, which departed the north a year later.[156] In 1729, however, while a number of ships ill-suited to the task were manned to meet the increased demand, those that normally made the journey were often overcrowded. Provisions at times ran out with disastrous results. Charles Clinton, who traveled aboard the *George and Ann*, recounted a frightful journey that took nearly five months and cost one hundred men, women, and children their lives. Clinton lost a son and a daughter halfway through a trip in which whole families perished.[157] Another ship, leaving after the *George and Ann*, spent twenty-two weeks at sea and "had thrown seventy-five people over board which died by the Way."[158] One ship foundered and sank off Cape Cod.[159] The migrants of 1729 often experienced "commonly long and miserable Passages, occasioned probably by the Unskillfullness of the mariners."[160]

At these times, when demand outstripped the supply of shipping, passengers found themselves at the mercy of unscrupulous captains and agents. The men and women on board the *Jenny* signed on to sail from Derry to New Castle. The master of the ship, however, decided to head to Virginia.[161] Some passengers suffered from mean provisioning. On one such voyage, only two months at sea the passengers "had no fresh Water but what they saved when it Rain'd or Snow'd." To survive, they had to "mix Rum, Salt Water and Lime Juice for their Common Drink."[162] Even if captains brought along enough food and water, a few of them tried to enrich themselves at the expense of their passengers. Sarah Fulton, for instance, complained that on her arrival in Pennsylvania, "John Findly on Shipboard in their Voyage to this Province had Illegally Obtained an Indenture from the sd Petitioner for the term of four years contrary to His promises and Agreement with Her in Ireland."[163] By 1729, therefore, the frenzy to leave had grown to such an extent that Ulster Presbyterians were willing, in the words of an Irish newspaper, to undergo "all the Tryles, Hardships, and Dangers of the Seas, by Storms, Shipwracks, Turks and Pyrates, to be Starved, or cast away by the Villany of Ship Masters."[164]

Hardship alone, however, does not explain the "madness." By this time, a network for passengers had been well established, and large numbers of arrivals began writing back, telling their friends and relatives of the allure of Pennsylvania. As more and more men and women made their way to the colonies, news arrived back home, making the temptation to leave Ulster irresistible. A government official complained that in letters emigrants told their friends and relatives, "Here the rents are soe small they can hardly be called such, noe Tythes nor Tythemongers, noe County cess not parish taxes, noe servitors money, groats, nor Bailifs corn. . . . These and the like expressions," he concluded, "I have red in severall of their letters, at the same time setting forth that all men are thereon a levill and that it is a good poor mans country where there are noe oppressions of any kind whatsoever."[165] Letters laid out the attractions of America often in inflated terms, in much the same manner as shipping agents did. But the news from friends and relatives, contemporaries suggested, did "very much affect the minds of the people."[166]

The vision of the New World contained in letters and reports drew a stark contrast between Ireland and America. As James Murray, a migrant from County Tyrone, declared, "God has open'd a Door for . . . Deliverance." In a letter to his former minister, Murray gushed over America. "This is a bonny country," he exclaimed, "and aw Things grows here that ever I did see grow in Ereland." In the Middle Colonies, he continued, "we hea Cows, and Sheep, and Horses plenty here, and Goats, and Deers, and Racoons, and Moles, and Bevers, and Fish, and Fouls of aw Sorts." With labor scarce, "a Lass gets 4 shillings and 6 Pence a Week for spinning on the wee Wheel." Religion flourished as well. Murray told his minister that in America ministers received their stipends. Moreover, even a great number "of the Native Folks of the Country turn'd Christians."[167] In America, prospective migrants learned, they would be "free from all those oppressions and impositions which they are subject to here . . . that there they have no tythe (or task masters, as they call them) to vex or oppress them, nor are they troubled with vexatious suits and prosecutions in the spiritual courts, nor laws which render them incapable of serving their King and Country." In America, "they will be intitled to share in those liberties and priviledges which they think are the natural right of every good subject."[168] The antithesis of all that was wrong with Ulster, Pennsylvania represented what one migrant called "a large land of Liberty and Plenty."[169]

By the following year, the "strange humour" had run its course. "We have an Account from the North of Ireland," the *Pennsylvania Gazette* reported in 1730, "that the Transportation of People to Pennsylvania, was now like to be at an End, the Plenty of Corn having induced them to think of remaining in their own Country."[170] The harvest of 1729 surpassed expectations. The following year witnessed a bumper crop. Linen and yarn sales had rebounded, and rents again stabilized. But from this point on, America became a refuge. The expansion of the Ulster Presbyterian world across the Atlantic in the early years of migration ensured that when hardship visited the province, men and women—with and without means—would try their luck in America.

The timing, extent, and tenor of the movement between 1718 and 1729 would also have implications for those who traveled to America. After a series of economic crises, most migrants, although free, would arrive with little money. They also left during a crucial moment for their church, a period during which congregants battled one another over subscription, challenged the role of church discipline in a time of economic change, and despite asserting their Britishness, still had to contend with religious and political discrimination in a confessional state. Most significant, migrants had created a vision of America that appeared as a negative image of Ulster. As they boarded ships, many no doubt envisioned a New World that would deliver them from the many problems they suffered. Their imagined America seemed to offer economic opportunities they had come to expect, religious freedom they had never enjoyed, and the unity they had lost.

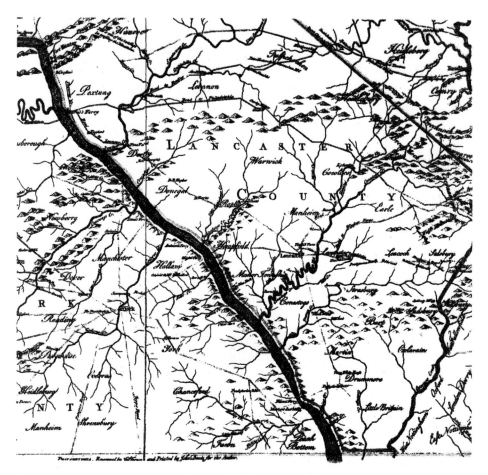

Nicholas Scull's Map of Pennsylvania (1760), detailing the "Upper End" settlements along the Susquehanna of Pextang (Paxton), Derry, Donegal, and Hempfield; and the "Lower End" settlements further south along the river of Drummore, Little Britain, Nottingham, Colerain, and Londonberry. Courtesy of the Edward E. Ayer Collection of the Newberry Library.

"The Very Scum of Mankind"

SETTLEMENT AND ADAPTATION
IN A NEW WORLD

As the ships that had left Belfast and Derry entered Delaware Bay, their passengers were, a contemporary noted, "inexpressibly happy."[1] To be sure, once they had, as one migrant put it, "Discovered Land on the Continent of America," they also experienced a mixture of relief and excitement. After weeks at sea, the steady traffic plying the Delaware to and from the growing city of Philadelphia must have been a welcome sight.[2] On passing Reedy Island, where the bay narrowed to the river, they first caught a closer glimpse of their New World. On both sides of the river, they beheld "large stretches of even country with woods." Looking west in the distance, if the day were clear, they could make out "many high mountains, especially the Blue Mountains" covered with "tall and exceedingly beautiful cedar trees." Coming from a land crowded with farms and short of timber, the immensity of what they saw before them, no doubt, astonished.[3]

After disembarking onto the narrow pier in New Castle, the newly arrived parted company with the few destined for four years of servitude, as well as the linen and trade goods bound for Philadelphia. Carrying their worldly belongings, migrants moved through a narrow bustling alley into the town's main square. For a major immigration port, the town appeared rather bare boned. New Castle only had "one great street which makes an elbow att right angles." The few structures, all brick and "built after the Dutch modell," included two houses of entertainment, Griffith's and "Curtis's att the Sign of the Indian King," as well as two public buildings, a courthouse and an Anglican Church. Just to the north of the church, to their right as they emerged from the packet alley, also stood a small, one-story Presbyterian meetinghouse, whose minister, George Gillespie, had migrated from Scotland.[4]

These men and women, who had left Ireland in search of land and toleration, found both in the New World. Many would soon inhabit the vast, remote—and seemingly unpeopled—woods in the shadows of the Blue Mountains they had caught sight of from the Delaware. Moreover, the congregants of New Castle's meetinghouse, no more than a stone's throw across a narrow common from the Episcopal Church, suffered under no disabilities and paid no tithes. But first impressions often deceive. The woods, to be sure, contained land for the taking. But many people already lived there, and clearing the land would entail years of backbreaking work. And although toleration had become a hallmark of the colony, allowing men and women of varied creeds from all over Europe to practice their religion in peace, the arriving migrants passing through New Castle for the wilderness filed past the last church they would see for some time.

Indeed, isolation on the frontier defined the migrants' first years in Pennsylvania. Without the benefit of ministers or elders, Ulster's migrants lived a rough-hewn existence. Settling miles west of any other European group, they encountered thickly wooded stretches of land connected by Indian trails. Far from markets and towns, they had to rely on barter for trade and could not attend the province's provincial courts. Living in a world of—to their eyes—strange-looking Indians and hard-drinking traders, life took on a violent, unrestrained tenor. Disputes, some trivial and some weighty, often led to bloodshed. Beyond the reach of roads, the only goods they had in abundance were linen, which had little marketability, and liquor, which had too much. Here on the frontier far from New Castle, migrants faced the prospect of fashioning a community with their misfit neighbors and with few social controls.[5]

To make sense of their New World, Ulster's migrants adapted older traditions. Old World experiences served both as a prism to understand the New World and a tool to act on it. Many relied on the only recognizable institution they encountered, the Presbyterian Church, to bring order to their communities. Soon after arriving on the frontier, some Ulster settlers assembled themselves into congregations, pushed for the establishment of their own presbytery, and tried to impose the Confession of Faith on the church, many of whose members had no such tradition. No doubt, the impetus to do so, in part,

100

stemmed from their experience as dissenters in Ireland. As a people coming with nonconformist traditions, they viewed Old World practices such as subscription as a means to give the group some distinguishing characteristics in a tolerant society. But ultimately, the push for subscription arose from a need for order in chaotic settlements on the frontier. In such a New World, the polite discourse of Ireland's New Lights made no impression, and those migrants who had espoused such views in Ulster abandoned them in America.[6]

THE earliest migrants arrived in a colony noted for its diversity. Swedes, Dutch, and Finns, who had established themselves decades before Quakers began settling the region in 1682, peopled the lower counties of Pennsylvania. German pietists, invited by the colony's founder, William Penn, to populate the colony, streamed in in the years following the earliest Quakers and established Germantown in the shadow of Penn's city of brotherly love. And of course, Indians, including Delawares, Susquehannocks, and members of the powerful Iroquoian Five Nations had inhabited the region long before all others and continued to control whole swaths of land under the nominal jurisdiction of officials in Philadelphia.[7] As Ireland's migrants disembarked in New Castle, further north in Philadelphia shiploads of German-speaking Palatines streamed into the city. At taverns throughout the colony, a contemporary noted, patrons could expect to encounter "a very mixed company of different nations and religions. There were Scots, English, Dutch, Germans, and Irish." Religious groups included "Roman Catholicks, Church men, Presbyterians, Quakers," and a number of German sects.[8]

Although attuned to the sights and sounds of a plural world, established Pennsylvanians grew alarmed at the scope of migration in the years Ulster's men and women began arriving. "We shall have a great mixt multitude," declared Jonathan Dickinson, a prominent Quaker, in 1717, "which put us upon thinking how to Deale by them."[9] The same year, Isaac Norris, another grandee, declared, "Some thinking people here are a little shock'd to see such great numbers of foreigners come in and set down."[10] By the 1720s, men of such stature feared that the swarms of Irish and Germans would transform the province beyond recognition and imperil their position in society. The province, the provincial secretary of the colony, James Logan, claimed, was "invaded by those shoals of foreigners the Palatines and strangers from the North of Ireland that crowd in upon us." The incessant flow of migrants stressed both resources and patience. Because of the number of Palatines entering the province, "these colonies will in time be lost to the Crown," he lamented. In a similar vein, he cautioned the Proprietors that "there are some grounds for the common apprehensions of the People that if some speedy method be not taken, they [Ulster migrants] will make themselves Proprietors of the Province."[11] In 1729, Benjamin Franklin wondered why in particular Irish migrants continued "to come to these Parts of the World" whose inhabitants held a "Disrespect and Aversion to their Nation." Ever subtle, Franklin warned his fellow Pennsylvanians of the noted "Impenitency" of the newcomers, suggesting that "The Small Pox spreads here."[12]

Despite these fears, many believed German migrants would assimilate. After time, the initial shock of their strange language, customs, and appearance gave way to a respect for their orderliness. To be sure, some believed the Germans would never fit in, claiming that the settlement of Palatines led to "the disquiet of the Inhabitants of the Province" by their refusal "to yield Obedience to the lawful authority of this Government." But this view proved the exception. As "aliens," the government obliged them "to take an Equivalent to the Oath of Allegiance to the King and to promise fidelity to the Proprietors of the Province to live peaceably and to conform to our Laws." By 1707, the pietists from Germantown had forsworn their allegiance to "foreign" powers and promised to be good subjects to the British monarch. Similarly, new arrivals clamored for naturalization, and year after year, migrants took oaths professing their desire to become English subjects by adoption. Patrick Gordon, the governor of the province, considered them "a very industrious People, and have hitherto been of advantage to this province." Another contemporary believed that "they behave themselves very respectfully to the Government, and pay their Taxes . . . and they are, for the most, a very sober and honest People." One of the proprietors, Thomas Penn, argued that the "Dutch" would "certainly by degrees loose their attachment to their Language, and become English, and as they acquire property I dare prophecy will become good Subjects." Indeed, so confident was his brother John of the ability of Palatines to acculturate over time that he concluded "we ought by no Means to Debarr their coming over," because "when settled these will Esteem themselves Pennsylvanians."[13]

While elites prophesied that the Palatines in time would "be as good Subjects to His Majesty, and dutifull Tenants to the Proprietors," most held out little hope for migrants from Ulster. Unlike the Germans, these people seemed to "have little Honesty and less Sense."[14] To begin with, English settlers, like their fellow subjects in England, harbored deep suspicions of the "Irish," regarding the term with distaste. "Last week," the *Pennsylvania Gazette* reported in 1730, "an Irish Servant Man . . . deprived himself of his Testicles . . . tis said he perform'd the Operation with great Judgement, and is like to do mighty well." Popular accounts portrayed the Irish as anything but sober and industrious. In fact, drawing from prevailing English prejudices, Pennsylvanians regarded the Irish as comic and criminal. Newspapers carried reports from Ireland such as a wedding at Antrim during which the nuptials preceded the cracking open of a "Hogshead of Whisky" in the high street. The drunken crowd "at every Bumper huzza'd" amid "Piping, Dancing, broken Bones, and other Demonstrations of Joy." The ocean crossing did not relieve such idiocy. The *American Weekly Mercury* recounted how an Irish-born field hand, angry with another for throwing "rotten eggs" at him, attacked his assailant with a sickle. Despite the help of a "*Hibernian*-Quack," the man died.[15]

Pennsylvanians believed the Irish "capable of the highest villainies." Newspapers detailed how they counterfeited the province's notes, hoping to flood the currency market. One Irishman, the *Pennsylvania Gazette* revealed, "ravish'd a Child about 6 Years old." According to a pamphleteer calling himself "Roscommon," immigrants faced the challenge of accommodating to a people who "wickedly toil to make the World believe, that we are a Clan of *Kidnappers, Pickpockets, Knaves, and Villains*."[16] Moreover, these men and women seemed clannish. "Some of the more ignorant Sort," the *Pennsylvania Gazette* read after a migrant was tried for murder, "have been so indiscreet as to give threatening Words against Authority, of what they would do in case any *Irishman* should be executed."[17] They were, a contemporary noted, "the very scum of mankind."[18]

Such stereotypes, although rooted in prevailing prejudices, were not far off the mark in describing life in many early Ulster settlements. Ulster's men and women, like other European migrants, settled together in clusters in Pennsylvania. Some moved to Jersey, a number went south into the Lower Counties, and still others found their way to Philadelphia. Most, however, traveled toward the western areas of Chester County, "the back parts of the Province as far as Susquehannah," or the sprawling region called Conestogoe.[19] Here, James Logan set aside land for those "who formerly had so bravely defended Derry and Inniskillen."[20] According to contemporaries, the Irish could not be "restrained . . . from settling any where from among themselves," and did not "mix in their settlements." Logan believed that they "chose to sitt down together there on a view of having in time a settlement of so many families of [their] own Profession of religious Principles as might be requisite to form a Religious Society."[21]

In fact, they had little choice. Although the vast majority of migrants paid for passage, contemporaries described them as "beggardly."[22] While these migrants lacked both land and money, Logan had an uncommon interest in both. As a principle supporter of the trade with Indians, Logan worked with both English merchants and fur traders, lending money and providing trade goods on credit.[23] As provincial secretary of the colony, Logan's duties included supervising the colony, looking after the interests of the proprietor, and supplying settlers with land. Although he viewed the trade as a means to accelerate settlement, at this time he did not have a free hand in granting migrants land.[24] After the death of the founder of the colony, William Penn, members of his family contested the will. The land office, therefore, remained closed as Ulster's migrants arrived. Because of "a Dispute among the family about the Right to the Estate," Logan informed a friend in London, "the agents could not venture to grant any more Lands."[25] Logan also had to contend with the "Claims of Maryland" on land "now in our Possession between Delaware and Susquehannah." From the founding of Pennsylvania, the proprietors of Maryland, the Catholic Calverts, argued that Penn had misinterpreted his charter. Much of the land he claimed for Pennsylvania, the Marylanders believed, lay under the jurisdiction of Maryland, including Philadelphia, three lower counties, and a swath of territory west of the Susquchanna River. Both problems, as Logan saw it, hamstrung the proprietary interest in the colony, whose wealth depended on the ability to rent and sell its lands. More important for Logan, these issues confounded some of his moneymaking ventures.[26]

Logan, however, found a way to settle these people and enrich his coffers. In 1719, he laid out large tracts to James Letort, Peter Bizaillon, and Moses Combs, traders in his employ, along the Susquehanna River and the Chickeselunga Creek.[27] Logan also speculated, buying a few tracts for himself in the region, under the auspices of the proprietary interest, and setting some aside for his political allies. By 1720, Logan held more than 1,400 acres of land on "Chicasolunga Creek," and James Steel, Isaac Norris, and Peter Garner an additional 2,800.[28] Logan then settled the first Ulster migrants immediately to the west and south of his traders on generous terms, hoping their presence would attract those better able to pay. The earliest Irish settlers had to put little or no money down for rights to the land. Logan only required that they pay quitrents or yearly taxes.[29] That migrants had little money did not matter. Logan could not offer them secure land tenure in any event. Most, therefore, occupied land unpurchased from Indians or tracts without warrants.[30] Although Logan and his cronies did not realize an immediate return on their settlement policies, they hoped that "more Industrious and able Persons will still remove further, such idle trash being generally the frontiers of an Improving Colony."[31]

A decade later, as even more migrants from Ulster landed in the colony, Logan continued his settlement policy. He steered most of these newcomers toward the "lower end" of the frontier along the disputed border with Maryland, further south along the river to the settlement of Nottingham or what would be known as the township of Dromore.[32] These migrants, even poorer than the earlier arrivals, represented a longer-term investment for Logan. In this area where, according to Logan, "no Lands can honestly be sold till the dispute with Lord Baltimore is decided," he hoped to plant enough men and women under the auspices of a Pennsylvania government to claim the area for future settlement.[33]

Other migrants continued to stream into the upper end, though without Logan's formal blessing. Few had the necessary money to purchase land, equip farms, and construct homes. With few alternatives, most, in the words of Logan, tended to "own on any sortt of vacant Land they can find without asking questions," often pretending to pay "but not one in twenty has any thing to pay with."[34] By all accounts, they picked "remote" or "Wilderness" areas, establishing themselves without, as one provincial official put it, "Grant or license."[35] Even if they had the money, renting lands in the east attracted few because, as one migrant explained, "We having been, before we came here, so much oppressed and harassed by under Landlords in our own Country, from which we, with great Losses dangers and difficulties, came, with the chief and principal view of being, in this foreign world, freed from such oppression."[36] Although Logan complained publicly, he did nothing to evict squatters. By 1729, only Conestogoe Manor, 17,000 acres surveyed by Logan for the proprietors, divided the enclaves on the upper and lower ends.

On arriving at places near the Susquehanna, migrants often "marked" good land "under pretence of keeping them for their friends in Ireland, or for their Children." Therefore, the region quickly became an Irish haven, attracting new arrivals. After completing their terms, indentured servants moved to the frontier. Patrick Boyd, for example, left Germantown, where he served James Logan, for established Ulster settlements, where he worked as a fur trader.[37] The region also drew those who had migrated to other regions. In 1733, John Kyly, a runaway servant from Rhode Island, described as an Irishman "with a great Arse," was suspected to have reached Pennsylvania. Four years later, three Irish migrants—"a woman burglar and two murderers"—fled Virginia where they had migrated for Conestogoe to hide among their own. People who had migrated to New England in 1717 and 1718 moved to Pennsylvania in the 1720s and 1730s. Even Irishmen serving in the British army who deserted sought out these communities.[38]

Pennsylvania's vaunted "mixt multitude" made little impression on the early migrants. Even reaching the regions Ulster's men and women settled presented problems. The area along the Susquehanna to which they moved lay "about Seventy Miles Distance almost directly West" of Philadelphia.[39] As the crow flew, maybe; however, prospective settlers followed weaving paths, laid out by Indians and traders and some no wider than a horse, through "vacant land."[40] Most, no doubt, traveled along "Old Peter's Road," a trail blazed by the trader Pierre Bizaillon that led to a trading post along the Conoy Creek just north of the Chickeselunga.[41] The upper end, a contemporary remarked, was "a wild and dreary region," where travel was a "laborious task" and newcomers often lost their way.[42] The closest European settlers— Mennonites from the Palatinate and Switzerland and French Hugue- nots—lived miles to the east. In 1722, the provincial authorities di- vided the township of Conestogoe in two. The region to the east of Pequea Creek contained these and other continental migrants, or "Dutch Inhabitants." West Conestogoe, on the other hand, contained a number of traders and a great many Irish migrants. Two years later, the authorities renamed the township "Donegal" in deference to the Irish origins of these people.[43]

Nonetheless, what appeared from the Delaware as a "remote land where everything is as yet wild and wooded," in fact, was home to an array of peoples.[44] Colonists inhabited a world peopled by Indians, including Delawares, Susquehannocks, Shawnees, Conoys, and mem- bers of the Iroquoian Five Nations. Indeed, the lower Susquehanna Valley had become by the early eighteenth century a center for Indian refugees fleeing tribal, imperial, and intercolonial rivalries. Originally, the region had been settled by Susquehannocks who feuded with their neighbors to the north in Iroquoia. Traumatized by wars, they banded together with Senecas. Collectively calling themselves "Conestogas," they centered their lives in a trading village on Conestogoe Manor just south of Donegal. Around the same period, Shawnees from the south and west and Conoys from the Potomac Valley appealed to Pennsylvania authorities for leave to resettle in the area. Moreover, by the early eighteenth century, bands from the Five Nations established a presence in the region, further north along the Susquehanna in the village of Shamokin. They also traveled through Ulster enclaves, leaving the headwaters of the river to battle Catawbas and Cherokees in the south.[45] North of Paxton—"the northern limit of the Proprietar- ies' land"—was a "country populous with Indians."[46]

Moreover, the lands that migrants settled abutted the homesteads of traders. Hard drinking and savvy in Indian ways, traders moved back and forth between Philadelphia and the Ohio Valley to exchange

European goods and rum for peltry. Others established stores in the Indian towns dotting the Susquehanna Valley. After the initial settlement of Logan's charges, a number of traders such as the English migrant Jonah Davenport and fallen Quaker Edmund Cartlidge continued to build homesteads in Donegal, which they used as staging areas to trade and treat with the tribes that moved through the region. Traders did not enjoy a good reputation from provincial officials or the people with whom they traded. They drank too much and relished fighting. Some cheated Indians after plying them with rum. Local Indians complained that in general they "would lie, cheat, and debauch their Women, and even their Wives, if their Husbands were not at Home."[47]

In this region along the Susquehanna, settlers fashioned a rough-hewn existence out of the woods. In Donegal, although contemporaries judged the land "exceeding Rich" on which crops could grow "without the Help of any Dung,"[48] Ulster's settlers confronted a dense forest described as "pritty high and woody"[49] with only a few cleared "barrens," small patches burned by the Indians in search of game. Officials claimed migrants stymied their investment plans by "barking" trees "without falling them."[50] If they did so, migrants had good reason. Alexander Mitchell, who left Ulster in 1719 and settled a plot of land, erected a cabin and with an axe could clear no more than one acre of trees his first year. Eventually, he managed to clear twelve acres of "plough land" and six or seven for meadow. The task took him thirteen years.[51] On these lands, settlers from Ulster raised wheat, rye, barley, Indian corn, and hemp. Grain went to John Galbraith's house, an Ulster settler who came to the region in 1721 before building a saw and gristmill along Donegal Creek, where he sold whiskey.[52] Most also grew flax, from which they spun yarn to weave into linen.[53]

In such conditions, the earliest settlers scratched out a precarious living. While migrants may have had land, they had little else aside from livestock, Indian corn, and crude farming implements. One settler in 1721 owned no more than five shillings' worth of household goods. Another who died eight years later had a little linen, one mare, a cow, a plow and axe, and two shirts. Joseph Cochran's prized possessions included a Bible, "old bedding," and "iron utensils." Robert Middleton, one of the earliest arrivals, counted only three guns, two iron pots, and a bed and sheet as household items. Settlers ate out of wooden bowls and, if they were lucky, earthenware. They made their own sheets and clothing and constructed their homes out of notched logs from the trees they felled to clear the land.[54]

Indeed, the only material they had in abundance was linen cloth. A visitor to the region noted that the inhabitants "chiefly cultivated British grain, as wheat, barley, and oats." They also raised "a great deal of flax, and in every house here the women have two or three spinning wheels a going."[55] By 1729 Alexander McConnell owned but two shirts and a pair of britches, but had yards of linen cloth as well as flax and wheels.[56] Robert Mackemore, whose estate amounted to £25, had forty yards of linen upon his death in 1734.[57] As in Ireland, nearly all migrants had cloth, wheels, or looms. While few specialized in linen production, even those skilled in other trades, such as the tanner Joseph Work, owned all the tools of the linen trade.[58] All, however, did not weave. John Allen, for example, had not acquired looms or tackling. In 1733, he died with fifty yards of linen in his home, a spinning wheel, twelve spindles of yarn, and a smoothing iron.[59] Linen production, therefore, still maintained by a gendered division of labor, remained a defining feature of migrants' lives. But while in Ireland elaborate structures emerged to market linen, none existed on the Pennsylvania frontier.

In fact, trade in the community was done by barter. In 1726, John Galbraith petitioned the court at Chester to brew beer. He wrote that a tavern was "requested by the neighborhood, for their public and common advantage," arguing, "A great quantity of barley is raised and malted, which by reason of the great distance from a market, without public-houses here, will turn to no account, to their great loss."[60] These inhabitants of "the upper part of the County of Chester" complained of a lack of a "highway" and that because "Trade and Commerce among our Selves [was] mostly by way of Barter, Money cannot be Supposed plenty."[61] Although the community at Donegal had tanners, carpenters, smiths, and weavers, and others who did such odd jobs as bailing hay for neighbors, few could raise money for their services. James Mayes, for example, owed more than £130 for work done by fellow migrants when he died in 1734.[62] Ulster's settlers claimed they were "honest and industrious . . . tho poor." This condition, they argued, stemmed from their remoteness "so far back from markets, whereby we are incapacitated from raising money out of our produce," as well as the "poverty and brokeness of much of our Lands."[63]

Because of the settlers' distance from any town, few disputes in these enclaves went to court. To be sure, those who had reason to move about the region, such as the trader James Patterson and itinerant weaver John McDowell, were summoned to court.[64] But between 1717 and 1729, only one group of Ulster-born residents on the frontier had a writ issued for another to appear at the court of common pleas in Chester. In 1726, the court ordered James Macky to answer a charge for £21 he owed to James Moore, James Cochran, and Cornelius Rowen. Macky and the plaintiffs apparently settled out of court, for the case never went to trial.[65] Nor did Donegal's inhabitants often testify or appear as defendants in criminal cases. When the quarter session summoned Joseph Cochran to appear in August 1725 as a witness in a case, he asked to be excused because, as he put it, he was "very unfit for so long a journey," one that would take him "three weeks on foot." In the same case, another pair of witnesses complained that even on horseback the trip took "three days comeing down and three Days going back."[66] The settlers from Ulster, therefore, had created a society literally beyond the reach of the law. The residents of Donegal complained of "the Great Distances we live from the County Town where elections and courts are held, and Publick Offices kept." They acknowledged that because of their isolation, "The arm of Justice is weakened." They were, they declared, "Deterred by want of Ready cash, to bear the charges of a Journey of Eighty or a hundred Miles to the County Jail." In these circumstances, going to court "makes the Recovery of a small Sum more detrimental than the loss of it."[67]

With taverns and no courts, violence and drunkenness became mainstays of the community. Too often "hurt with liquor," colonists lived lives noted for their brutality.[68] Even at house-raisings, a "case of Difference or Quarrel" could turn into a bloody fight. At such events, men competed with one another to see who could notch logs the fastest. On one such occasion on the lower end, a sore loser taunted the winner, telling all within earshot that he had "rotten lungs" and "a stinking Breath." "Stinking or not," the winner replied, "I have beat you." After each called the other "a lying son of a Bitch," one threatened to pull the other "down by the Nose." Finally, after drinks were passed around, a brawl ensued. What had started as an argument between two men became a free-for-all with relatives and friends of each joining in the fray.[69] Even traders, hardly known for their sobriety, complained of young men from "Denegall" fighting at "Drinking Bout[s]."[70] Women, too, were partial to the bottle. In 1734, for instance, after a number of Donegal women enjoyed an evening of boisterous drinking, one witness to the event spread a story of how Elizabeth Ross "reeled and staggered like one drunk." The gossip led to a feud among a number of families.[71]

Scenes such as these did not go unnoticed by provincial officials. The provincial council noted in 1727 that "in remote Parts of this Province" colonists "sometimes have proceeded to Acts of Violence," particularly in the township of Donegal, where "one John Scott being with his Wife and Children in peaceable Possession of a House, which he had built, were not only ousted by Force but their house was pull'd down before their Eyes."[72] Logan lamented "the Conduct of my Countrey men from the North of Ireland, on the numerous and heavy complaints brought to me of their Voilence and Injustice to each other, such as this Province till their arrival, was very much stranger to." Of all the inhabitants of the province, he considered them "the most unjust and Cruel to each other."[73] "Without a speedy Regulation which will admit of no Delay," Logan pontificated, "they will quarrel amongst themselves and commit such outrages as no force against them will be sufficient to quell or appease." Officials were right to point out, as Isaac Norris had, that it was easier to "Preach righteousness, plead law or advance Reason on board a Pyrate, or to a nest of Banditi" than to police or restrain Donegal's inhabitants.[74]

Nevertheless, Ulster's migrants did create some semblance of community in the region, which surprisingly included their trading neighbors. Traders were a dangerous lot to cross. The people of Donegal and Henry Hawkins learned as much in 1724. Hawkins's misfortunes began as soon as he arrived from England as an indentured servant. Although he was hoping to learn the gunsmith trade, his time was purchased instead by the hard-drinking trader John Burt.[75] Burt had no inclination to teach Hawkins the fine points of mending a gun.

Hawkins claimed he was "forced" to help Burt in the trading business, and as a first assignment was sent to Philadelphia to procure trade goods with Jonah Davenport. Although Hawkins tried to remain in Philadelphia, Davenport brought the reluctant man back to Donegal. By now, Burt had little use for the complainer. He sold Hawkins to John Harris, who turned him over to Davenport. Davenport then "sold the said Sevt to an Indian called Chickoekenoke," who "carried the said Hawkings some hundred miles back in the woods."

Hawkins's troubles were only beginning. Chickoekenoke returned and asked for his money back. While Davenport and the Indian haggled over their bargain, Hawkins tried to fetch James Mitchell, an early migrant and justice of the peace for the area, but to no avail. Before Hawkins could reach Mitchell's, Davenport grabbed him before a group of Donegal women and tied him to the tail of his horse, dragging the poor servant "a considerable way through a thick muddy Swamp."[76] When officials in Philadelphia got word of the incident, they were appalled. Even James Logan, who had set Davenport up in the trading business and allowed him to settle three hundred acres in Donegal, believed that Davenport would confront "an uncommon severity from his neighbours."[77]

In Donegal, however, traders and colonists from Ulster got on well. Two Ulster migrants, Andrew Galbraith and Randall Chambers, far from punishing Davenport, put up £30 bail each to ensure his appearance at court.[78] Moreover, in the same month a grand jury summoned Davenport, the "inhabitants of Donngall" drew up a petition in support of Davenport's application to remain a licensed trader. Thirty-six settlers of Donegal declared that he "behaved himself honestly in all his dealings with us and so farr as we know (excepting an accident with Henry Hawkins) has been a good master to his servants." Years later, Davenport, poor but well respected, died at Patrick Campbell's tavern in Donegal.[79] A number of migrants from Ulster also entered the trade, such as Patrick Campbell, Lazarus Lowry, and James Patterson. Some who did not do so established close relationships with their trading neighbors. Joseph Cochran, for example, lent money to Jonah Davenport and French Canadian James Letort.[80] And James Galbraith witnessed the will of Huguenot trader Isaac Miranda.[81] After Davenport's death, Donegal's inhabitants continued to look out for his family, as did a saddler who bequeathed his estate to Jonah's sons John and William.[82]

Community also encompassed the region's Indians. No doubt, the large numbers of European migrants settling in the region caused resentment. Logan claimed that many settlers from Ulster had "no regard to Indian claims." Local tribes complained that they had little choice but "to behold their Lands invaded by Swarms of strangers that they have an aversion to for the Irish are generally rough to them." So widespread was the problem that the Conestoga Indians presented Quaker officials with presents of skins and from year to year "engage[d] them to assist in composing any Difference that may arise between the Irish people and these Indians who intend to live and dye where they are now settled."[83] At times relations between the groups grew tense. In 1722, an argument over rum between trading brothers Edmund and John Cartlidge, based at Conestoga, and Sawantaeny, a Seneca, that led to the murder of the Indian, almost unleashed a frontier conflagration. Six years later, the Pennsylvania frontier again nearly erupted in warfare. Rumors spread of Conestogas readying to attack Shawnees. Traders talked of groups of eastern and western Indians preparing to "lift up their Axes . . . against the Christians." In that year, tales of bloody run-ins between borderers and Indians whipped colonists into a frenzy. Only a treaty at the Indian town of Conestoga averted war.[84] Although tensions soon eased, officials warned Ulster settlers not to have anything to do with neighboring Indians. The government and traders instructed Indians, especially those apt to be "too unruly," "not to come amongst or near to the English Settlements" on the upper end.[85] For their part, few Ulster settlers even entered Indian cabins "to which nothing we think could tempt any white people," as a contemporary put it.[86]

Although Logan claimed Donegal's inhabitants remained insensible to "Resentment of those Peoples," in fact, relationships emerged.[87] Some traders, to be sure, won the respect and admiration of Indians, such as Thomas McKee, whose wife "was brought up among the Indians" and spoke "but little English."[88] And some of those from Donegal who did not enter the business drank and traveled with Indians, including Edward Dougherty, who kept "an ilgoverned Tipling House" where he sold rum to Indians,[89] as well as John Maccabee, a servant to a trader in Donegal, who ran away from his master into the woods with an Indian named Toby.[90] One migrant claimed that, as a rule, inhabitants over time became "well acquainted in the woods," as well as "the Manner and Customs of several Nations of Indians."[91] Some found little to distinguish between the two groups. Indeed, as one missionary to the region put it, little separated Indians and the "nominal Christians" they lived around along the Susquehanna. Both drank too much "strong liquor," and each were "ill examples" to the other.[92]

In this chaotic New World, the American Presbyterian Church had little to offer the group. The stern discipline so sorely lacking within Ulster settlements was not a central feature of the American Presbyterian Church. To be sure, the church had the formal structures of the church in Ulster, with organized congregations, presbyteries, and a synod, but whether these institutions would follow more closely the New England consociational model or the strict hierarchical framework of the Synod of Ulster or the Church of Scotland remained unclear.[93] The threadbare Presbyterian system offered little help for directing the religious life of migrants. Few established congregations existed in the colony in the years migrants began arriving, about ten or so in all, and none in the areas men and women from Ulster had settled. Moreover, the tiny church was suffering from a shortage of clergy even before the migrants landed in New Castle. Although they attempted to organize themselves into congregations, settlers had little money to build meetinghouses or attract ministers, nor the direction of a well-organized presbytery to order church life.[94] As early as 1721, Donegal's settlers requested the services of a minister from the Presbytery of New Castle. Over the course of five years, no less than five ministers preached at Donegal from time to time. But again the isolation of the group stymied attempts to supply the community. One minister had to make a sixty-mile roundtrip journey to supply the people. On one occasion, a minister failed to keep his appointment with the settlers of Donegal because he lost his way in the woods. Finally, in 1727 they secured a minister.[95]

In the New World, migrants also encountered an alien church. Although Ulster native Francis Makemie established America's Presbyterian Church in the late seventeenth century, the church little resembled the one they had left behind. In Pennsylvania, Presbyterians suffered under no disabilities, as they did in Ireland. No Ascendancy "as by law established" collected tithes or passed laws disabling dissenters; indeed, in a province where toleration prevailed, the term "dissenter" was meaningless. Moreover, unlike the Irish Presbyterian Church, the American church included people of diverse national backgrounds and theological traditions. The descendants of New England Puritans, Welsh migrants, Scots, a few Germans, and Irish Presbyterians met together at presbyteries. The Presbytery of New Castle, representing congregations on the backcountry, contained ministers serving men and women on "Welsh tracts," Irish settlements, and New England–style congregations, and called men for the ministry from New England colleges, Scotland, and Ireland.[96]

The men and women who sailed from Ulster referred to "this American world" they encountered as a "Wilderness" of "Hardships and difficulties." Poverty-stricken and beyond the reach of larger society, they considered themselves inhabiting a "foreign world," a place one migrant described as "among strangers not knowing how to trust any, [and] in danger by the heathen."[97] Migrants lamented the uncertainty they had happened upon. While they settled among those of their persuasion, the poor structure and alien nature of the American church threatened to dissolve the bonds that tied them together, as well as to leave many unchurched. Within their frontier enclaves amid groups of "wild native Indians" and hard-drinking traders, "Monstrous Swearing, whoring Sabbath breaking drunkeness [were] all common."[98] Because of "Circumstances of these parts," some wondered, "how many poor Souls are scattered to and fro in the wilderness, under awful Danger of perishing for Lack of Vision . . . which may render both themselves and their posterity miserable Pagans."[99]

MANY of Ulster's migrants believed they could acquire the "vision" to negotiate the new context they encountered by adapting Old World traditions. At the most basic level, the Irish church provided a model of discipline settlers could use in America. Churchmen and a number of lay people early on made the adoption of Old World ecclesiastical traditions a priority for the survival of the group in Pennsylvania. After securing a minister, Donegal's inhabitants constructed a log meetinghouse a few miles east of the Susquehanna along a small tributary of the Chickeselunga in the midst of the earliest settlers.[100] Next, ministers sought to mold the Presbytery of New Castle, the presbytery nominally responsible for Ulster enclaves, into an institution similar to those they had left. By the mid-1720s, the presbytery began a practice of "visitations," moving its meetings around the congregations under its jurisdiction to question the people and ministers regarding their responsibilities to one another, check the session books, and hear witnesses in disputes.[101]

To bring order to their settlements, settlers then clamored for the establishment of a presbytery of their own. In 1732, the Synod of Philadelphia created the Presbytery of Donegal, responsible for all congregations west of Fagg's Manor. These included lower-end congregations going up in Nottingham, Brandywine, and Octoraro and those on the upper end at Donegal, Derry, and Paxton. As such, the Presbytery of Donegal ministered mainly to Ulster migrants. Within a few months of its creation, the prebytery decided that its members "shall go in circuit, and sit in the several Congregations within our Bounds."[102] Because money was tight, the Presbytery of Donegal requested that its members take up collections to pay those ministers whose congregants could not and provided poor relief for "Objects of Charity" within its bounds.[103] With a focus on organizing the settler communities, church bodies made it clear that those who did "not Join themselves" to a congregation "by neglecting to congregate themselves within the Societies of Gods people are guilty of too great contempt."[104]

In the absence of other courts, the church tried to police its own. Once a minister was installed at Donegal, the session heard cases, such as those regarding drunkenness and fornication.[105] Soon after the erection of the new presbytery, Donegal's minister, James Anderson, asked the members to condemn the "profane and needless Spending in a publick house" he saw too much of. "Many of our perswasion," he reckoned, "Spend more in a year this way unprofitable both to themselves and to their families."[106] Sessions laid out rules for allowing miscreants to join others at the Lord's table, including evidence of repentance and appearance before the whole congregation on successive Lord's Days.[107] The sessions showed little reluctance to assert their control over the affairs of congregants. For example, when William McKinney, accused of drunkenness in New Londonderry, ignored the session's discipline, the body considered it "our Duty publickly to Declare him to be no Regular Member of the Church of Christ, and to have no Right to the Distinguishing communion and privileges of the visible church with us, unless he will comply."[108]

Members of the Presbyteries of New Castle and Donegal turned a necessity into a virtue, stipulating that the congregational sessions, not the official courts, hear cases of disciplines. In 1729, three Irish-born ministers from frontier congregations sponsored an overture "to prevent going to Law, in Cases of Civill differences; which is recommended to all Members, and the Members to all their Congregations." While the more cosmopolitan Presbytery of Philadelphia considered and rejected a similar move—indeed, members of that body considered it "allowable . . . to have Evidences sworn before a magistrate" used at an ecclesiastical court—the Presbyteries of Donegal and New Castle chastised their members who thought of seeking redress in any court outside the session or for debating one another in the press. Whereas Ulster's Presbyterians shunned Irish ecclesiastical courts because of their objection to the confessional state, in Pennsylvania they took the same line to avoid "Exposing our holy religion . . . to ridicule and contempt before the world."[109]

Some also pushed for subscription to the Westminster Confession of Faith. Before 1729, the various presbyteries did not require ministers or people to subscribe to the Confession. But some had broached the subject earlier. In 1724, the Presbytery of New Castle recorded its first voluntary subscription. Within two years, it had become standard procedure for candidates to subscribe and to declare "subjection to this Presbytery."[110] No one advocated subscription for the entire American church until John Thomson, an Irish-born minister serving the lower-end congregations of Chestnut Level and Middle Octoraro, did so in 1727. By 1729, a number of ministers followed Thomson's example, submitting a proposal to use the Westminster Confession of Faith as the terms of ministerial communion. At the synod session that year, the so-called Adopting Act passed, requiring ministers to subscribe but allowing them to make distinctions between necessary and essential doctrines and those they viewed as peripheral. Modeled on the Irish Pacifick Acts of 1720, an attempt to chart a middle course between the two feuding parties within the Synod of Ulster, the measure enabled probationers to state beliefs in their own words. Despite the exceptions allowed by the Adopting Act, by 1732 the Presbyteries of New Castle and Donegal mandated unqualified subscription to the Westminster Confession of Faith.[111]

The act of 1729 proved a far cry from the unqualified subscription many proposed because such measures met with stiff resistance, mainly from a group of non-Irish ministers led by Jonathan Dickinson. A descendant of New England Puritans, Dickinson and his Welsh and American-born colleagues argued that subscription to any creed represented a "bold Invasion of Christ's Legal Authority." Critics of subscription contended that the Scriptures alone were "the only outward Test to try Doctrines by," and as such, the imposition of creeds represented a "bold invasion of Christ's Royal Power, and a rude reflection upon his Wisdom and Faithfulness, for proud Worms to make any Addition to that perfect Pattern, which he has given us." To this argument, Dickinson added examples from history, some far removed, others closer to home. "Imposing and subscribing Creeds," he suggested, "was both an Inlet to Papacy, and a continual Engine of Papal Tyranny." If this did not sway the subscriptionists, he pointed out that "we need not look so far back, nor go farther from Home, than the Country where you and I were born, to find brightest Examples of this kind." He continued, "The Presbyterian Church in Ireland, subsisted some Ages in Peace and Purity . . . had not the Fire of Subscription consumed their glory; and this Engine of Division broke them to pieces, disuniting them in Interest, in Communion, and in Charity."[112]

Those leery of subscription also viewed the move for the Confession as an ethnic strategy and decried it as such. Dickinson argued that although the Irish tradition may have called for subscription—to the detriment of the Irish church, he added—New Englanders, from whom he descended, had "continued from the first Foundation Nonsubscribers." "Many of my audience," Dickinson claimed, drawing a distinction between his people and the Irish, "are the Posterity of those who left their delightful Country and pleasant Habitations, [and] crossed the Atlantick with their Families. . . . to fly from the Imposition of these Things." Jedediah Andrews, a Philadelphia minister, explained that the Confession was "Recommended by all the Scotch and Irish members present," and that they would "certainly carry it by numbers." As he saw it, while these members demanded subscription, "all the English and Welsh" opposed it "to a man." "Some say," he lamented, "the Design of this Motion is, to spew out our Countrymen."[113]

Andrews's fears had some substance. Scottish ministers, as Andrews alleged, supported the move. Indeed, George Gillespie, a Scottish-born minister, first broached the subject of the need for "the better carrying on in the Matters of our Government and Discipline." Serving the people of the established Delaware River town of New Castle, Gillespie had protested the lenient treatment of a frontier minister charged with fornication by his presbytery. After the synod upheld the decision of the Presbytery of New Castle to suspend the wayward preacher for four weeks, Gillespie "entred his Protest and Dissent," and demanded the synod minutes be "altered or annulled," suggesting that the church needed a better set of institutional structures for discipline to overrule erring presbyteries and to ensure a godly ministry. Although his plea fell on deaf ears, Gillespie became a strong supporter of later attempts for subscription.[114]

Nevertheless, Irish-born ministers differed with Scots such as Gillespie over the meaning of the Confession. John Thomson claimed that his support for subscription did not stem from a devotion to Scottish practices. Although he considered himself "to be the Seed and Offspring of it [the Church of Scotland] in Matters of Religion," he declared that America's Presbyterians were "an intire Church of our selves, so as not to be a Part of any particular Church in the World."[115] Moreover, Ulster-born ministers split with their Scottish colleagues over the importance of ministerial morality. In 1738, Gillespie complained that the Presbytery of Donegal treated Richard Sancky, an Irish-born probationer, "with too much Lenity," after he was suspected of plagiarizing sermons. Although the presbytery "rebuked" Sancky for his actions, it did not "see any ground to suspect him of unsoundness in the faith."[116]

The presbytery's failure to discipline Sancky could be interpreted as an ethnic strategy to safeguard Irish-born ministers. To be sure, Ulster's settlers preferred ministers from Ulster. By the mid-1730s, acceding to the wishes of the laity, the Irish-dominated Presbytery of Donegal accepted probationers only from Ireland, rejecting anyone whom they referred to as "strangers." In 1735, a number of congregants from Brandywine refused to consider any ministers for their vacant pulpit except "some of those young Gentlemen who are lately arrived from Ireland." Although suffering a shortage of young men trained for the pulpit, the presbytery encouraged an Irish-born ministry. In September 1736, the members of the presbytery refused to license "Mr Williams lately from England" because he was "likely to doe harm to our interest." Three years later, they likewise rejected a university-trained probationer from New England.[117]

The preference for an Irish-born ministry, however, had less to do with ethnic solidarity than with sound principles. The ministers of Donegal, in fact, worried that the church was "in Danger of being imposed upon" by Irish-born ministers who harbored latitudinarian ideas. Fearing that the American church was heading the way of Ulster's church, Thomson contended that "All our Brethren's Arguments . . . are all borrowed from the new-light Men, or Non-subscribers in the North of Ireland; they are as like them as one Crow's Egg is like another, or rather as an Horse-shoe is like a Mare's, remove the Shoe, and it changeth its Name."[118] Ministers from the upper and lower ends had fought for the expulsion from the synod of one such man, Samuel Hemphill, in 1735. In 1734, Samuel Hemphill from Strabane arrived in Pennsylvania, subscribed to the Confession, and a year later accepted a call as an assistant to Jedediah Andrews in Philadelphia. His sermons soon caught the attention of Benjamin Franklin. He delivered, Franklin wrote in his *Autobiography*, "with a good Voice, and apparently extempore, most excellent Discourses, which drew together considerable Numbers of different Persuasions, who join'd in admiring them." He continued, "Among the rest I became one of his constant Hearers, his Sermons pleasing me as they had little of the dogmatical kind, but inculcated strongly the Practice of Virtue, or what in the religious Style are called Good Works."[119]

Soon a storm erupted over the new latitudinarian message. As one Presbyterian put it, "Never was there such a Tryal known in the American world."[120] In 1736, less than a year after Hemphill began preaching, the synod brought him up on charges. Members of a synod commission considered it their duty "courageously to resist the Torrent of Irreligion, which seems to threaten the Destruction of the Christian World," particularly "the Growth of Error and Infidelity." George Gillespie, a Scottish-born minister, warned of the allure of "meer Morality," suggesting it could "allow of no Religion but Natural Religion; that is that Religion which is known by Nature's light only."[121] From both sides, Hemphill encountered critics who saw his ideas as dangerous innovations and his incendiary attacks on the Presbyterian system as reproachful. John Thomson became his most vehement opponent, a man who, Franklin believed, was "able to outdo the Jesuits themselves, in Subterfuge, Distinction and Evasion." At the instigation of Thomson and with the full cooperation of Dickinson, the synod stripped Hemphill of his office for both heterodox beliefs and plagiarism.[122]

By Irish standards, Hemphill's sermons contained little new material. Indeed, they differed little if at all from, in Franklin's words, those of an Irish "New-Light Man." Franklin, who published a number of pamphlets in support of Hemphill, went so far as to show how Hemphill's ideas met with the approval of the leading Irish dissenting minister of the age, Joseph Boyse, a Dublin Presbyterian and ally of Abernethy and nonsubscribers from Ulster. But in America, the arguments of an Abernethy had little appeal. With the support of what Franklin dismissed as a "Priest-ridden Laity" on the frontier, the subscriptionist party—"Creed-Imposers," as he called them—worked to ensure the New Light did not get a foothold in the New World. Ministers had little trouble holding Hemphill up as "a Scare-crow to the People," portraying him as a "Missionary sent from Ireland to corrupt the Faith once delivered to the Saints."[123] The Hemphill episode demonstrated the futility of ministering to Presbyterians in Pennsylvania on Irish New Light terms. In the colony, where Irish migrants found themselves a poor people in a tolerant context, appeals elevating the rights of conscience over revelation or championing the rights of dissenters for a full enjoyment of civil liberties they were entitled to as British subjects had no meaning.

To be sure, other ministers also came to the New World with unstayed principles. The number of Irish subscribers roughly equaled that of nonsubscribers who traveled to Pennsylvania. Of course, those who backed the measure in Ulster had little reason to contest it in America. But nearly every minister who out of conscience refused to subscribe in Ireland also pushed for ironclad subscription in the synod of Philadelphia. Robert Jamison and James Martin had arrived by the 1736 session and voted with the majority. The rest who left Ireland by 1740, including Francis Alison, subscribed upon presenting their credentials to the synod and lent their support to a 1741 overture that again mandated subscription without qualification. Only John McDowell, who presented himself before the Presbytery of Donegal in 1736, left no record of his stance of subscription in America.[124]

Like Hemphill, McDowell supplied a Philadelphia congregation—in his case a new erection—for two months in 1736 before disappearing from the record. The others, however, served in frontier meetinghouses. Jamison and Martin presented their credentials to the Presbytery of Donegal before setting out for the lower counties. John Craig, Francis Alison, Samuel Cavin, and Samuel Thomson obtained their licenses to preach through the Presbyteries of Donegal or New Castle and headed for congregations on the lower end. The need for qualified ministers often trumped checkered pasts. Indeed, some even assumed Irish-trained ministers would "fall into Business among some People in the Country."[125] Therefore, all those who switched positions on crossing the ocean did not minister in established, cosmopolitan areas but along the frontier.[126]

By 1736, ministers from these areas pressed for ironclad subscription. Before the synod of 1736, members of the Presbytery of New Castle complained that some people "have been stumbled and offended" by the use of "ambiguous words or Expressions," and affirmed that "we all with one accord firmly adhere to the same sound doctrine which we and our forefathers were trained up in." They explained that, in particular, residents from the upper end in Derry and Paxton pushed the issue of subscription further by arguing that "many Persons of our Perswasion both more lately and formerly have been offended with some Expressions or Distinctions relating to our receiving or adopting the westminster Confession and Catechisms." The people advocated subscription "without the least Variation or Alteration" as proof of a "firm attachment to our good old received Doctrines." If any opposed, Thomson and his colleagues thought themselves "obliged in Conscience" to encourage a rupture of the synod. "I am sure that Truth and good Conscience is infinitely preferable to any Peace or Unity that can be had without it," claimed Thomson.[127]

Coming from a kingdom in which they had defined themselves by their role as a dissenting people to a tolerant, plural society, many Ulster migrants wondered what would distinguish them from other European settlers. To be sure, like all English-speaking Presbyterians, they were a people "whose language would not allow them to join with the Dutch or French churches, and whose Consciences would not allow them to join in the service of the English Church." To make sense of this New World and their place in it, they attempted to recreate a church based on "their own . . . way of worship," and Ulster's migrants employed Scottish practices honed in an Irish context to adapt to life in Pennsylvania.[128] For as one Ulster Scot argued, without distinguishing characteristics that set them apart from others—the role, for instance, dissent played in Ireland—"we are thereby no more united together as one particular Church, than to all other Christian Churches in this World."[129]

But as Thomson claimed, he and his followers were not "biggotted" to the Confession "by a kind of Nationality." Rather, they supported subscription as part of program to add "Systems and Doctrines" to a church increasingly peopled by men and women on the frontier.[130] While in Ireland subscription served to buoy the dissenting church in a confessional state, in Pennsylvania the Confession represented an "external Bond of Union," a visible marker of an Ulster "Zion" migrants had fashioned in the Pennsylvania wilderness. Although subscription had its origins in Old World traditions, the push to impose the Confession did not emerge as an ethnic strategy, but arose in response to the plight of frontier settlers reeling from poverty, drunkenness, and violence, searching for stability. Of course, nearly all of the ministers serving Ulster migrants came from Ireland. But they understood their role less as defenders of Irish or Scottish ways than as "Watchmen of the Church," guardians of discipline and order in isolated communities.[131]

THE curious interaction of the familiar and unfamiliar bounded the lives of migrants. To be sure, Ulster lay a world away from Pennsylvania. In Ireland, northern Presbyterians used subscription to buoy the dissenting church in a society transformed by the market; in America some saw the measure as a means to make sense of toleration and isolation. In such a place, the polite discourse of Irish New Lights had little appeal. But as in Ireland, this "vision" too would be contested. The push to resurrect old ways did not arise in response to the ethnic or religious "other," but from the peculiar plight of frontier inhabitants. The Confession, presbyteries, and sessions added some certainty and order to the violence, poverty, and chaos gripping migrant enclaves. As men such as James Logan realized, however, isolation would come to an end and with it much of the foundation for the adaptation of Old World ways.

"Melted Down in the Heavenly Mould"

RESPONDING TO A CHANGING
FRONTIER

AT THE MOMENT some of Ulster's migrants pushed to impose the Confession, a young Irish-born minister, Gilbert Tennent, began proclaiming a searing message of salvation. Moving throughout the Middle Colonies, he thundered about the "Terrors of an enraged God," a stern judge who would, Tennent warned, "tear you in Pieces, except you repent."[1] At the heart of the appeal of the "New Side" lay an attack on "the general and lamentable Security that prevails so exceedingly among the children of this generation." Ministers such as Tennent decried the false security that comforted most, indeed nearly all, of Pennsylvania's Presbyterians. The gravest challenge he faced was bringing the message to those who "contented themselves with a dead form of Piety, resulting from a religious Education, and historical Faith; instead of seeking after the Power and Life of Christianity." Far from a message of order, Tennent's was a stern warning to what he saw as a world asleep. "Awaken then, you sluggish Souls," he bellowed, "and strive to enter the strait Gate."[2]

Many souls were "melted down in the heavenly Mould" during the Awakening, as one revivalist put it.[3] The call for a vital piety broke frontier congregations, and ultimately the American Presbyterian Church, in two, leading one minister to proclaim that New Side ideas were "tearing us in Pieces like Birds of Prey." Because of the work of "Ringleaders of our Divisions and the Destroyers of good Learning and Gospel order among us," congregants ousted ministers and families divided. "Disorderly Itinerations," some lamented, "and Preaching through our Congregations," destroyed order, "by which (alas for it!) most of our Congregations thro' weakness and Credulity, are so shatter'd and divided, and shaken in their Principles, that few or none of us can say, we enjoy the Comfort, or have the Success among our people, which otherwise we might, and which we enjoy'd heretofore."[4]

The appeal of vital piety among Ulster's migrants arose amid a frontier transformed by economic changes and demographic shifts. By the 1740s, as congregations disintegrated, the frontier isolation that had defined the early years of settlement had come to an end. By this time roads connected enclaves to frontier entrepots tied into the growing city of Philadelphia, and from thence to a larger Atlantic world of trade. Peddlers moved throughout the countryside, and courts appeared nearby. Population in the region grew, pushing up land values and leading to the movement of Indians from the area and the arrival of "strangers" in and around Ulster enclaves. With these changes, places like Donegal were becoming more like regions to the east and less like frontier backwaters. Many, especially those who owned substantial amounts of land, grew prosperous, while for others, in particular the young, opportunity was declining. As Tennent and others like him, trained in the colonies and younger than their pro-subscription brethren, lashed out at the consolidating vision premised on creedal orthodoxy and elaborate church structures, they were speaking to the concerns of these people less settled and less tied to stability of place than those more established.

The Great Awakening for Ulster's migrants, therefore, amounted to a debate over order and the meaning of change within their communities. The campaign to impose the Westminster Confession of Faith and Irish church-like structures on the church to bring coherence to chaotic frontier congregations appeared to be working. Indeed, a semblance of order came to areas mired in chaos. But with the construction of roads, growth of trade, and the opening of Ulster migrant enclaves, provincial institutions and increased economic activity, not sessions or presbyteries, created more stable social relations. Indeed, many showed little reluctance to ignore church institutions with the arrival of courts and trade. Nonetheless, as some embraced a vital piety that spoke to the changing realities of life on the frontier, others invested Old World practices created to make sense of isolation, such as subscription, with greater meaning. When Ulster's migrants and their sons and daughters encountered new groups and a wider world, no single vision of the group triumphed. Rather, contentious divisions, opening along the lines of how individuals experienced a changing frontier, defined relations within the group.[5]

"WE HEAR from Lancaster County," the *Pennsylvania Gazette* reported in April 1741, "that during the Continuance of the great Snow which in general was more than three Foot deep, great Numbers of the back Inhabitants suffer'd much for want of Bread." Winter that year was unusually brutal. Because of "the Severity of the Cold," the *Gazette* recounted, "Fodder is very scarce," and the Delaware River was "all Ice towards the Sea as far as Eye can reach." The newspaper's account focused on the hardship caused by the freak blizzard, especially for the residents of the upper end. It found that "many Families of New-Settlers for some time had little else to subsist on but the Carcasses of Deer they found dead or dying." Although "they had given all their Grain to their Cattle, many Horses and Cows are dead." One person perished, "a young Woman in Derry Township" who froze to death trying to reach her home. Clearly, by this time, life within frontier enclaves remained harsh.[6]

The story of death and dearth obscures the transformations that were taking place along the upper and lower ends of Pennsylvania's frontier. During the 1730s, Pennsylvania experienced a re-immersion into a British Atlantic world of trade. Philadelphia grew into a leading American port in the 1730s, as demand for Pennsylvania's goods increased in Europe and along the American coast. Agricultural products grown in the province's fertile hinterland, such as wheat and hemp, spurred trade, which led to the erection of market towns on the frontier, entrepots connecting Philadelphia with frontier settlements. In 1729, inhabitants of the upper parts of Chester County complained to the provincial council that "no Care is taken of the high ways; Townships are not laid out, nor Bridges built, when there is an apparent Necessity for them." Citing the distance to county courts and need for a jail, they requested "Erecting the Upper part of the Province into a County, called the County of Lancaster." The Town of Lancaster, founded in 1730, provided a local market for grain and hemp and also a number of services tying the frontier to the Atlantic economy. Lancaster merchants purchased surplus produce and livestock, sent these to Philadelphia for the Atlantic markets, and sold manufactured goods produced locally and in Great Britain.[7]

From the time of the founding of Lancaster, the settlers in Ulster migrant enclaves recognized the advantages of and clamored for inclusion within the expanding economy. Citing the "hardships and Inconveniencys they lye under for want of a Road to Meeting House, Mill and Lancaster Town," settlers set to surveying roads. As early as 1732, the men and women of Donegal Township petitioned a Lancaster County court to build a road from the "Meeting house in Donegal to the Town of Lancaster." Indeed, during the 1730s inhabitants in many Ulster settlements requested roads citing "Convenience" and "the Necessity of a Road to Mill and Market." In the following years, migrants on the lower end also petitioned for highways connecting Conestoga, Dromore, Octorara, and Nottingham to Lancaster.[8]

Over time, networks became more elaborate, reaching new areas and further integrating older ones. Already by 1734, Donegal's settlers asked to run their road to the remoter still "Townships of Peshtank Derry . . . from Benjamin Chambers Mill on Sasquehanah att Kihtotoning . . . by the Most Convenient way to the Town of Lancastr." Derry's settlers petitioned for an additional route from their meetinghouse "Until the Same Shal fall Conveniently into the Road leading from Peshtank to Lancaster." The Paxton road was then extended further "to the Presbyterian Meeting house and from thence to the Kings Road Westward." In some cases these roads proved inadequate for increased traffic. Inhabitants at Hempfield, a settlement on the banks of the Susquehanna just south of Donegal, found they needed a more "Ready and Convenient Road from Pexton to the Town of Lancastr. then that already laid."[9] The days of isolation had come to an end.

Such networks brought trade to the region. Into the 1740s, settlers still relied on barter. John Roan, a Presbyterian minister on the upper end, for example, recorded payments in kind for his services. Congregants paid him with saddles, wheat, shoes, liquor, cloth, and flax, or by doing chores or knitting stockings. In 1747 and 1748, for example, David Johnston made payments in liquor, "in stilling," twice by working "at the Chimney," and by reaping and mowing. But throughout the 1740s, nearly two-thirds of Roan's congregants made each payment in cash. Roan also recounted how congregants made trips to merchants in Lancaster and that two peddlers, one Ferguson and James Elder, regularly came from the town to places like Donegal, plying their wares.[10]

The road to Lancaster also allowed Donegal's residents to move out into a wider world. As soon as Lancaster County's courts met in session, Donegal's inhabitants wasted little time in attending. At the first quarter session held at nearby Conestogoe, eight Ulster migrants served as grand jurors and heard a case of assault arising between Robert Allison and John Dunbar.[11] Within two years, Donegal's settlers regularly brought suit against one another, finally finding a legitimate outlet for years of pent-up disputes. At the court of common pleas in August 1731, for example, four cases involved Ulster migrants suing one another. Six months later, Lazarus Lowry, an Ulster-born fur trader, requested that six of his neighbors appear to answer charges, and for next three years he attended the court either as a plaintiff or defendant in a number of cases.[12]

The Presbyterian Church complained "at the litigious Law-Suits that are maintained among Professors of Religion, so contrary to that Peace and Love which the Gospel requires."[13] In 1734, a Paxton man brought suit against another for his failure to deliver lumber for the construction of the minister's house. Session members were amazed that one of their own would "hasard a breach in the Congregation for the sake of so smal a trifle." Before long, the Presbytery of Donegal was complaining of settlers throughout congregations resorting to using county courts to handle disputes, moves through which "so many deliberately to Chuse to sacrifice the peace of Christs Chh to their own privat interests and humour."[14] The Presbytery of Donegal even went so far as "to proceed to publish the sentence of excoiaon" against "Lasorous Lowry" for his "obstinacy."[15]

But this move did not stop Lowry or others. Less than six months after Lowry's excommunication, the court ordered Patrick Black to appear for a charge of debt. Black claimed that because he had "long been a prisoner and suffered great hardship having no effects to answer his condition," he asked to "make satisfaction by servitude." The court demanded Black serve his creditor, John Boyle, for a year and a half. Another plaintiff charged that Black owed him money also. On top of his time to Boyle, Black had to serve another two years. Undeterred by the judicial system, Black brought a suit at the next session against the weaver John McDowell.[16] By 1735, as many as ten cases per session involved settlers from Ulster migrant enclaves suing their own.[17] So popular had civil courts become that in 1734 one resident of Donegal declared that "there was no need of session or Judicatories." Justices of the peace could "doe all and rule all."[18]

Although session members complained, they had some difficulty adjudicating disputes arising from debt or trespass, the two most likely reasons cases came before civil courts. Elders and ministers found themselves in the uncomfortable position of arbitrating disputes over "Lines between . . . Plantations" and contracts.[19] In one such instance, Thomas Dobbins entered a complaint against a member of the session, Hanse Kirkpatrick. Dobbins argued that Kirkpatrick was guilty of "Breach of Bargain, declaring that Hanse had sold him his flax-seed at 4 s 10 d p Bushel, and afterwards would not let him have it at that price." Dobbins contended that Kirkpatrick agreed to the price but reneged once he found a better deal down the road by the mill. "Because it was so much under the price of flax-seed at the Landing," Kirkpatrick felt justified in ignoring the prior contract. Clearly, the session had some grounds to adjudicate the dispute. Both parties were, after all, members of the same congregation, and a public feud brought scandal to the whole congregation. Yet the conflict also required the members of the session to make judgment on the actions of people and affairs outside their nominal jurisdiction. The offense took place outside the bounds of the parish near the "Landing." Moreover, the third party was not a member of the congregation. Despite these issues, the session judged the bargain with the "stranger" valid, finding that "it appeared that Hanse had at least understood the Bargain so as that he was to have the advantage of the rising of the Market: whereon he was clear'd."[20]

Even issues involving moral lapses at times intersected with market imperatives. When in 1741 the lower-end session of New Londonderry "had to deal with some persons on account of their being guilty of the great and scandalous sin of Excess of strong Drink," members argued that such practices tended to "corrupt and Debauch the Land, and make bad men worse." In this instance, however, the session admitted that "it has been generally at Publick Vendues they were guilty of this Evil." Drink no longer merely blackened men's souls and the congregation, but also "Elevat[ed] men beyond the sober solid Exercise of their reason . . . that they may get the better prices for their Goods, and get advantage to themselves from the others incapacity and folly." Such actions smacked of "fraud and injustice." The session ordered that "when any of you may see cause to make such publick sales, you would not comply with this pernicious custom of giving Intoxicating Drink, but look on it as an unjust and sinful method for advancing your own gain."[21] As a censurable offense, Sabbath-breaking at New Londonderry also took a back seat to economic imperatives. "On a certain Lord's day morning," William Penny "found his neighbour, Robert Turner's cattle in his field of green oats." Angered by the loss to his crop, Penny "did designedly turn them into sd. Robt Turner's own field of oats and corn." The session concluded that Penny's actions were "very sinful and offensive." But the session did not chastise him for breaking the Sabbath, but found instead that his crime was "highly aggravated by being done on the Lord's day."[22]

As sessions competed with civil courts for the attention of congregants, elders and ministers showed some reluctance in disciplining wayward congregants. To ensure disputes remained within the congregation, session members at times acted more like arbiters than judges, hoping to avoid stepping on too many toes. At Middle Spring, for instance, a few congregants claimed that after a wedding Samuel Leard was "not fully capable to sit straight on his horse," an unexceptional accusation in session meetings. Although three witnesses attested to his state and the amount he drank that night, Leard asserted that he suffered from ill health, not drink. The session found no grounds for censure. Another member of the congregation, Thomas Finley, learned from this episode. When his turn came to stand before the session for public drunkenness, he pleaded a case of "cholic." Again, the session did not convict.[23] Similarly, the Middle Spring and Big Spring sessions met together in 1745 to resolve "a scandalous and riotous Quarrell wherein some Members of each congregation were concern'd." Instead of calling the malefactors before the session to face its judgment, members tried brokering a deal between the two groups, a preemptive strike to bring a stop to needless conflict. At issue was not censure of one group or another, but arbitration because each side feared the other "going to the justices."[24] Apparently, the threat of civil courts inspired more fear than the justice of the session. In the 1720s, a resort to civil courts would have been both unwarranted and nearly impossible.

The campaign to refit chaotic communities with Old World institutions and practices, therefore, was not working as planned. This proved to be the case at the most contentious congregational squabble the Presbytery of Donegal encountered in the 1730s.[25] In 1734, a few congregants from the lower-end settlement of Nottingham complained to the Presbytery of Donegal against "John Kirkpatrick and some adherents, for Endeavoring to Make a rupture in the Session, and destroying the interest of Christ in the Congr." After one congregant told Kirkpatrick "he should stand for the Cause of Christ according to truth and the light of his conscience," Kirkpatrick and his followers "had gone up and down the congrn" accusing their minister, William Orr, of asserting "in his Publick doctrine . . . that it was a damnable notion which some intertain of Election." Another congregant, John Moor, claimed Orr preached "false doctrine" and declared "that he thought it not agreeable to what he had been taught, and further he owned that he had said that Mr Orr had raked Hell for his Sermon." Following close on the heels of the Hemphill affair, a charge of heterodoxy was sure to catch attention.

However, the issue at first involved money. Kirkpatrick and Moor refused to pay for the erection of a new meetinghouse because they were "difficulted about a Bond they stand bound in for building the meeting-House which should have been paid before now, and for which they are in Fear of being troubled." They also "laboured under some Difficulty, with Respect to an obligation wherein they stand bound to make good Mr. Orr's maintenance, from which . . . they desired to be released." Caught in this bind, they found problems with Orr's doctrine.

Soon the problem escalated. When Kirkpatrick and his followers failed to sway the rest of the congregation to depose Orr, they resorted to mean-spirited tactics. A year after the affair began, a "Mrs Robinson" accused Orr of adultery. Not to be outdone, David Kennedy, a supporter of Orr, claimed that Mrs. Robinson sailed with him from Ireland and that "she was drunk on board, and that it was supposed she was drunk at New Castle." Moreover, Kennedy continued, "he heard some persons on board [claim] . . . that Mrs. Robinson was a witch." The backlash against Orr's detractors led the presbytery to fear that "there is a design and Combination of several persons . . . that they are intending to strike and abuse sd Jon K etc. with Clubs and stones in a tumultuous manner." Robinson at last refused to come before an unyielding Presbytery of Donegal, "but that she would declare what she had to say before a Justice of the Peace." Among the charges Kirkpatrick's detractors claimed the presbytery ignored was his accusation that Orr was in the habit of "vomiting on horse-back after drinking."

Because the session had lost control of the process, the presbytery and the synod responded to the charges. Although, the members of the presbytery made clear that Orr remained "firmly attached to the doctrine of predestination and free grace as held by us and contained in the Westminster Confession," they agreed with Kirkpatrick that his preaching tended toward heterodoxy or, as they put it, "rash Arminianism." The synod likewise found that "by Reason of his natural Temper, he is something liable to act with an Appearance of too great an Air of Imperiousness," but refused to loose him from his charge. Kirkpatrick also received a mild reprimand. The presbytery rebuked Orr's enemies for causing a "rupture" within the congregation. And the synod, backed by the large numbers of ministers from the Presbytery of Donegal, asked Kirkpatrick and his adherents to "acknowledge their rash and impudent Manner of Discoursing of Mr. Orr's Doctrine representing it as false and erronious."

Although the synod and particularly the Presbytery of Donegal found the tone of charge and countercharge reprehensible, the fear of division determined their approach to the affair. Both bodies attempted to keep the peace. Although the synod implored each side to "industriously for the future to take Care and not to repeat past Matters of Controversy, but bury all in Oblivion, and endeavour by all proper Means to assert and cultivate true Christian Charity and Affection," Kirkpatrick and his followers paid little attention. They continued to intimidate Orr with new charges. Orr never obtained the demission that he had requested from the Nottingham congregation. Infuriated with the presbytery and synod for refusing to come down harder on his detractors, he denounced both as "a company of Damn'd Hipocrites" and, according to the synod, "did soon after disorderly desert the Bounds of that Presbytery as a Fugitive of Discipline." The synod ordered "that his Name be rased out of the Catalogue."

A few months after the scandal broke, the Presbytery of Donegal noted the "deep concern we observe, that this cong, which hath Subsisted since its formation, with so much remarkable force and unanimity, should become now a field of intestine division, of unnatural and irreligious debate." Nor did Nottingham prove the exception. Within many congregations, ministers sensed "an Evil Spirit that seems, Alas for it!, to have got dreadfully possession of a great Many of our persuasion, and Especially of our own Country men in these parts of the World."[26] Far from an overarching vision that would allow the group to negotiate a difficult New World, consolidation proved rickety in practice.

The problems that sessions and presbyteries encountered reflected deeper patterns of change gripping Ulster enclaves during this period. Increasingly, a number of settlers had sufficient resources to employ servants, and, in some cases, to purchase slaves. The 1750 tax assessment for Donegal recorded ten servants held in the township. In the same year, the settlers just to the north at Paxton had thirteen servants. In addition, taxpayers in Paxton owned forty-two slaves. Although the Donegal return lists no slaveholders, by the late 1730s a number of settlers had purchased slaves.[27] John Stuart counted as his own a "melatow wench named Joan." And George Stuart, an early migrant who had an estate valued at £572, owned "one negroe girll." Indeed, the greatest slaveowner in the area was the minister, James Anderson, who held a "negro wench" named Dinah, a "negro man" called Pline, and a three-year-old girl called Bell. Listed as his "additional inventory" was "a Negress Childe of two months old" valued at £2.[28]

With the opening of Donegal society, Anderson and some of his neighbors had prospered. In addition to owning slaves, Anderson ran a mill and a ferry service from one of his two sizeable holdings across the Susquehanna, owned a fine clock, furniture, and £40 worth of books.[29] His experiences were not exceptional. Good roads ensured that surpluses could be marketed and that homespun gave way to consumer goods. For example, on the lower-end, Susann McCain left "the last year of her time" to a servant maid, as well as four hundred acres of land, and seventy-seven bushels of wheat and ninety-three bushels of barley at the mill to her sons.[30] By 1739, one settler had acquired an oval table with six walnut chairs, four wigs, and "a walnut bed stead with a poplar board at the head of it." His crop surplus amounted to sixty-six bushels of rye.[31] Even Thomas Wilson, who died in 1746 and whose estate totaled £48, left his heirs a walnut table, bedside, and a chest with lock and key.[32] And while Joseph Work, not worth much more than Wilson, owned three feather beds, three chests, and table linen,[33] the carpenter James Murray had by 1747 buttons of silver sewn onto his coats and wore a silk hat.[34] By the late 1740s, settlers had purchased such items as quilted petticoats, silver teaspoons, snuff-boxes, and silver buckles and clasps from merchants in Lancaster and peddlers in the region.[35]

As Donegal began to change, James Logan's investments finally began to pay off. To begin with, Logan had a free hand to grant land titles. By 1732, the land office was back in business, and Thomas Penn arrived to press the family's claims. In the summer of that year, he sailed to Pennsylvania to bring some order to proprietary affairs in the colony. Within a few months of his arrival from London, Penn began a campaign to evict squatters on proprietary land, court potential buyers, collect back rents and quitrents, and put a stop to the practice of selling "improvements." While Logan ignored the practice earlier, with Penn's arrival, policy changed. " 'Tis true some of them [from Donegal] applyed to the Commissioners before their Settlement," Penn argued, "whereas others went without thinking that formality Necessary." Some, he continued, "settled 12 or 15 Years, have paid no Consideration for that favour, [and] neither think they ought."[36]

Moreover, through a policy of bargaining and coercion, Pennsylvania officials obtained more land for settlement from the Indians in the lower Susquehanna Valley. "Our Commissioners," Governor Gordon had declared, "would never allow any survey to be made [west of the Susquehanna], not only on Account of our Agreements with our Indians but also of that made with Maryland." Despite Gordon's directive, settlement was taking place by the beginning of the 1730s. In 1731, the proprietors learned that "people from the North of Ireland . . . have run over the back parts of the Province as far as Susquehannah and are now to the further disaffection of the Indians, passing over it." The Presbytery of Donegal in 1732 was already ministering to "the people west of susquehhana," on land unpurchased from Indians.[37] A Conestoga by the name of Civility reminded the governor that "itt being in our road in our hunting . . . no person should Settle on that side of the river without our Consent."[38] By the late 1730s, Indians in the region admitted, "We know our Lands are now become more Valuable." "It is very true," an official informed representatives of the Six Nations, "the Lands of late become more Valuable, but what raises their Value? Is it not intirely owing to the Industry and Labour used by white people in their Cultivation and Improvement?"[39]

The growing presence of European migrants presented leaders in Philadelphia with a difficult choice: either stand by old promises made to Indians or support migrants who promised to enrich the colony's coffers. They chose the latter. In 1736, at Conestogoe, in what would be the last treaty council held there, the Six Nations agreed with provincial officials to cede the lower Susquehanna, both east and west banks, for white settlement. The Six Nations did not suffer from the bargain; rather, Conestogas and Delawares did, the peoples who inhabited the region. With the treaty, the once vibrant trading village of Conestoga declined in significance. Trade moved further west to the Ohio Valley and the focal point of Indian/colonist relations shifted to the village of Shamokin further north on the river and dominated by the Six Nations.[40]

Finally, the border dispute with Maryland was reaching a resolution. In 1731, Governor Gordon sent an angry letter to the proprietary governor of Maryland. "I am . . . credibly informed," Gordon intoned, "that some Persons of Maryland having obtained Grants from your Offices have pretended to lay them over the River Susquehanna."[41] Gordon's fears were not misplaced. The government of Maryland in that year began sponsoring a policy of settling its own inhabitants on the rich, disputed land. As part of their strategy to claim the territory west of the river for Maryland, instigators tried to woo German settlers away from their allegiance to Pennsylvania, offering them title to land and protection. To press their claims, Maryland officials sent Thomas Cressap, a carpenter by trade and a Catholic, to intimidate settlers allying themselves with Pennsylvania. Cressap settled in an area west of the river, and north of four hundred men who paid taxes to Pennsylvania. A year later in 1732, Cressap and a band of Marylanders attacked traders, stealing the horses of the Ulster migrant James Patterson. In 1735, Cressap began a reign of terror in the region, assaulting settlers and burning their crops. In that year, his band rode to the home of "one Murphy," and "Sett on to burn his fences" and "the Crop of Corn he had put in the ground." Later that year, Cressap attacked another settler who had "sowed a field of the said Tract of Land on the West side of the said River with Wheat." Cressap's tactics involved hitting Pennsylvanians where it hurt—their surplus produce for market. "The Intention of the said Cressap," wrote John Wright, the Lancaster County sheriff, "to prevent [the settler] . . . from reaping his field and carrying off his Grain, was abundantly manifest by his the said Cressap's having brought Sundry Waggons with him in which he prepared . . . to carry off the said Grain."[42]

The land now meant a great deal. James Patterson implored "all the People thereabouts to stand up Manfully for Pensilvania against the Marylanders." For his own part, he "would fight to the Knees in Blood before he should loose his Plantations on either side of the River." He had his chance in 1736. In the summer of that year, two hundred men from Maryland—described as "a Number of Irish Papists, in Arms"—"with Beat of Drum and Sound of Trumpet" crossed the river near Hempfield and "demanded the Dutch," those who "declin[ed] to be Subject to the Government of Maryland, and turning to the Proprietors of Pennsylvania." An Ulster migrant and owner of a saw and gristmill, Benjamin Chambers, rode to Donegal where he met a number of residents at a houseraising, imploring the men to help repel the Marylanders. With Chambers's help, the Irish-born Samuel Smith, the sheriff of Lancaster County, raised one hundred fifty men, most from Donegal Township. Although no battle ensued, these measures led to a series of raids and counterraids, culminating with the arrest of Cressap in his cabin. When the Pennsylvanians surrounded the cabin, they "were Answer'd by Cressap with Oaths and Imprecations, calling the sd Sherif . . . and Company, Damn'd Scotch Irish Sons of Bitches, and the Proprietor and people of Pensilvania Damn'd Quakering Dogs and Rogues." While Cressap wondered "why they wou'd ffight for a parcell of Damn'd Quakering Sons of Bitches," Samuel Smith explained, "a Discovery had been lately made of a Design sett on foot by the Government of Maryland, for dispossessing several Families."[43] As one Donegal settler contended, "Great Numbers of the Inhabitants of these parts of the sd County of Lancaster who had been threatened with the Extreamest Severities, cou'd scarce expect to be safe any longer in their Possessions." A number of settlers had by this time a stake in society and the commercial economy. They stood to lose too much by standing by.[44]

With these issues close to resolution, in 1735 Logan took out a patent for four hundred acres adjoining John Galbraith's land to the west. He did not sit on the holding, but in a short time conveyed it to Jacob Hertzler.[45] Beginning in the early 1730s, Germans such as Hertzler began moving into the Donegal area. In 1733, John Heer and Peter Musselman requested "a parcel of Land, the former at Checasalunga and the other near Dunagall . . . so that if the Land be clear of other claims it may be survey'd."[46] As the fur trade moved further west, traders also conveyed land to Germans, as did John Combe, who sold a tract along the Susquehanna to Christian Breneman in 1739.[47] In some cases, Germans purchased substantial amounts of land. A year after Heer and Musselman made their request, together three others bought more than 1,000 acres for the settlement of their people.[48] In 1735, Germans purchased at least 550 additional acres along the Chickeselunga.[49]

As the pace of change quickened, Logan, ever on the make, ordered one of his agents to "warn the Irish off Fagg's Manor" on the lower-end and have the tracts surveyed for sale.[50] He also decided the time had come for settling "about Ten Thousand acres of Conestogo Manor." He parceled this land to his friends, who then turned a tidy profit by selling it to German-speaking Mennonites. The "Dutch" now inhabited the area between the enclaves on the upper and lower-ends.[51] Moreover, by 1750 Donegal contained almost as many settlers from the Palatinate as from Ulster, and in the area immediately west, which had been unoccupied in the 1720s, Germans outnumbered all other groups.[52]

Although some in Donegal protested the transformation, others took advantage of it. Amid these demographic changes, a group of settlers refused to allow surveyors into the area. One surveyor laying out plots on a proprietary manor in 1741 encountered Ulster settlers who snatched his compass and declared that "if the Chain be spread again," they "wou'd stop it." "It is as much as man's Life is worth," the frightened surveyor reported, "to go amongst them, for they gather'd together in Companies, and go in Arms every Time they Expect I am any where near there about, with full resolution to kill or criple me."[53] Others pleaded with Logan "that the Dutch may not be allow'd to settle between them," even if they were the "best bidders."[54] In particular, some lamented that "some unstay'd People having an Inclination to remove from thence" were acting with regard to their "private interest only" by "disposing of their Improvements" and allowing "strangers" into the region.[55] But despite complaints, a number of settlers began selling out to Germans, as did Collum McCurry, who in 1736 deeded one hundred acres of his plot adjoining John Magee's farm to Jacob Moyer.[56]

As Indians left the upper end and more migrants streamed in, the population in the region exploded from fewer than 30,000 in 1710 to more than 100,000 in 1750. Land became more valuable, in some areas rising in value threefold over the period. Moreover, available acreage was dropping.[57] By 1750, the largest landholder in Donegal held only 300 acres. Most held 100 or so, a far cry from the years of early settlement when some held 700 acres and few less than 250.[58] For those starting out, therefore, such as sons of early migrants, opportunity in the region was declining.

By the 1740s, the sons of early settlers began clashing with their fathers. On his deathbed, James McMichael willed to his eldest son John a "pair of Mens Books and one shilling." To his other son, James, he bequeathed "one Blue Coat and a pair of checkered Trousers and one shilling." They received nothing else. The farm he left to his wife, and on her death to his four daughters.[59] Similarly, John Hill received from his father, James, "two Pounds ten shillings which is in his own hands and Oweth me." Hill also refused to set aside anything for his other boy. His unborn child, if a boy, was to receive the farm. If not, it went to his daughter Mary.[60] Donegal resident Alexander McNutt left to his "well beloved son Robert McNutt as much Gray Cloth as will make him a strait coat" and one shilling to his other son, James.[61] Fathers had good reason to disinherit their boys. Sons, it appears, showed little interest in working their parents' farms. Patrick Carr stipulated that his son not inherit until he proved his worth by clearing some land.[62] Similarly, David Foster offered his son William "two full years, bedd and Board," provided he helped with the harvest.[63] James Patten went so far as to leave his sons with a ewe and a cow and to bequeath his holding to his servant "if he proves good."[64]

Undoubtedly, with land going in Virginia for a fraction of the price near Donegal, leaving the region looked more appealing than working the family farm. With rising land values and the opening of the trans-Susquehanna frontier after the defeat of the Marylanders and the Indian treaty of 1736, movement began to the south and west. Because many held land without title, they sold "Improvements" much as they had sold tenant right in Ireland to pay for passage. Although authorities frowned on this and did not record the practice in official records, they recognized its validity.[65] By doing so, those with few resources could "make Merchandize" of the land they worked and use the proceeds to purchase cheaper land elsewhere.[66] For example, after the death of an early settler, James Mitchell, his son sold the land and improvements he inherited to Henry Musselman and left the region.[67]

In a similar situation, James Magaw from Paxton implored his brother John to "Come up soon" to a new settlement west of the Susquehanna. Magaw, who held no taxable property in Paxton by 1750, his wife, Jane, and their young children made the trip across the Susquehanna to Monaghan in three days, crossing the river at Harris' Ferry.[68] "I think we will like this part of the country," he told John, "when we get our cabbin built." His letter spoke of the economic possibilities the new region offered, especially for a man with a young family. "There is plenty of timber south of us," he gushed. Even before the Magaws had constructed a home, they had "planted some corn and potatoes." James Magaw decided to build a cabin near John McCall, Alick Steen, and John Rippey, fellow travelers from Paxton.

"We have 18 cabbins built here now," he informed his brother, "and it looks like a town; but we have no name for it." He also requested guns because, as he put it, "there's a good wheen of ingens about here." James Magaw ended his letter by asking his brother to "Tell Billy Parker to come up Soon and bring Nancy with him. I know he will like the country."[69]

Despite the upheaval of the period, a number of the earliest settlers learned to adjust to the changes taking place. As Germans were moving in many sought to legalize their holdings. In 1734, one of Logan's agents, James Steel, wrote that "From some Conversation I had last night among our Friends, it was thought expedient . . . to make the Surveys about Dunagall." The inhabitants, he added, "are very desirous to have it don."[70] Many had worked the land for years without warrant or survey, such as Alexander Work, who had lived on his plot for thirteen years before bothering to legalize his claim.[71] With Penn's estate settled and the land office back in business, a number of the earliest arrivals, those holding the greatest amount of land, requested warrants for their tracts to have their claims recognized.[72]

Though they haggled with Logan and the proprietors, settlers realized they had a stake in the region where they had fashioned a comfortable existence. As Thomas Penn pressed the earliest migrants to make good on promises they had made to Logan for land, they bristled at the amounts he was seeking for unpaid quitrents and taxes. They negotiated Penn down to accepting "the half penny rent," far below the amount he sought. "They desire also," an agent informed Penn, "that this favour may be Extended to all the inhabitants new and old now settled in Donegal, which are of their congregation and also to Extend to six or eight of the Old settlers in the Edge of Derry Township."[73] Yet they came to terms. Legal title to land now mattered, and some did their best to discourage newcomers from setting up without it. When, for example, "a gang of Scotch Irish" squatted in Conestogoe Manor and "threatened to hold it by force of arms,"[74] Andrew Galbraith, a substantial landowner, accompanied a group of officials who "pull'd down and burnt 30 of their Cabins."[75]

A number of settlers also learned to cooperate with the newcomers. Joseph Work, an early settler, lent money to his German neighbors, as well as borrowed from "Ould Hartman and Felix Muller."[76] Relations with other groups were not always so cordial. On one occasion, after a dispute over money, Archibald McNeal "swore and cursed" at one settler to whom he had lent a small sum, leading the borrower to declare that "the Society of Presbyterians were as bad Devils as ever came out of Hell and that he would make Examples of them, and would root them out." As for their ministers, "he would riffle them."[77] In November 1743, Ulster and German settlers confronted one another in court at least ten times. Six months later, twelve cases involved disputes between members of the two groups. But these involved trespass and debt, not only highlighting the issues dividing the two groups but also revealing moments of meaningful interaction and growing proximity.[78]

The proximity of other groups meant that men and women often inhabited two worlds, one bounded by the meetinghouse, the other not. In 1743, for example, after Esther McClosky accused a fellow congregant on the lower end of fathering her illegitimate child, she admitted that Christopher Stoop, a German she met at a fair at New Castle, was the father. She tried to convince the session she had been raped by Stoop, but the session soon learned that she consented to his advances. Outside of chastising her, the session could do little. Its members had no power to induce Stoop to marry the woman.[79] This new plural world also made for some fascinating developments. In 1747, Robert Patterson, who had moved from Donegal to the Town of Lancaster, instructed his wife that on his death "my body shall be interred in ... the Grave Yard belonging to the Germans or Dutch Calvinists Church." After setting aside money for his family, Patterson left the rest to "the Presbytery of Dunnegall ... to forward promote and propagate the Gospell."[80]

By the time Patterson revealed his divided loyalties, the upper end was becoming a place of extremes. Settlements like Donegal and Paxton were now inhabited by men such as John Magaw who held no taxable land, had young families, and were willing to strike out elsewhere for opportunity. At the other end of the spectrum were men such as Andrew Galbraith, early migrants to the region who owned either slaves, servants, or mills, and worked substantial amounts of land. Galbraith, who had arrived before 1720, began serving as the coroner of Lancaster County, a justice of the peace, and an assemblyman during the 1730s. By 1736, he legalized a claim to three hundred fifty acres adjoining the meetinghouse. Galbraith was among the first to petition the Presbytery of New Castle to supply Donegal with a minister and served as an elder in the congregation. Evicting squatters and pressing for the claims of Pennsylvania against Cressap, according to James Logan, he had "always Shewn a readiness to oblige" the Proprietors and was "a good man."[81] At this time, Galbraith and others like him on the upper end would put their weight behind sessions, the Confession, and order. Men like Magaw, on the other hand, would turn their backs on the consolidating vision. The Great Awakening both revealed and exacerbated these growing tensions within migrant enclaves.

THE first signs of a new emphasis on vital religion appeared in the synod of Philadelphia in 1733. In that year, Gilbert Tennent presented an apparently innocuous overture. "To use some proper means to revive the declining power of godliness," he argued, "the synod do earnestly recommend . . . to take particular care about ministerial visiting of families, and press family and secret worship, according to the Westminster Directory." He also recommended "to every Presbytery, at proper seasons to inquire concerning the diligence of their members in such particulars."[82] A committee of six reviewed the petition and saw nothing objectionable. Indeed, the overture seemed to call for a reemphasis of measures already under the jurisdiction of each session, that elders would travel throughout the bounds of each parish checking into possible scandal. As for the allusion to "the declining power of godliness," such a phrase raised few eyebrows for a people accustomed to such jeremiads in Ulster and America.

In the following year, Tennent's tone became more insistent. At a meeting in 1734, while ministers from the Donegal and New Castle Presbyteries presented a proposal calling for an annual examination of all presbyteries to ensure that each enforced subscription, Tennent, apparently stung over the way in which synod members had interpreted his overture of the previous year, restated his appeal in no uncertain terms. Tennent proposed that "due Care [be] taken in Examining into the Evidences of the Grace of God in them [ministers], as well as of their other necessary Qualifications," claiming that the Westminster

Confession of Faith also made allowances for checking the spiritual state of the clergy. Tennent's overture placed his subscriptionist brethren in a bind. They had little enthusiasm for the thrust of Tennent's petition, but his petition invoked the Confession of Faith, which they saw as the cornerstone of their program of ordering the church. They did not scruple with anyone who in one way or another reinforced the centrality of the Confession. Yet the overture represented a new departure. Appointing "godly men" to the ministry, as one minister argued, meant not only finding those with sound principles, but also encouraging "such as are experimentally acquainted with the renewing and sanctifying Grace of God in their own souls." Members agreed "not to admit . . . loose careless or irreligious Persons," a standard qualification for admission to the ministry, and certainly less than the ringing endorsement for which Tennent had hoped.[83] Nonetheless, within two years Gilbert Tennent's brother Charles was licensed by the Presbytery of Philadelphia to preach once he had subscribed to the Westminster Confession of Faith and was "examined . . . as to the evidences of the Graces of Sanctification in his Soul."[84]

At first, many did not recognize what was afoot. John Thomson called this new concern for the "graces of sanctification" a "new-fangled Stir about Religion" and a "spiritual Frenzy." He and his colleagues from the Presbytery of Donegal made little sense of the new habit of "crying out . . . at Sermons." Francis Alison dismissed the whole notion of looking into a person's inward state. "The heart," he argued, "is not under human cognizance; declarations of experience may be, or not be, what men feel." He added that "no man can judge whether they feel, or not"; moreover, "this practice has no authority from Scripture." Alison also claimed such a sensibility was unprecedented, "not known in Holland, Scotland, nor Ireland, nor was ever heard of in our Prebys south of Philada." Some saw the revival spirit as a foreign-sounding fashion enjoying a warm reception in more cosmopolitan areas. John Craig, born in Antrim and educated at Edinburgh and who considered himself "steady to the Presbyterian Principles and against all Innovation," saw Tennent's new preoccupation as inspired by "one Mr. Freelinghouse a Low Dutch Minister."[85] Finally, the conversion of the minister Alexander Craighead to Tennent's message led many to fear that the to-do smacked of rising antinomianism.

In 1736, a number of Craighead's congregants complained that he had barred his own wife from the Lord's table and began preaching in Tennent's style. Perplexed by his behavior, the Presbytery of Donegal found him so "exceedingly unreasonable, that we cannot forbear suspecting 'that he is under some dreadful delusion of Satan, if not a delirium in his head."[86] During this period, the frenzy seemed a distant curiosity, affecting only Dutch Reformed congregations and scattered Presbyterian congregations in New Jersey, such as Tennent's, but few beyond this. None believed these unconnected outpourings of the spirit formed the start of a general revival. Parishes on the frontier remained untouched, and as long as they did, no concerted opposition to revival sprang up.

The Awakening, though, soon moved closer to home. In 1738, two years after frontier ministers had secured ironclad subscription to the Westminster Confession of Faith as the terms of ministerial communion, a troubling conflict arose within the Neshaminy congregation in Bucks County, Pennsylvania, of William Tennant, father of Gilbert and Charles. In 1738, some members approached the Presbytery of Philadelphia, threatening to establish a new, rival congregation. They complained of Tennent's new insistence on "new birth." They further requested that Francis McHenry, a probationer from Ireland, serve as their minister. McHenry had little enthusiasm for vital religion. Although the presbytery found him "well-qualified . . . esp. as to his Knowledge and Orthodoxy in Divinity" and noted that he had subscribed to the Confession of Faith, in the estimation of some members, "he gave a modest but satisfactory account of his Experience of the Sanctifying Influences of the Spirit on his own Heart." This drew fire from Tennent's supporters in the congregation. For the first time, the presbytery acknowledged the existence of two well-defined "parties" within a congregation, divided over the issue of piety. Ministers and elders from the surrounding areas settled for a compromise. Each group was to pay its chosen minister. In order to allow two ministers to work in the congregation, the presbytery listed McHenry as an "assistant" to Tennent. Such middle-ground solutions, however, would prove increasingly difficult to broker.[87]

The first skirmish within the synod erupted over the issue of education. All of Pennsylvania's Presbyterians took seriously the proper preparation of young men for the ministry. From the earliest years, Presbyterians had filled their pulpits with men trained abroad or, in some cases, at Harvard and Yale. But demand far outstripped supply. As a generation of American-born Presbyterians began coming of age, all hoped promising youths would decide to fill the ranks. There was a catch, however. Relying on European and New England universities to produce men prepared for the ministry proved both costly and inconvenient. Few could afford to pay for an American-born youth to travel to, lodge, and study in Scotland. Yet, with the number of congregations proliferating, especially on the frontier, the need for ministers showed no signs of abating. Because William Tennent had had some success preparing his sons for the ministry, other young men approached him to train them. After educating a few esteemed ministers, such as Samuel Blair, Tennent founded his own school at Neshaminy in 1735, contemptuously dubbed the "Log College" by critics. Tennent's Log College graduates studied a curriculum similar to those trained in Scotland. Students received a classical education stressing theology, biblical exegesis, and knowledge of Latin and Hebrew; indeed, his graduates rivaled those educated in Scotland.[88]

Early on, ministers trained in Scotland and licensed in Ireland did not question the ability of men schooled by William Tennent. By 1733, the synod had admitted to the ministry four men who had studied under Tennent without so much as a whisper, including Gilbert Tennent and Samuel Blair. They appeared competent. Yale had even awarded Gilbert Tennent an honorary M.A. to recognize the quality of the education he had received from his father. More important for the members from the Presbytery of Donegal, all were at least born in Ireland and, therefore, most likely subscribers. But a number of ministers discerned a troubling trend. All of Tennent's students advocated "enthusiasm." Students were tested on the inward working of grace on their souls. John McMillan, for example, schooled at one such academy, found that "while there the Lord poured out his spirit on the students, and I believe there were but a few who were not brought under serious concern about their immortal souls." The great English itinerant, George Whitefield, saw these academies less as places of learning and more as a means of instilling a new type of preaching and theology, one that rejected the ways of "false dead-hearted Preachers . . . who hold the Form of found Words, but never felt the Power of them in their Souls." In particular, he praised the Log College as a "school of the old prophets." As the only American Presbyterian institution of higher learning, it looked to many more like a hatchery for vital religion than a training ground for orthodox ministers.[89]

With the religious winds within the synod shifting, some ministers began scrupling the educational rigor of the Log College. In 1739, a majority of ministers agreed that "every person who proposes himself to Trial as a Candidate for the Ministry, and who has not a Diploma or the usual Certificates from an European or New-England University, shall be examined by the whole Synod . . . This we trust will have a happy Tendency to prevent unqualified Men from creeping in among us." There was little radical about this overture. For years, ministers and elders from the Presbytery of Donegal had rejected candidates, some with superb qualifications, because they had not received their training in Scotland and served as probationers in Ireland. Such a move, therefore, ensured that frontier inhabitants could vet prospective ministers under the guise of educational achievement in hopes of attracting orthodox ministers to fill frontier pulpits. But the decision to use the power of the synod to restrict licensure amounted to an infringement on the rights of presbyteries to ordain and inspect candidates. Although the overture provided a growing opposition to revival with added insurance, it also gave William Tennent a strong leg on which to dispute the move.[90]

Tennent would have none of this. He and his allies claimed their candidates for the ministry measured up to the exacting standards of European education, but they refused to suffer the insult of parading them before the synod, especially since those who had credentials from Ireland did not have to undergo this process. To press their claims, Tennent and his colleagues tried to license one of his graduates, Welsh-born John Rowland, within the Presbytery of New Brunswick without sending him before the synod for examination, hoping that the synod would have to recognize the right of presbyteries to ensure candidates measured up. Tennent then asked him to preach before his congregation. The settlers at the congregation of Maidenhead and Hopewell followed suit. A problem soon arose. Both congregations fell within the bounds of the Presbytery of Philadelphia. Although the presbytery found that the people had "Liberty, with proper Restrictions . . . to call any orderly and regular Candidates in order to have a Tryal of his Gifts," its members tried to nip the incipient controversy in the bud. Rowland, the presbytery found, had not "complied with the order of the last synod relating to the Examination of Students by a Com.ee," and, in fact, "was hastily passed over in his Tryals by the Pry of New-Brunswick." To make matters worse for Tennent and Rowland, a number of congregants of Neshaminy, no doubt members of the McHenry party, saw this as an opportunity to discredit William Tennent further. They lodged a formal complaint "of a late action of Mr. Tennent, viz. His bringing into his Pulpit Mr. John Rowland." For his part, Tennent "justified the action, and after disclaiming the authority of the Presbytery. . . . He contemptuously withdrew."[91] By crossing presbytery lines without permission and refusing to countenance the synod's position on the matter, Rowland transformed an infraction into a crisis for the church. If he could breach the bounds of the Presbytery of Philadelphia with apparent impunity, he could do the same at Donegal or New Castle, both of which still contained vacant pulpits.

Battle lines began to emerge. At issue, though, were not the merits of education in America or even of vital religion; rather, something more fundamental was at stake. Every major tenet for which the New Side stood represented the antithesis of the consolidating vision. For one thing, members of the New Side considered creeds irrelevant to their message of vital religion.[92] Certainly, Gilbert Tennent and the Presbyterian New Side took issue with the growth of formalism. He objected to those who, like Samuel Hemphill, "cry up Morality as sufficient, while they neglect the positive Duties of divine Worship," arguing that such people walked with "the *Legs of the Lame*."[93] Subscription as a means to check heretics like Hemphill he saw as useful, and he had subscribed to the Westminster Confession of Faith as a licentiate. However, he differed with his fellow Ulster-born Presbyterians on its significance. Far from central to his beliefs, the Confession was, to him, marginal to salvation, and he scoffed at those who held it as the touchstone of faith. Tennent argued that many of his contemporaries "have never had any more than a Speculation and historical

Knowledge of the Necessity of an Interest in him [Christ]." Formal learning did not lead to Christ, conversion did. In fact, a preoccupation with creeds led to a dead religiosity. Those who "cry up the positive Duties of divine Worship," he contended, "for all your pharisaical Show, Grimace and Ceremony, neglect Morality and the Duties you owe to your Neighbour." This tendency appeared as perilous as Hemphill's heresy, remaking men into "graceless Persons," as he called them, "that having had the Privilege of a Religious Education, can chatter by Rote more orthodoxy. . . . tho' their State towards God be not a whit better."[94]

From the beginning of their ministries, revivalists also spurned parochialism and denominational biases. Gilbert Tennent gloried in the fact that his converts included "Negroes and Indians."[95] Similarly, George Whitefield was wont to say "Don't tell me you are a Baptist, an Independent, a Presbyterian, a dissenter, tell me you are a Christian, that is all I want."[96] Each New Light, Samuel Blair proclaimed, "love[d] all good Men, where ever he finds them, of whatever Denomination, whether Conformist or nonconformist; and holds agreeable and sweet Fellowship with them, notwithstanding their different Sentiments in some Things." Universalist sentiment led Gilbert Tennent and his followers to contribute, along with Baptists and Moravians, to the construction of a nondenominational tabernacle in Philadelphia for George Whitefield. Because New Side preachers placed an emphasis on the individual's path to God and not membership in a particular church, ecumenism defined the thrust of the Awakening. "Persons of almost all Denominations," Tennent enthused, have "been wrought on by the Word."[97]

Itinerancy, however, presented the gravest threat to those intent on order. Itinerancy was nothing new to Ulster's settlers. From the time the earliest settlements were established, presbyteries sent their ministers to many congregations that did not have a pastor. Following this established pattern, members of the Presbytery of New Brunswick ordained ministers, most of whom received their education at Tennent's Log College, without a specific charge; however, some of them preached in areas under the jurisdiction of other presbyteries. New Lights realized they were hitting a raw nerve by sending itinerants into the bounds of congregations with established pastors. Blair argued that Old Lights contested vital religion because "it is like to make a mighty inroad on us," adding that Old Lights took little notice of revivals as long as they were "kept within due Limits without disturbing our Borders."[98] What the opponents of the New Light found alarming was exactly what attracted men such as Blair to the ministry. Tennent believed his opponents fought his message not so much because of theological principles but because of their fear of opening a Pandora's box of chaos. "Partly thro' Ignorance of the Nature of vital Religion, and partly thro' a native Enmity against it, and partly thro' fear of losing their Credit . . . by its Spread near their Borders," a number of ministers and people began a campaign to crush Tennent and his followers.[99]

As conflicts continued to flare up, a group of ministers soon coalesced around opposition to the new style of religiosity. To a man, they had pushed for subscription to the Westminster Confession of Faith as the terms of ministerial communion.[100] They included every cleric from the Presbytery of Donegal and most from the Presbytery of New Castle, men such as James Anderson, John Elder, Francis Alison, and John Thomson. All ministered to men and women in frontier enclaves. With the exception of Samuel Blair at Fagg's Manor, every New Light tended to have greater success in more cosmopolitan and established areas such as New Brunswick and Bucks County, where prosubscription arguments held little sway. Here was the heartland of antisubscription forces, led by Jonathan Dickinson. The lines that divided subscriber from nonsubscriber and moderate subscriber, therefore, became the gulf that separated the New Side from the Old Side. Blair proved the exception to the rule in another significant way. Unlike every frontier Old Light, Blair did not receive his education in Scotland, nor did he serve as a probationer in Ulster. Like the Tennent brothers, he too migrated at a young age and decided to enter the ministry once in the colonies. The only member of the New Side who had spent his formative years in Ireland and obtained a degree from a Scottish university was Gilbert's father, William, a convert from Anglicanism. Region, and ultimately age and experience, determined which ministers "converted" to or were "enraged" by Tennent.[101]

These ministers, who had at first viewed far-off revivals without much alarm, then attempted to keep them beyond their enclaves, now saw the potential of an invasion of their territory, both spiritual and geographic. One minister, who railed against the itinerants "invading his charge," declared, "Whether thou be a Minister or a Member of a Congregation, that is guilty of any of *these divisive Ways* . . . may the *Omnipotent Spirit of God* prick thee in the Heart." Preachers moving about, unconcerned with denominational distinctions and creeds "advanceth Satan's Interest, and will open a Door to Disorders and Confusions." He warned all to "beware of Wolves," not only at the door but within it, those who were "pulling down the Hedge and Wall of the Government and Discipline of *Christ's Church.*" The newly organized Old Side saw in every innovation of the New Side a serious threat to the vision of the group they had created.[102]

To preempt the possibility of such men spreading New Light ideas in their own bounds, in 1738 the synod's ministers from Donegal and New Castle Presbyteries overtured that "no Minister belonging to this synod shall have Liberty to preach in any Congregation belonging to another Presbytery . . . after he is advised by any Ministr. of such Pres that he thinks his Preaching in that Congregation will have a Tendency to procure Divisions and Disorders." Again, the enactment provided Donegal's ministers with an impregnable defense: if an itinerant crossed into the presbytery, even a minister miles away could invoke the act to have the trespasser removed. By doing so, members from Donegal hoped to insulate their people from itinerants trained by William Tennent until they could fill vacancies with ministers from Ireland whom they found more agreeable to their principles. Through their ability to control the synod, this well-defined and well-organized group again thwarted the New Side.[103]

To defeat a group that had nearly achieved control of the synod and through it could manufacture a way to hamper the cause of revival, New Lights changed their tack and drove their message into the heart of frontier enclaves. They chose to go to the lower-end congregation of Nottingham. After the Orr affair at Nottingham, the pulpit remained vacant. The Presbytery of Donegal supplied the congregation from time to time, but not frequently enough. On some occasions, congregants attended services at Blair's meetinghouse at Fagg's Manor twenty miles away. Some even invited Blair to preach at Nottingham, which drew fire from the Donegal Presbytery. On March 8,

1740, Gilbert Tennent visited the congregation to deliver a ground-breaking sermon, in which he lashed out at the "letter-learned and regular Pharisees," who left the people, he argued, as "Sheep having no Shepherd."[104]

In his sermon, "The Danger of an Unconverted Ministry," Tennent implored the people to ignore their ministers, men who were "Moral Negroes so white in the Mouth" who tried to stop anything that "comes near their Borders, and interferes with their Credit or Interest." Because of "Bigotry to human Invention in religious Matters," Old Lights in these areas thwarted the work of true religion to the point that "a Work of Conviction and Conversion has been so rarely heard of." Hitting on all the themes that he knew enraged his opponents, Tennent epitomized the many changes that were gripping Ulster enclaves. "What a sad Security reigns there," he lamented.[105] These "carnal ministers" or "dead drones," as he called them, who ministered to men and women within congregations near Nottingham, "serve to keep better out of the Places where they live; nay, when the Life of Piety comes near their Quarters, they rise up in arms against it, consult, contrive and combine in their Conclaves against it, as a common enemy." Old Lights, he bellowed, could only offer reasons for opposing vital religion, "gilded with the specious Names of Zeal, Fidelity, Peace, good Order, and Unity." He implored congregants to move beyond their "parish-line," arguing that "it is lawful and expedient to go from them to hear Godly Persons."[106]

Intrusions into these areas continued. In 1739, Whitefield made his first appearance in Pennsylvania. On his arrival, Tennent erupted over the possibilities. "Your Sermons," he wrote Whitefield, "have much confirmed the Truth of Christ, which had been preach'd here for many Years in the *Dutch* and *English* Languages."[107] The Tennents prevailed on him to preach in their meetinghouses. Whitefield visited these and other New Light strongholds before departing. A few months later he returned. This time, Gilbert Tennent enlisted Whitefield in his strategy to undermine the base of his detractors. "I rode towards *Nottingham*," Whitefield recalled, "in company with Mr. *Tennent*, Mr. *Craighead*, and Mr. *Blair*, all worthy Ministers." He was, as he claimed, invited by "some of the Inhabitants who had a good Work begun amongst them, some time ago, by the Ministry of

Mr. Blair, Mr. Tennent, and Mr. Cross, the last of which had been denied the Use of the Pulpit by one of his Brethren, and was obliged to preach in the Woods."[108] No doubt, many regarded him with hostility, especially the "*Pharisaical* letter-learned Brethren," chief among whom was James Anderson of Donegal, who challenged Whitefield on points of doctrine.[109] Nevertheless, with Whitefield's arrival, revivals broke out on the lower-end.

"Divisions, Distractions, and Convulsions"[110] gripped Ulster migrant communities. John Craig found himself in the uncomfortable position of ministering to a congregation in which a few families "looked on me as an opposer of the work of God." Some even called for itinerants "to come and preach and convert the people of my charge and free them from Sin and Satan and from me a Carnal wretch."[111] Patrick Campbell and a number of the earliest settlers from Donegal brought charges against Hamilton Bell, a minister with New Light leanings, for "telling one Night how to lye with a woman without her having a Child," leading Bell to declare that "if he knew who told such Stories on him, he would whip them like new Negroes."[112] At the same time, congregants from Derry and Paxton charged John Elder with "false Doctrine" once he prohibited any New Lights from preaching to his people.[113] While some congregants at Brandywine complained "of Mr Blair's intruding into their Congregation," others called for the overthrow of the Old Side minister Samuel Black because he "disliked . . . the field preachers," and seemed "to oppose the work of God's appearing in the land in our day, and speaking diminutively of Some Minrs."[114] With the Awakening, it was not uncommon, as one minister put it, to be "Reproached by some of my own People and Nation."[115]

The Old Side, however, fought back. To combat a group "sowing the Seeds of Division among People,"[116] the Presbytery of Donegal declared "that all the members of this Pby shall, in order to remove the Jealousies which we understand have spread themselves among some of our people, subscribe the Westminster Confession."[117] With the subscription controversy, the Confession served as an idiom of assent, a visible Old World marker of stability. With the Awakening, it also became a creed of resistance. The Donegal ministers also reasserted discipline. But in this case, the sessions were to impose sanctions for inviting the spread of vital religion. They did so through, in the words of Gilbert Tennent, an "extraordinary Act or Canon fram'd by the Presbytery of *Donnegal,* which *ipso facto* excommunicates, or deprives of Church Privileges, all of their People that go to hear any of the Itinerant Preachers."[118]

The debate over the Great Awakening tore the church apart. Ministers such as Thomson and Elder who had tried to turn the church into a bulwark of stability for the group and the Confession into its keystone confronted a younger group of Ulster settlers such as Tennent, educated in the colonies and intent on undermining the strategies of their elders. "I cannot comprehend," a stunned Thomson declared, how New Lights could "justly claim the Denomination of Presbyterians, while they avowedly preach and act contrary to the very plan of Church Government contained in the Confession and Directory, from whence we have the Denomination of Presbyterians."[119] The two visions could not coexist. In 1741, the old guard ousted the New Side from the synod of Philadelphia. Tennent and his New Side brethren acquiesced before a "Narrowness and Bigotry" that stemmed from a belief that "all God's Ministers and People are coop'd up within the Verge of any one particular Denomination."[120] The New Lights left the synod, along with Dickinson and the New England party, allowing Old Lights to proclaim themselves—in a Pyrrhic victory—"the true *Presbyterian Church* in this Province."[121]

Similar forms of mass revival had flourished in Ireland and Scotland in the years before Ulster's migrants left for the colonies. Indeed, Presbyterians in Scotland and Ulster had long traditions of sacramental feasts that drew many from around the countryside to a single meetinghouse.[122] While these origins may explain why Scots in cosmopolitan New Jersey and some of Ulster's migrants found the services surrounding the revival experience appealing, alone they cannot account for the nature of divisions within frontier congregations. In fact, the splits within communities reflected the ways in which settlers experienced change during the period. As a rule, inhabitants on the lower-end, areas in which migrants had settled later, occupied fewer acres, and had a more difficult time obtaining deeds to land, embraced the Awakening. When Tennent traveled to Nottingham on the lower-end to deliver a sermon castigating the Ulster-born Old Lights, he received a warm welcome; indeed, in a congregation where Samuel Blair enjoyed much success converting sinners, many received his message with great "enthusiasm." The *Pennsylvania Gazette* reported, "The Presence of God was visible in the Assemblies, especially at *Nottingham* and *Fagg's Manor*, where the People were under such deep Convictions, that by their Cries they almost drown'd his voice."[123]

But communities on the upper end divided. In 1754, settlers from the region presented a call to John Elder, "promising all due subjection, submission and obedience to the Doctrine, Discipline and Government and Ordinances" of the church. The pro-subscription migrants considered themselves "Deeply Sensible of the great loss and Disadvantage we and ours may sustain In regard of our souls and spiritual Concerns by our living in such a Condition in this Wilderness." By this time, however, settlers no longer lived in a wilderness. In fact, of the twenty-one men who signed the petition requesting the services of the Old Light and who appeared on tax assessments, nine owned slaves. Six others employed servants. Few held less than one hundred acres of land, and four of the petitioners held more than two hundred. These men who requested Elder were the leaders in the community, those who had flourished with the opening of southeastern Pennsylvania and had the greatest stake in stability.[124] And in Elder they found a man who shared their views on slavery. "The Negroes the Progeny of Ham," he bellowed to his congregation, "are the servants of servants and their Country the Market of Slavery."[125]

As contemporaries noted, such settlers as a rule did not embrace vital piety. Tennent argued that the Great Awakening shattered the hold of such an "adulterous Generation" on the church. Revivals, he contended, attracted "Some aged persons, some middle-aged, Multitudes of young People in the Bloom of Life, as well as many little Children."[126] A profile of those who supported a New Side minister from the upper end bears out Tennent's observation. Of the congregants who contributed to the stipend of the upper-end revivalist John Roan, none owned slaves and most held fewer than one hundred acres of property.[127] New Side partisans, though on average less prosperous, were in all likelihood more recent arrivals to the area, younger than their Old Light neighbors, and the wayward sons who witnessed declining opportunities in southeastern Pennsylvania. Attuned to the increasingly plural world they inhabited and more mobile than an older generation of better-established settlers, those in the "bloom of life" had less a stake in the status quo in areas transformed by demographic pressures and in Old World traditions such as the Confession. Challenging social and spatial boundaries and established social relations, the Awakening enabled those with fewer resources to make sense of a rapidly changing frontier.[128]

Francis Alison remembered the period of the Awakening as "an era of heat and ignorance." "In their warmth," he lamented, "our brethren thrust out some into the vineyard, that do our Society no great honor."[129] But in reality, the frontier regions that Alison and other Ulster-born ministers served encompassed many societies. Most, no doubt, considered themselves Presbyterian, but this term embraced varieties of experience, ranging from the subscriptionist views of a Patrick Campbell, to the pro-revival spirit of a Samuel Blair, to the indifference of a Lazarus Lowry. Frontier communities by the 1740s also included an older generation rooted in a place with a stake in stability but which also learned to adapt to a plural environment, and another group, younger and threatened by socioeconomic change but willing to take advantage of new opportunities.

For the people of places such as Donegal, the Great Awakening represented less a moment of ethnic triumph or the conclusion to a transatlantic process of identity formation than a time of bitter division over the meaning and extent of change in Ulster migrant communities. The encounter with the "other" did not occasion an expected ethnic response, but ambivalence. Some retrenched, reasserting cultural traditions such as the Confession to keep revivalists at bay. Others embraced the New World of mobility and diversity that itinerancy represented. Far from canonizing a single vision for the group, the period of profound change called for a number of responses. If anything united Ulster's migrants in the New World, it was shared experience in a changing region, an identity that drew on a useable and contested past and underscored the dynamism defining their lives.

CHAPTER SIX

"The Christian White Savages of Peckstang and Donegall"

SURVEYING THE FRONTIERS OF AN ATLANTIC WORLD

During these formative years, patterns of adaptation had emerged that had profound implications for the subsequent experience of Ulster's New World settlers. Chief among these was ongoing movement. By 1750, the upper and lower ends of Pennsylvania's frontier had become migration depots, as thousands moved to, from, and through the southeastern section of the colony. As places like Donegal became more settled, some of the sons and daughters of original settlers struck out south for the back parts of Virginia. Others crossed the mountains to take their chances on Indian lands to the west and north. New arrivals from Ulster, immigrants fleeing famine and a failing linen economy for a promising New World, added to this land-hungry, giddy multitude. After working as indentured servants on the upper and lower ends of the Pennsylvania frontier, many of these men and women would also head to new backcountry regions.

Later generations of Ulster Presbyterian settlers made sense of an ever-changing frontier by adopting the practices and traditions the earliest migrants had employed in their years of settlement. In no instance was this dynamic more evident than in the continuing religious experience of Ulster's men and women in America. Just as those on the edges of frontier society had embraced a vital piety to make sense of change, new immigrants from Ireland in similar straits flocked to hear New Side preachers. Although such revivals enjoyed little success in Ulster, on the American frontier they continued to attract the young, mobile, and poor. While new arrivals to Pennsylvania faced the challenge of assimilating to codes of behavior in a settled society, those moving south confronted a wilderness beyond the reach of law and church. But those who left Pennsylvania for Virginia in the 1750s also followed established patterns of adaptation. As their mothers and fathers had, settlers in the Shenandoah Valley pleaded with Presbyterian Church officials to send ministers and help in organizing congregations in the scramble to bring order to frontier chaos. In a short period of time, economic and social change gripped this new frontier in much the same way it had the old. As the construction of roads to places like Donegal and Nottingham and thence to Philadelphia tied Virginia into a greater Pennsylvania, some prospered, while others did not. In these circumstances, evangelical piety flared up once again, leading to an awakening reminiscent of the earlier one that had struck the Pennsylvania backcountry. Once again, divergent visions of the reformed Protestant tradition armed those trying to make sense of a rapidly changing world with the means to do so.

Legacies from the past, however, were not static blueprints; they represented tools that people reinvented in new contexts. Take the case of those who remained in southeastern Pennsylvania. By the 1760s, these men and women achieved elusive unity after years of socioeconomic and religious strife. They overcame division by rallying around a familiar concept, Britishness. Ulster's Presbyterians, of course, had employed the discourse in the past at critical junctures, such as in the years after the Glorious Revolution and during the push to repeal the Test Act. The 1750s and 1760s presented similar challenges for the group in America. In these years, the frontier was in disarray. As British and French armies engaged in history's first global war, settlers on the upper and lower ends withstood raids by vengeful Indians from the west. After the conclusion of the Seven Years' War, men and women along the Pennsylvania frontier bore the brunt of an Indian confederacy intent on rolling the region of white settlement back to the east. Like most colonists in the years immediately after the war, settlers in Ulster enclaves—wealthy and poor, Old and New Side—celebrated their participation in a larger empire and confirmed their attachment to a unifying Britishness. But for these people holed up in small forts in times of danger on a bleeding frontier or fleeing east from dispossessed Indians, British liberty took on new, troubling meanings. Britishness underscored a right to life and property, a liberty that negligent government officials alienated at their own peril. For frontier settlers, however, the unifying logic of such concepts could also justify the slaughter of Indians both hostile and friendly. The experience of Ulster's settlers in Pennsylvania during the years of frontier warfare, therefore, revealed both the liberating and frightening implications of rights discourse.

AFTER more than a ten-year lull, migration from Ulster to America resumed on a large scale in 1740. During the 1730s, the Irish economy rebounded from the troubles of the late 1720s. Exports of linen rose to new heights, offsetting increased rents and food prices. The cottier system, sustained by middlemen renting smaller tracts to weavers, continued to spread as tenants devoted more time to spinning and weaving and less to farming. But by 1739, the short-lived prosperity came to an end. In that year, the winter proved especially harsh, potato and grain crops failed, and exports of linen slumped. With food prices skyrocketing, famine overtook many, especially those with little land. Five years later, the harvest again fell below expectations. As a series of hardships struck the province, many elected to take their chances in the New World. With a transatlantic system in place and migration an established strategy to escape economic misfortune, such a decision, while no doubt difficult, became easier. Unlike those who left in earlier years, however, few of these men and women had the necessary money to purchase fares to America. Most, therefore, signed on as indentured servants.[1]

In September 1740, the *Pennsylvania Gazette* ran an advertisement for the master of the ship *Mary Ann* from Belfast. The ship had arrived in Philadelphia with "a parcel of likely Men and Women servants" and a "great Variety of White and Check linens." The men, the newspaper reported, "are for the most part Tradesmen." The following spring, more ships from Ireland loaded with servants landed in Philadelphia. Although the numbers did not approach those of the late 1720s, the specter of many poor peopling the province set off another round of alarm. The governor of the province, for example, asked the legislature to establish "a Hospital or Pest-House" to quarantine new arrivals. But the anti-immigrant din never reached the levels of the late 1720s. In Pennsylvania, demand for servants from Ireland outpaced supply. Indeed, men of means complained at the time of any practice that acted as "a Discouragement to the Trade of Importing White Servants."[2]

Many of these new arrivals moved to the frontier, either when back-country inhabitants purchased their time or after they satisfied the terms of their indentures. If the earliest migrants proved an elusive lot, their servants were nearly invisible. Viewing the records of the time, we know them as miscreants, troublemakers in increasingly stable communities. Newspapers ran notice after notice with rewards for Irish runaways.[3] One Lancaster County "servant maid" ran away on four occasions. Another man tried twelve times.[4] The penchant of servants to flee even vexed the earliest settlers from Ulster. A court, for example, required John Bayly to "serve the Revd. Mr. John Elder . . . for the Term of one year and 6 months over and above the time specify'd in his Indenture . . . for run away time and expenses."[5] Courts punished servants for fornication, bearing illegitimate children, and more serious offenses. On rare occasions, magistrates sent immigrants "imported" to the province back to New Castle if they proved "Impotent Person[s] . . . likely to become chargeable to this County of Lancaster."[6]

Some proved more trouble than they were worth. One runaway from West New Jersey, John McCoy, who assumed the name John Ryan in the Susquehanna Valley, was arrested for assaulting a woman "with the Intention to Ravis." He received twenty lashes, a £5 fine, and had to serve an additional four years of time.[7] Another servant, John Reed, committed "assault and battery upon a Certain Violet the Slave of George Stevenson."[8] Servants also could inspire fear in their masters. One Lancaster County settler reported that he was in constant "Terror and fear" of his servant William Downine, "he being a Rude ill natured and Insolent fellow."[9] A lower-end servant from Ireland, Robert Jones, went so far as to murder Henry McIntyre, his master, with a spade.[10]

Such episodes, of course, proved exceptional. Most servants served out the time of their indentures, if not happily, at least quietly. In fact, new arrivals fit themselves into reigning patterns of interaction. The presence of wayward men and women in increasingly stable frontier societies did not set new terms of social relations, but followed patterns established a generation earlier by the first migrants to people the frontier. As adaptable as the first settlers from Ulster, new migrants quickly learned how to get ahead in the New World. Many did so most visibly by embracing the revival spirit.[11]

Evangelical religion did not take root in Ulster in the years it swept through the Middle Colonies. To be sure, Scottish Seceders, those ministers who had left the Church of Scotland over the issue of patronage and who tended to favor a vital piety, established a following in Ulster. In 1736, a number of families petitioned a Scottish separatist presbytery to send a minister "who would preach the Gospel not in wisdom of men's words, but in the purity and simplicity thereof." Six years later, more Ulster Presbyterians called for such ministers.[12] But northern dissenters did not request the services of Scottish ministers to touch off a general awakening or, for that matter, because they contested the relationship between the Synod of Ulster and the state. Rather, some Presbyterians looked to Scottish separatist movements, such as Seceders or Covenanters, as buffers against the further spread of Irish New Light ideas. As congregations and presbyteries continued to experience divisions during the 1730s and the appeal of New Light ideals grew within the synod, the notion of separation and a renewed emphasis on Gospel purity struck a responsive chord.[13]

Some of those migrating in the 1740s harbored such views. A few ministers traveled between small congregations of Covenanters in Ulster migrant enclaves in these years, preaching a message of the virtues of holy isolation. Ministers, such as the evangelical-turned-Covenanter Alexander Craighead, warned their charges to have nothing to do with "opposers," those "who do not joyne to the Reformed Religion."[14] But these movements had little appeal in Pennsylvania where no established church existed and where latitudinarian ideas had no significant following. Indeed, over time, some of those who joined separatist churches on the frontier abandoned them in favor of New Side congregations. In 1745, for example, four men and women who had "join'd Mr. Craighead's party" requested admission to a New Light meetinghouse. Three years later, another group decided vital piety served them better on the frontier than separatism.[15]

Like earlier migrants, new arrivals used the available cultural materials of their New World to assert some control over their lives. Of course, they employed familiar forms to do so. Each generation of

Ulster Presbyterians made sense of change by adapting practices from the Reformed Protestant tradition. However, in certain contexts some facets of Reformed Protestantism worked better than others. The consolidating vision had broad appeal in both Ireland and America. But just as the Irish New Light vision drew little support in the colonies, Scottish separatist traditions were better suited to the Old World. In the New World, evangelical piety stressing mobility, youth, and permeable cultural boundaries continued to allow those threatened by demographic shifts to carve out meaningful cultural space on the frontier.

INDENTURED servants also learned that movement offered the surest way to better their chances on the frontier. After serving out their indentures, many of these men and women joined the sons and daughters of an earlier generation of migrants on the road to Virginia. In 1752, Thomas Penn reported that former servants "were such as having Large Familys that could not Settle near them [earlier migrants] in Pennsylvania; they removed enough for themselves and their children to settle together."[16] Around this time, many headed south along the eastern slope of the Appalachians, or the "Great Wagon Road," as it came to be called, to the back parts of Virginia. A large number settled in the Valley of Virginia or the Shenandoah, nestled between the Blue Ridge Mountains to the east and the Alleghenies to the west. Officials from the colony encouraged the movement, inviting migrants with promises of cheap land and legal title. Magistrates also tolerated squatters. In much the same way James Logan had believed that Ulster's Presbyterians would provide a sound buffer to western Indians and land-hungry Marylanders, Virginia's colonists hoped a new generation of seasoned migrants would people the Shenandoah Valley to protect the east of the colony from hostile Indians and safeguard the colony's claim to lands further west of the valley.[17]

Such insurance had its costs. From the moment they arrived, settlers alarmed established colonists. The wealthy planter William Byrd II likened these newcomers to "the Goths and Vandals of old."[18] One step ahead of the civilizing influences of the law and the church in an undeveloped wilderness, "beggarly Irish Presbyterians," as Charles Woodmason, an Anglican minister from Virginia, put it, seemed "Ignorant, mean, [and] worthless." They were "the Scum of the Earth and Refuse of Mankind." Echoing the sentiments of Pennsylvanians in 1729, Woodmason observed that "they delight in their present low, lazy, sluttish, heathenish, hellish Life, and seem not desirous of changing it." He added that "both Men and Women will do any thing to come at Liquor, Cloathe, furniture, etc. etc. rather than work for it— Hence their many Vices," ones he enumerated as "gross Licentiousness, Rudeness, Lewdness, and Profligacy."[19]

But by the 1760s, conditions began to change along the southern frontier. As Philadelphia continued to develop as an important Atlantic-trading center, settlers from Virginia began sending their surpluses up the wagon road. In the same way that Chester and Lancaster Counties had experienced change a few decades earlier, settlements in western Virginia quickly took on the trappings of settled societies. Some of those who traveled from or through Pennsylvania to the south prospered with the transformation, establishing themselves as a new backcountry elite. Others did not fare as well, especially those coming of age, and many would set their sights on yet remoter areas where land was cheaper and opportunity beckoned. The tumultuous frontier process once again created a group of young, mobile men and women, less prominent and hungry for land.[20]

As the exodus south grew in scope, Presbyterian officials tried to incorporate the new settlers into the church. Both the Old Light Synod of Philadelphia and its New Side counterpart in New York sent ministers to newly settled regions, either supplying settlements or establishing congregations in Virginia. In 1745, the New Side synod, judging "the Circumstances of Virginia," saw "a wide Door opened for the Preaching of the Gospel in these Parts with a hopeful Prospect of Success." Similarly, four years later, the Synod of Philadelphia decided to "Supply the Inhabitants of Virginia by two Missionaries who are to be out Eight Weeks."[21] Old Siders John Craig, Samuel Black, Alexander Miller, and John Thomson had established new congregations in the Great Valley by the 1740s. Around the same time, New Lights such as John Roan from Donegal and John Blair, the brother of the renowned itinerant Samuel Blair, also made their way south to preach from time to time.[22] Despite these efforts, the church up north could not keep pace with the movement south.

Already overwhelmed by numbers, the Presbyterian Church faced significant obstacles in fulfilling the needs of the people south. In 1758, the Old and New Side factions put aside many of their differences and reunited in the Synod of New York and Philadelphia. Although strong partisan sentiments remained among both members and congregants, unification dulled the excesses of both camps. Governing bodies instructed ministers heading south "to study in all their Publick Administrations and private Conversations to promote Peace and Unity among the Societies." Missionaries were to "avoid whatever may tend to foment Division, and Party Spirit" to "promote true Religion and Not Party Designs."[23] The decline of evangelical zeal in favor of orderly and polite relations no doubt slowed the advance of vital piety in the south, offering little solace to those hungry for salvation.

The plan of the reunited synod for evangelizing the south reflected the new turn in relations. Falling back on a formula that had worked in Pennsylvania in the first years of settlement, ministers decided to put their efforts behind church building. In 1754, the synod recognized "the great Importance of having those Congregations properly organized." The "Congregations to the Southward" were instructed to appoint elders, install discipline, and adjust the lines between parishes so "in their after conduct" they could "proceed to obtain the Stated Ministry." The synod from the north "had their interest much at heart," assuring the people in Virginia that its members would "neglect no opportunities of affording them proper candidates and supplies to the utmost of our power."[24] Before the church would minister to the men and women further south, its institutions would have to be put in place. Such a process promised to be time-consuming.

The people living further south had little patience for such an approach. Searching for stability in a world transforming before their eyes, they expected a rapid response the church to the north could not provide. Baptist missionaries, however, could. Preachers from New England hoping to win souls traveled into Virginia as settlers ventured to the frontier of the colony. And they enjoyed much success. In one sense, the New England evangelical tradition championed by Baptist itinerants gained a substantial following in Virginia because the established Anglican Church failed to comprehend the needs of poor settlers in the west of the colony.[25] But for Pennsylvania's Presbyterians who moved to the unchurched valley, Baptists promised the benefits of vital religion without institutional trappings or delay. Baptists favored an independent form of church government and, therefore, did not have to answer to any formal church hierarchy. The congregation of believers, they argued, formed the bedrock of the church. Moreover, they required no formal education for ministers. Congregations did not need the directive hand of presbyteries or sessions to organize or to choose a minister. This variant of the Reformed Protestant tradition was well suited to a world of rapid change and continual movement, allowing people to absorb the shock of transformation and to come to terms with dislocation.[26]

By the time Baptists won souls to Christ, Ulster society in America had become a culture of movement. The scramble in search of cheaper land in the wake of wrenching demographic change had become not only a distinguishing feature of the group but also the most dependable way to get ahead on the margins of the Atlantic world. The initial movement from Ulster to the Pennsylvania backcountry gave birth to conditions that encouraged a great many people to push on further south. New waves of immigrants from Ireland gave this movement a relentless logic that would not stop with Virginia. As yet another wave of immigrants from Ireland reached Pennsylvania in the early 1770s, many men and women would press on to the Carolinas. Others would seek their fortunes west of the mountains in Kentucky. The frontier process first seen in southeastern Pennsylvania also revealed the protean nature of vital religion and ways in which it related to mobility. Less encumbered by formalities than the Presbyterian Church, the Baptist Church proved the ideal religious institution for the frontier. Responsive to need and allowing for community autonomy, Baptists would triumph first among those Ulster settlers moving south and, a generation later, among those in Kentucky.[27]

THE Presbyterian Church faced another hurdle in the years Baptists gained a foothold in the South. During the 1750s and 1760s, ministers refused to supply settlements in Virginia. This failure stemmed from frontier conditions throughout this period. In 1756 and the following year, ministers from the New Side Synod of New York could not make their way to Virginia because of "The Difficulties and Dangers of the Times." After reunion, the united synod reported the same problem. From 1759 through 1764, a crucial period of time during which Baptists grew in influence, missionaries failed to make their appointed rounds. Throughout the mid-1750s and into the 1760s, Indian war parties closed the road south from Pennsylvania to all but the hardiest souls. The "mission to the Frontier," members of the church lamented, was "entirely frustrated by the breaking out of Indian War."[28]

The unfettered movement of settlers to new regions played a large part in unleashing frontier warfare. Beginning in the late 1740s, a number of settlers from the upper and lower ends moved north and west over the mountains. As one official put it in 1750, "Numbers of the worst sort of Irish had been to mark places and were determined to have gone over the Hills this Summer or in the Fall." Such forays to stake out choice land angered Indians, who once again faced the prospect of dispossession, which led to "Quarrels between the Indians and the Trespassers."[29] The attendant problems of unlicensed traders and disease followed settlement west. In 1751, a county court indicted John McAlister for carrying "Quantities of Rum and other strong Liquors above the Quantity of one Gallon amongst the Indians at their Towns and Beyond the Christian inhabitants." Two years later, the same court brought charges against eleven such settlers.[30] The proprietors and their agents saw no way to keep the frontier quiet except "to get the Indians to burn the Log houses" of squatters.[31]

Officials in Philadelphia feared the incessant push for Indian lands would move tribes into alliance with the French to the west.[32] The native groups to the west and north had good reason to embrace the French cause. North of the Blue Mountains lived Delawares incensed over fraudulent land deals such as the infamous "Walking Purchase" of 1737. West of the Appalachians in the Ohio Country other bands of Delawares and Shawnees had settled after losing their lands along the Susquehanna with the Treaty of 1736. In Ohio, the motley collection of peoples experienced a spiritual, economic, and military renaissance, enabling them to emerge from the shadow of the Six Nations.

Over the hills, therefore, lived powerful Indians with good reason to hold a grudge.[33]

When Britain and France went to war over their empires in North America, the disaffected Indians struck back. After hostilities broke out in America in 1754, the Shawnees cast their lots with the French, and soon the Delawares in Ohio followed suit. Neither needed much encouragement to burn homes and scalp settlers on the Pennsylvania frontier. Indeed, most of the five hundred scalps and two hundred captives taken to the French at Fort Duquesne during the first few years of the war came from Pennsylvania.[34] Refugees flooded back to Donegal and Paxton, where the trader John Harris turned his home into a fortified armory.[35] In 1755, those living over the hills retreated to Carlisle, where they erected five forts. After two women were taken prisoner, frontier settlers sent urgent requests to Philadelphia, asking "all well thinking Christians . . . to assist us who are in Eminent danger of falling into . . . [the] Merciless Barbaritys" of "Delawar and Shanny Indians."[36]

The pleas fell on deaf ears. The Quaker-dominated provincial assembly refused to raise a militia. The proprietor, John Penn, argued that the government should take steps to defend the frontier, but he refused to tax proprietary lands to do so. Representatives from western counties were unable to resolve the deadlock. Quakers enjoyed a disproportionate share of representation in the assembly from their control of Philadelphia, Chester, and Bucks Counties. The eastern counties and city of Philadelphia sent twenty-six representatives to the provincial assembly; the equally populous five western counties sent only ten.[37] Eventually, as pressure from the frontier increased, a bill passed the assembly to raise £55,000 to equip a militia and construct a string of frontier forts. And in 1756, the governor of the colony declared war on the western Indians despite the scruples of the assembly, leading Quakers to desert the legislature en masse. But such measures proved insufficient. Only in 1758, after British troops took Fort Duquesne, cutting off Indians in Ohio from the east, did the raids cease. Months later, in a decisive battle on the Plains of Abraham above Quebec, General James Wolfe defeated the Marquis de Montcalm, bringing an end to France's New World empire.[38]

No sooner had the frontier quieted down than tensions flared up again. In 1763, as an Ottawa war chief named Pontiac led an assault against the British garrison at Fort Detroit, the Indians of the Ohio Country renewed their attacks on the frontier, leading to another frenzied round of movement east.[39] Once more, "Carlisle was become the barrier" of the colony, the *Pennsylvania Gazette* reported, "not a single Individual being beyond it."[40] Again, the assembly and governor failed to respond. With little hope for assistance, settlers from Donegal, Paxton, and outlying regions took matters into their own hands, forming into companies to patrol the mountain passes from the west. Only after they did so did the government agree to contribute funds for arming seven hundred men for the "Defence and protection of the Frontier Inhabitants, whose Ruin and Destruction the vilest Race of Savages seem at this time to threaten."[41] The "Paxtang Rangers," as they were called, operated under the leadership of John Elder, the minister of Paxton. Elder had his men stand watch in the area and led a group north of the hills to Wyoming where hostile Indians had killed a group of settlers from Connecticut.[42] Pontiac's War, however, came to an end before the Rangers had an opportunity to confront their enemies from the west.

With Britain's victory over France, American colonists lit bonfires in Boston, Charleston, and Philadelphia. As never before, they proclaimed themselves Britons, loyal subjects of King George and members of a vast, unrivaled Atlantic empire. In much the same way the Glorious Revolution created a unified state encompassing the British Isles, the Seven Years' War achieved similar results but on a far wider scale. A notion of British rights and liberties united the Protestants of England, Scotland, and Ireland with colonists in America in a state system straddling the ocean. Therefore, in 1763 the defeat of Catholic France had a galvanizing effect for British Protestants, even those far from London in the American colonies.[43]

But settlers along the frontier found little to celebrate. To be sure, these "Frontier Inhabitants" declared their attachment to the empire. "To a Man," they regarded themselves "loyal Subjects to the best of Kings, our rightful Sovereign George the Third," professing their allegiance "to his Royal Person, Interest and Government." Like other provincial Americans in a British empire they viewed themselves as

"Free-Men and English Subjects," Protestants who through birth and loyalty enjoyed rights rooted in Britishness.[44] But the wars had revealed as never before their marginal status in Pennsylvania and their impotent voice in an empire that they believed they had a significant hand in fashioning and defending.

It took little more than hearsay to set them off. Just before dawn on December 14, 1763, a group of Paxtang Rangers, perhaps fifty in all, rode to a settlement on Conestoga Manor where a small group of Indians lived. The Rangers had heard that the settlement housed a number of Indians who had aided western Indians with information about frontier settlements and that one in particular, Bill Sawk, had murdered white settlers. The raiders found six Indians there, murdered them, and burned their cabins. The rest were away that morning, as an official put it, "to sell brooms."[45] On hearing of the attack, authorities placed the fourteen survivors in the workhouse at Lancaster for their protection. Two weeks later, the frontiersmen "collected together at a tavern on the Donegal Road," and through ice and snow arrived at the workhouse to complete their butchery. They entered the workhouse, witnesses recounted, armed with rifles, tomahawks, and scalping knives, and murdered all fourteen. The Lancaster massacre was particularly savage. A man from the town saw two children "of about the age of three years, whose heads were split with the tomahawk, and the scalps taken off." A number of women met similar fates. One man's legs "were chopped with the tomahawk, his hands cut off." The murderers also discharged a rifle into his mouth "so that his head was blown to atoms." Incensed, the proprietor offered a reward for the capture of the ringleaders and planned to try the culprits in an eastern county.[46]

After the Lancaster affair, these "Paxton Boys," as they were now called, learned that Quakers in Philadelphia were rounding up vulnerable Indians in and around the city to avert another tragedy. Enraged that Quakers seemed to care more for Indians than for the frontier settlers who had suffered for nearly ten years, the Paxton Boys, now numbering more than two hundred, set off for Philadelphia. They made quite a sight dressed in blanket coats and moccasins. "I have seen hundreds of Indians traveling the country," recalled David Rittenhouse of Philadelphia, "and can with truth affirm, that the behav-

iour of these fellows was ten times more savage and brutal than theirs."
They walked through Germantown thrusting "the muzzles of their
guns through windows, swearing and hallooing." They grabbed pas-
sersby "without the least provocation; dragging them by their hair to
the ground, and pretending to scalp them."[47] Even some Quakers
armed themselves, readying for the invasion of the city. Conflict was
averted when Benjamin Franklin headed a delegation to meet the
leaders and listen to their demands. Promising to raise the grievances
of the Paxton Boys before the government, Franklin convinced the
restless frontiersmen to return to their homes.

By all accounts, the Paxton Boys comprised those buffeted by demographic change in southeastern Pennsylvania. "Few of them were men
of any property," a witness observed.[48] They came from that stratum
of frontier society—"the lower Sort of People," as a contemporary put
it[49]—little better-off than the servants working in and around Donegal
and Paxton. Critics lampooned them as "a Parcel of ragged Arse tatter-
demalion Fellows" with such names as "O'Haro" and "O'Rigan." The
murderers, another detractor swiped, were but "an ignorant and en-
thusiastick *Mob*" of Presbyterian traitors.[50] Sympathizers conceded that
the Paxton Boys drew their support from the lower ranks of society.
"I know not of one person of prudence or Judgement," John Elder
admitted, "that has been any wise concerned in it but [the murdering]
has been done by some hot headed ill advised persons." While others
had moved south to seek out better lives, the Paxton Boys and an
"enraged multitude," as Elder put it, had stayed behind, growing into
a violent underclass in an increasingly mobile and plural landscape.[51]

Benjamin Franklin pulled no punches in describing the group's
marginal status in the colony. He dubbed them the "CHRISTIAN WHITE
SAVAGES of *Peckstang* and *Donegall*." Through their brutality they appeared more savage than Indians and any "poor unenlightened *African Negroe*," all of whom could distinguish the guilty from the innocent. The Paxton Boys lacked such elementary understanding. "If an
Indian injures me," Franklin asked, "does it follow that I may revenge
that Injury on all *Indians*?" By Paxton logic, "The only Crime of these
poor Wretches seems to have been, that they had a reddish brown
Skin, and black Hair." A people who considered themselves loyal Prot-

estants had in fact, Franklin argued, brought "Disgrace" to both "Religion" and "Country."[52]

But to their supporters, the Paxton Boys appeared quite different. Invoking the popular series of Whiggish writings, "Cato's Letters," one apologist argued that the government through its negligence had denied men and women on the frontier "a Right to *demand,* and to *receive* Protection," the just privilege of all "*free born Subjects of Britain.*"[53] If the men of no property conspired to march, men of property understood the conditions that compelled resistance. John Elder had warned authorities to move the Indians from Lancaster. He also tried to stop the attacks when he learned what was afoot. But although he considered the massacre of innocent Indians "barbarous and an aberration in its' nature," he believed that the Paxton Boys had good reason to stand up for their rights. Elder thought that the group was made up "by such I imagine as suffer'd much in their relations by the Savages committed in the late Indian war."[54] Justifiably, "the Inhabitants are so exasperated against" the negligent Quakers.[55]

The Paxton Boys conceded that they were "Flying in the Face of Authority," but argued that they did so out of "Necessity." They claimed that although they lived far from centers of power, "we have an indisputable Title to the same Privileges and Immunities with his Majesty's other subjects." A powerful cabal, however, undermined their rights. "Such is our unhappy Situation," they exclaimed, "under the Villany, Infatuation and Influence of a certain Faction that have got the political Reigns in their Hand and tamely tyrannize over the other good Subjects." Airing broader frontier grievances, the writers from Paxton declared that inequitable representation amounted to an "infringement of our natural Privileges of Freedom and Equality." Trying individuals for offenses outside the jurisdiction in which they were committed also "manifestly . . . deprive[d] *British* Subjects of their known Privileges." Although inhabiting the empire's marchlands, they knew the discourse that defined Britishness. No government could "contradict the well known Laws of the *British* Nation, in a point whereon Life, Liberty, and Security essentially depend," even if upholding those rights entailed murdering a score of people from a "Perfidious" race.[56]

Confident in their rights, the frontiersmen felt justified in deriding any detractors. Stung by the barbs of Presbyterian treachery and Irish criminality, a minister asserted that those who had migrated from Ireland to Pennsylvania defined themselves by their "intire Renunciation of Popery," unlike the "Native *Irish* that trot in our Bogs" or, as he suggested, the colony's Quakers and Anglicans. As in the past, Presbyterian settlers had "brandish[ed] the Sword in the Cause of Christ." Invoking Locke, he argued that "I have considered myself in a State not of Nature, but of Society; not linked in with papal Power, as others are, but in the Service of *Christ.*" He issued a stern warning to a corrupt government. Any settler would "be obedient to Government, when they give me Protection," but, he added, "when I am not protected, nor can they expect me to be Obedient." Yoking British rights with the Protestantism that buttressed it, he declared that settlers had acted in the service of "Liberty and Truth." "If People," the minister concluded, "are rightly Principled for Government they would kill the *Indians*, because they murder us."[57]

The rights discourse employed by the Paxton Boys and their defenders once more served as a touchstone for group unity.[58] For some, a notion of British liberty could justify the murder of innocent Indians also living on the margins of a developing society, who conspired to keep settlers from land. For others, Britishness mandated inclusion in governing institutions and a just allocation of representation. The language that the Paxton Boys and their supporters used proved malleable enough to unite diverse interests through its invocation. Like other American colonists caught up in the tumultuous events of the 1760s and in much the same way their ancestors had done in Ireland in the 1720s, men and women from Paxton and Donegal viewed British traditions through the prism of their immediate needs and status in society. Such concepts which at one time and place could be used to confront a hostile Ascendancy and at another to justify the slaughter of a race of peoples proved explosive stuff, unstable elements on which to construct an empire.[59]

FROM the beginning of one British chapter in 1688 until the end of another in 1763, the three legacies of movement, Reformed Protestantism, and Britishness, which formed the content of Ulster Presbyterian identity, also shaped the contours of the Atlantic world. Through profound periods of change, moments during which men and women confronted larger forces and processes beyond their control, individuals appropriated and reinvented the discourses and processes that animated the larger world around them. They also continually pushed these traditions to new limits. Migration, of course, stretched the physical dimensions of the Atlantic world. Moreover, as men and women fastened upon different elements of a Reformed Protestant tradition, they demonstrated the multifaceted and protean nature of the religious impulse that underscored their rightful place as loyal subjects. Finally, their experience revealed the interpretive implications embedded in British conceptions of rights and that such notions could sustain or destroy an empire. No doubt, the elusiveness of Ulster's Presbyterians—and our inability to pin an identity upon them—stemmed from their dynamic ability to take advantage of the imaginative possibilities of their larger world as they struggled to make sense of it. And as their unfolding transatlantic story illustrates, although these people with no name moved along the margins of an Atlantic world, they also stood at its center.

❖ *Notes* ❖

INTRODUCTION

1. On migration within the English and British Atlantic worlds, see Alison Games, *Migration and the Origins of the English Atlantic World* (Cambridge, MA, 1999); Bernard Bailyn, *The Peopling of British North America: An Introduction* (New York, 1986); and Bailyn, *Voyagers to the West: A Passage in the Peopling of America on the Eve of the Revolution* (New York, 1986). The British Atlantic perspective or "new" imperial history owes much, of course, to the older imperial perspective of Charles M. Andrews and others. See Andrews, *The Colonial Background of the American Revolution: Four Essays in Colonial American History* (New Haven, 1931); and Richard Johnson, "Charles McLean Andrews and the Invention of American Colonial History," *William and Mary Quarterly*, 3rd ser., 43 (1986): 519–41. For a view of the state of the field, refer to the essays in Jack Greene and J. R. Pole, eds., *Colonial British America: Essays in the New History of the Early Modern Era* (Baltimore, 1984); Bernard Bailyn and Philip Morgan, introduction to *Strangers within the Realm: Cultural Margins of the First British Empire* (Chapel Hill, 1991), 1–31; and Jack Greene, "Interpretive Frameworks: The Quest for Intellectual Order in Early American History," *William and Mary Quarterly*, 3rd ser., 48 (1991): 515–30. Bailyn covers the origins of the new Atlantic history in "The Idea of Atlantic History," *Itinerario* 20 (1996): 19–44.

2. James Leyburn, *The Scotch-Irish: A Social History* (Chapel Hill, 1962), 330; Maldwyn Jones, "The Scotch-Irish in British North America," in *Strangers within the Realm*, ed. Bailyn and Morgan, 284.

3. Hector Crevecoeur, *Letters from an American Farmer and Sketches of Eighteenth-Century America*, ed. A. E. Stone (New York, 1986), 85. Historians have also defined the group in such terms. Carl Bridenbaugh, for instance, portrayed America's Scotch-Irish as "undisciplined, emotional, courageous, pugnacious, fiercely intolerant, and hard drinking, with a tendency to indolence." See *Myths and Realities: Societies of the Colonial South* (New York, 1966), 133.

4. James Anderson to Thomas Penn, 26 June 1733, Penn Physick Papers, VI, 29, Historical Society of Pennsylvania, Philadelphia (hereafter HSP).

5. John Elder to Colonel Joseph Shippen, 1 February 1764, John Elder Papers, Dauphin County Historical Society, Harrisburg, Pennsylvania. In fact, the name "Scotch-Irish," an eighteenth-century term of derision, did not gain general currency until the late-nineteenth century when real and imagined descendants of settlers from Ulster embraced it to distinguish a Protestant people from Irish Catholic immigrants streaming into the country. Moreover, migrants did not call themselves "Scots Irish." Historians created the sanitized name to reflect the origins of an American group that left Ireland but de-

scended from Scots. On the problems with names for the group, see Ned Landsman, "Ethnicity and National Origin among British Settlers in the Philadelphia Region: Pennsylvania Immigration in the Wake of *Voyagers to the West*," *Proceedings of the American Philosophical Society* 133 (1989): 170–74; Jones, "The Scotch-Irish in British North America," 284–85; and Leyburn, *The Scotch-Irish*, 327–34.

6. See John Elder to Edward Shippen, 4 August 1763, 1 February 1764, Elder Papers.

7. To call the Presbyterians, who had migrated from Scotland to Ulster over the course of the seventeenth century, "Ulster Scots" smacks of anachronism. The term, coupling ethnic and geographical designations, came into use in Ireland only after the eighteenth century. See Toby Barnard, "Identities, Ethnicity and Tradition among Irish Dissenters c. 1650–1750," and Raymond Gillespie, "Dissenters and Nonconformists, 1661–1700," in *The Irish Dissenting Tradition, 1650–1750*, ed., Kevin Herlihy (Dublin, 1995), 29–48, 11–28.

8. Linda Colley, *Britons: Forging the Nation, 1707–1837* (New Haven, 1992). This approach has been dubbed the "new" British history since the publication of two articles by J.G.A. Pocock. See Pocock, "The Limits and Divisions of British History: In Search of the Unknown Subject," *American Historical Review* 87 (1982): 311–36; and "British History: A Plea for a New Subject," *Journal of Modern History* 47 (1975): 601–21. His plea has been answered in studies too numerous to mention, but for a view of the state of the field, see A. Grant and K. Stringer, eds., *Uniting the Kingdom? The Making of British History* (London, 1996); R. Asch, ed., *Three Nations—A Common History? England, Scotland, Ireland and British History c. 1600–1920* (Bochum, Germany, 1994); S. Ellis and S. Barber, eds., *Conquest and Union: Fashioning a British State 1485–1725* (London, 1996); Brendan Bradshaw and J. Morrill, eds., *The British Problem, c. 1524–1707* (London, 1996); Brendan Bradshaw and Peter Roberts, eds., *British Consciousness and Identity: The Making of Britain, 1533–1707* (Cambridge, 1998).

9. Colin Kidd, *British Identities before Nationalism: Ethnicity and Nationhood in the Atlantic World, 1600–1800* (Cambridge, 1999).

10. Alan Tully argues that the term "ethnoreligious" underscores the nature of identity in Pennsylvania in this period. Sally Schwartz, on the other hand, claims that "religious" identification better captures the ways in which groups conceived themselves. Both forms of identity, however, no matter which label we choose, stood the test of time. Only shrewd Quaker management and an ethos of toleration, embodied in the principles espoused by William Penn, allowed such disparate groups to coexist peacefully. See Sally Schwartz, *"A Mixed Multitude": The Struggle for Toleration in Colonial Pennsylvania* (New York, 1987); Alan Tully, *William Penn's Legacy: Politics and Social Structure in Provincial Pennsylvania, 1726–1755* (Baltimore, 1977); and Tully, "Ethnicity,

Religion and Politics in Early Pennsylvania," *Pennsylvania Magazine of History and Biography* 107 (1983), 491–536.

11. Ned Landsman argues that Scots achieved a common ethnic identity in America, uniting around the revivals of the Great Awakening, which had their roots in Scottish traditions. See *Scotland and Its First American Colony, 1683–1765* (Princeton, 1985), 4, 165, 174–76, 184–85, 250; and Leigh Eric Schmidt, *Holy Fairs: Scottish Communion and American Revivals in the Early Modern Period* (Princeton, 1989). On the similar transformation among German-speaking groups, see A. G. Roeber, *Palatines, Liberty, and Property: German Lutherans in Colonial British America* (Baltimore, 1993), 6–7; and Aaron Fogleman, *Hopeful Journeys: German Immigration, Settlement, and Political Culture in Colonial America, 1717–1775* (Philadelphia, 1996), 11–12, 80, 89. The one exception to this general trend may be the Huguenots whose "rapid social and religious disintegration" in America bespoke the ways in which many of their traditions had been destroyed in the France. Refer to Jon Butler, *The Huguenots in America: A Refugee People in New World Society* (Cambridge, MA, 1983), 5. So prevalent has this model become that this sensibility seems to have animated almost all of Pennsylvania's migrant groups. Indeed, this form of identity defined the contours of social relations Pennsylvania, prefiguring the nineteenth and twentieth-century experience of immigrant groups. So argues Michael Zuckerman in "Introduction: Puritans, Cavaliers, and the Motley Middle," in *Friends and Neighbors: Group Life in America's First Plural Society,* ed. Michael Zuckerman (Philadelphia, 1982), 5–6; and "Farewell to the 'New England Paradigm' of Colonial Development," *Pennsylvania History* 57 (1990): 66–73.

12. Ian McBride, *Scripture Politics: Ulster Presbyterians and Irish Radicalism in the Late Eighteenth Century* (Cambridge, 1998); and McBride, "Presbyterians in the Penal Era," *Bullan* 1 (1994): 73–86.

13. Of the many groups inhabiting eighteenth-century Pennsylvania, no people have teetered more between visibility and invisibility. By one account, Pennsylvania's Irish put an indelible stamp on the American Presbyterian church and determined the direction of the Great Awakening, that moment of vital piety that swept through the colonies during the mid century. Almost immediately after the arrival of the first wave of migrants, as the story goes, settlers attempted to resurrect institutions that had sustained the group in Ireland, particularly a Presbyterian church structure and adherence to the Westminster Confession of Faith, the classic statement of British Calvinist orthodoxy. Many of these then championed a vital piety similar to that which had flourished in Ireland a century earlier. On these themes, see Marilyn Westerkamp, *Triumph of the Laity: Scots-Irish Piety and the Great Awakening, 1625–1760* (New York, 1988); and Elizabeth Nybakken, "New Light on the Old Side: Irish Influences on Colonial Presbyterianism," *Journal of American History* 68 (1982): 813–32.

Other interpretations, however, downplay the significance of the group. Carrying no distinctive traditions to the colonies, Ulster's migrants embraced Scottishness in the New World. The revival spirit and the Confession arose from Scottish, not Irish, ecclesiastical traditions. Although most on the frontier who supported Scottish church practices migrated from Ireland, their Irish background merits little explanation. See Landsman, *Scotland and Its First American Colony;* and Schmidt, *Holy Fairs.* Similarly, a group of historians has argued that the violence and pastoral nature of British "borderlands," encompassing Ulster, Scotland, and northern England, bred a xenophobia in America. See in particular, D. H. Fischer, *Albion's Seed: Four British Folkways in America* (New York, 1989), 605–782. For examples of this approach, refer to any number of works by Forrest McDonald and Grady McWhiney, including "The Antebellum Southern Herdsman: A Reinterpretation," *Journal of Southern History* 61 (1975): 147–166; and "The South from Self-Sufficiency to Peonage: An Interpretation," *American Historical Review* 85 (1980): 1095–1118. For critiques of this perspective, especially the ways in which it lumps peoples with distinct origins together, see Jones, "The Scotch-Irish in British North America"; R. Berthoff, "Celtic Mist over the South," *Journal of Southern History* 52 (1986): 523–46; Jack Greene, "Transplanting Moments: Inheritance in the Formation of American Culture," and Ned Landsman, "Border Cultures, the Backcountry, and 'North British' Emigration to America," *William and Mary Quarterly,* 3rd ser., 48 (1991): 224–31, 253–60.

14. For such a definition of the term for the early modern period, see J. H. Elliott, "Introduction: Colonial Identity in the Atlantic World," and Jack Greene, "Changing Identity in the British Caribbean: Barbados as a Case Study," in *Colonial Identity in the Atlantic World, 1500–1800,* ed. Nicholas Canny and Anthony Pagden (Princeton, 1987), 3–14, 213–66. Philip Gleason decried the ubiquitous and unquestioned use of the term—but not its ultimate utility—in migration and ethnic studies in "Identifying Identity: A Semantic History," *Journal of American History* 69 (1983): 910–31.

15. Nicholas Canny has been the most vocal on these points. See "The Attempted Anglicisation of Ireland in the Seventeenth Century: An Exemplar of 'British History,' " in *Three Nations,* ed. Asch, 49–82; and "Irish, Scottish, and Welsh Responses to Centralisation, c. 1530–c. 1640: A Comparative Perspective," in *Uniting the Kingdom,* ed. Grant and Stringer, 147–69.

16. Identity, the sociologist Anthony Giddens argues, varies over time in interaction with changing circumstances in *Modernity and Self-Identity: Self and Society in the Late Modern Age* (Cambridge, 1991). Refer also to *The Constitution of Society: Outline of the Theory of Structuration* (Berkeley, 1984). Stephen Cornell similarly believes that many theorists, and presumably historians, conflate the "content" of identity—such as religious or ethnic tradition—with identity itself. Without exploring context, content has no meaning. See "The Variable

Ties That Bind: Content and Circumstance in Ethnic Processes," *Ethnic and Racial Studies* 19 (1996): 265–89.

17. On this literature, see Nicholas Canny, "Writing Atlantic History; or, Reconfiguring the History of Colonial British America," *Journal of American History*, 86 (1999), 1093–1114. Also refer to the essays in Nicholas Canny, ed., *The Oxford History of the British Empire*, vol. 1, *The Origins of Empire: British Overseas Enterprise to the Close of the Seventeenth Century* (Oxford, 1998); and P. J. Marshall, ed., *The Oxford History of the British Empire*, vol. 2, *The Eighteenth Century* (Oxford, 1998).

18. A study of the transatlantic experience of this group with this approach may offer the best hope for reconciling the "new" British and Atlantic histories. So argues J.G.A. Pocock. "It is possible," he writes, "to imagine a narrative of this people acting and traversing in 'British' and 'Atlantic' history." Such a project "would investigate the discontents that led to considerable emigration from Ulster to the Alleghenies and elsewhere," a study that "would be both a history of this people as a presumed entity—a status some have sought to deny them—and a history of the archipelagic, Atlantic, and American complexes organized around the theatres of their successive actions in it." See "The New British History in Atlantic Perspective: An Antipodean Commentary," *American Historical Review* 104 (1999): 497.

Chapter One

1. Harman Murtagh, "The War in Ireland, 1689–91," *Kings in Conflict: The Revolutionary War in Ireland and Its Aftermath 1689–1750*, ed. W. A. Maguire (Belfast, 1990), 61–91.

2. T. W. Moody, F. X. Martin, and F. J. Byrne, eds., *A New History of Ireland*, vol. 3, *Early Modern Ireland, 1534–1691* (Oxford, 1976), 289–315.

3. S. J. Connolly, *Religion, Law and Power: The Making of Protestant Ireland* (Oxford, 1992), 33–40.

4. John Mackenzie, *A Narrative of the Siege of London-derry* (London, 1690), preface; George Walker, *A True Account of the Present State of Ireland* (London, 1689), 12; Walker, *A True Account of the Siege of London-derry* (London, 1689), 34, 41, 58.

5. A Full and True Account of the Beginning and Taking of Carrickfergus by the Duke of Schomberg, D/1409/1, Public Record Office of Northern Ireland, Belfast (hereafter PRONI).

6. Minutes of the Antrim Meeting, January 1688/89, February 1688/89, September 1689, November 1689, 452, 457, 461, 463, Presbyterian Historical Society, Belfast (hereafter PHSB).

7. Description of the Parish of Aghalow, 1693, Reeves Copy of Visitations made by Bishop William King, KH II 6, Armagh Public Library; Minutes of

the Laggan Meeting, September 1694, 58, PHSB; William Molyneux, "A Journey to the North," 7 August 1708, 10, PHSB.

8. C. S. King, ed., *A Great Archbishop of Dublin, William King, 1650–1729* (London, 1906), 32, cited in Raymond Gillespie, *Settlement and Survival on an Ulster Estate: The Brownlow Leasebook, 1667–1711* (Belfast, 1988), lxiii.

9. Mackenzie, *A Narrative of the Siege of London-derry;* Walker, *A True Account of the Siege of London-derry.*

10. John Morrill, "The British Problem," in *The British Problem,* ed. Bradshaw and Morrill (London, 1996), 19.

11. John Morrill, "The Sensible Revolution," and D. W. Hayton, "The Williamite Revolution in Ireland, 1688–91," in *The Anglo-Dutch Moment: Essays on the Glorious Revolution and Its World Impact,* ed. J. Israel (Cambridge, 1991), 104, 186; Alexander Grant and Keith Stringer, "The Enigma of British History," in *Uniting the Kingdom?,* 8–9; John Brewer, *The Sinews of Power: War, Money, and the English State, 1688–1783* (New York, 1989); Colley, *Britons.*

12. John Spurr, "The Church of England, Comprehension and the Toleration Act of 1689," *English Historical Review* 104 (1989): 927–46; W. A. Speck, *Reluctant Revolutionaries: Englishmen and the Revolution of 1688* (Oxford, 1988), 167–87; Richard Brown, *Church and State in Modern Britain, 1700–1715* (London, 1991), 109.

13. Ian Cowan, "Church and State Reformed? The Revolution of 1688–9 in Scotland," in *The Anglo-Dutch Moment,* ed. Israel, 163–83; W. Ferguson, *Scotland, 1689 to the Present,* vol. 1 (Edinburgh, 1968), 1–10.

14. P. Tesch, "Presbyterian Radicalism," and Ian McBride, "William Drennan and the Dissenting Tradition," in D. Dickson, D. Keogh, and K. Whelan, eds., *The United Irishmen: Republicanism, Radicalism, and Rebellion* (London, 1993), 34, 56. R. L. Greaves examines the role of the establishment in the Restoration period in " 'That's no good religion that disturbs government': The Church of Ireland and the Nonconformist Challenge, 1660–1688," in *As by Law Established: The Church of Ireland since the Reformation,* ed. Alan Ford, James McGuire, and Kenneth Miline (Dublin, 1995), 120–35. For the Presbyterian response, see P. Kilroy, *Protestant Dissent and Controversy in Ireland, 1660–1714* (Cork, 1994), 225–43.

15. J. Boyse, *Remarks on a Pamphlet publish'd by William Tisdal, D. D.* (Dublin, 1716), 15.

16. Memorial Relating to the Presbyterians in Ireland, Re: Imprisoning Minister in Drogheda, 1708, Wodrow Papers, T525, PRONI.

17. Petition of Francis Iredell, 25 August 1713, T 780/67, PRONI.

18. Presbyterian polemicist quoted in W. Tisdal, *A Sample of True-Blew Presbyterian Loyalty in all Changes and Turns of Government* (Dublin, 1709), 3. See J. Kirkpatrick, *An Historical Essay upon the Loyalty of Presbyterians in Great Britain and Ireland from the Reformation to the Present Year, 1713* (Belfast, 1713) for the Presbyterian plea of merit.

19. Henry Maxwell to ———, 9 April 1716, T 448/280, PRONI. Hayton, "The Williamite Revolution in Ireland," 199–201.

20. J. I. McGuire, "The Church of Ireland and the 'Glorious Revolution' of 1688," in *Studies in Irish History Presented to R. Dudley Edwards*, ed. Art Cosgrove and D. Macartney (Dublin, 1979), 147–49.

21. Connolly, *Religion, Law and Power*, 147, 309.

22. Ibid. 33.

23. Jim Smyth, "The Communities of Ireland and the British State, 1660–1707," in *The British Problem*, ed. Bradshaw and Morrill, 249.

24. Before the Revolution, England's government maintained an Irish policy of "drift." Elizabethan and Cromwellian armies had subdued the native Irish, but effective English rule proved ephemeral and inconsistent. An Irish Parliament legislated for the country without much English interference. Only the Crown, which ratified Irish bills, intervened in Irish affairs. The English Parliament, on the other hand, chose not to exercise its influence very often. See N. Canny, "The Marginal Kingdom: Ireland as a Problem in the First British Empire," in *Strangers within the Realm*, ed. Bailyn and Morgan 37. See also Canny, *Kingdom and Colony: Ireland in the Atlantic World, 1560–1800* (Baltimore, 1988); T. W. Moody and W. E. Vaughan, *A New History of Ireland;* volume 4, *Eighteenth-Century Ireland, 1691–1800* (Oxford, 1986), 8–16, 138–39; L. M. Cullen, *An Economic History of Ireland since 1660* (New York, 1972), 34–43; and Hayton, "The Williamite Revolution in Ireland," 211.

25. Moody, Martin, and Byrne, *A New History of Ireland*, 3:397–400, 443–44.

26. Jim Smyth, " 'Like Amphibious Animals': Irish Protestants, Ancient Britons," *Historical Journal* 36 (1993): 785–97.

27. William Molyneux, *The Case of Ireland's being bound by Acts of Parliament in England, stated* (Dublin, 1698), 97–98, 27, 170; Jonathan Swift, "The Fourth Drapier's Letter," in *The Drapier's Letters and Other Works*, ed. Herbert Davis (Oxford, 1941), 55. On Ascendancy patriotism, see J. G. Simms, *Colonial Nationalism* (Cork, 1976); Robert Eccleshall, "Anglican Political Thought in the Century after the Revolution of 1688," in *Political Thought in Ireland since the Seventeenth Century*, ed. D. George Boyce, Robert Eccleshall, and V. Geoghegan (London, 1993), 36–72; David Hayton, "Anglo-Irish Attitudes: Changing Perceptions of National Identity among the Protestant Ascendancy in Ireland, ca. 1690–1750," *Studies in Eighteenth-Century Culture* 17 (1987): 145–57.

28. T. C. Smout, N. C. Landsman, and T. M. Devine, "Scottish Emigration in the Seventeenth and Eighteenth Centuries," in *Europeans on the Move: Studies in European Migration, 1500–1800*, ed. Nicholas Canny (Oxford, 1994), 85, 87–88, 78–79.

29. For an extended discussion of the Scottish exodus to Ireland, see M. Perceval-Maxwell, *The Scottish Migration to Ulster in the Reign of James I* (London, 1973); and especially, W. Macafee and V. Morgan, "Population in Ulster, 1660–1760," in *Plantation to Partition: Essays in Ulster History in Honour of J. L.*

McCracken, ed. P. Roebuck (Belfast, 1981). On the growth of the Presbyterian system in Ireland, refer to R. Gillespie, "The Presbyterian Revolution in Ulster, 1660–1690," in *The Churches, Ireland and the Irish: Papers Read at the 1987 Summer Meeting and the 1988 Winter Meeting of the Ecclesiastical History Society*, ed. W. J. Sheil and D. Wood, 159–70 (Oxford, 1989); and R. L. Greaves, *God's Other Children: Protestant Nonconformists and the Emergence of Denominational Churches in Ireland, 1660–1700* (Stanford, CA, 1997), 160–72. Peter Brooke claims Ulster's Presbyterians constructed their identity as a people on this system. On the church and identity, *Ulster Presbyterianism: The Historical Perspective, 1610–1970* (New York, 1987), 60–62, 89.

30. Minutes of the Antrim Meeting, February 1687, August 1688, 389, 426, PHSB.

31. Minutes of the Presbytery of Killyleagh, 4 December 1728, D 1759/1D/10, PRONI.

32. See, for example, Carmoney Session Minutes, 12 May 1697, MIC/1P/37/4, PRONI.

33. Connor Session Minutes, 9 February 1706/07, PHSB; Minutes of the Presbytery of Down, January 1706/07, 7, PHSB.

34. T. McCrie, ed., *The Correspondence of the Reverend Robert Wodrow*, (Edinburgh, 1842), 2:239.

35. Robert McBride, *The Overtures Set in a Fair Light* (Belfast, 1726), 65; The Presbyterian Church of Ireland, *Records of the General Synod of Ulster, from 1691 to 1820* (Belfast, 1890), 1:34. Raymond Gillespie argues that northern "nonconformists" took such measures at this stage because they aspired to established status in "Dissenters and Nonconformists," in *The Irish Dissenting Tradition*, ed. Herlihy, 11–28.

36. Burt Session Minutes, 12 August 1696, Union Theological College, Belfast. All session minutes detail the elaborate preparations for the Lord's Supper as well as collections taken. For a good example, see Templepatrick Session Minutes, 15 August 1693, CR 4/12B/1, PRONI.

37. Templepatrick Session Minutes, April 1705.

38. Aghadowey Session Minutes, 8 June 1708, PHSB.

39. Minutes of the Antrim Meeting, February 1687/88, 389.

40. Aghadowey Session Minutes, 2 March 1707/08, 6 April 1708.

41. Daniel Mussenden's Book of Sermons and Themes, August 1704, D 1759/2B/2, PRONI.

42. Reeves Copy Book of Visitations of Armagh Made by Bishop William King, 30 August 1700, Armagh Public Library, KH II 6. Corporate liturgies reminded all, according to Raymond Gillespie, that "the church was not limited to one parish but comprised a wider Presbyterian community." See Gillespie, "Dissenters and Nonconformists," 25. Also see Westerkamp, *Triumph of the Laity*, 66–67; and Schmidt, *Holy Fairs*.

43. *A Discourse concerning Ireland and the Different Interests thereof* (Dublin, 1697/98), 34.

44. L. M. Cullen, "Population Trends in Seventeenth-Century Ireland," *Economic and Social Review* 6 (1974–75): 157–58.

45. David Hayton, *Ireland after the Glorious Revolution* (Belfast, 1976), 7–9.

46. Ibid., 8. Although Sean Connolly tries to resurrect the fallen reputation of the Church of Ireland, even he concedes that it "was an institution torn between an exalted vision of its potential role and a circumscribed, demoralizing, and, in places, sordid reality" (*Religion, Law and Power*, 171).

47. See 1725 session in The Presbyterian Church of Ireland, *Records of the General Synod of Ulster*, 2:82–84.

48. Sir Joshua Dawson to Southwell, 23 January 1712/13, T 780/48, PRONI.

49. McBride, "Presbyterians in the Penal Era," 73–86; Connolly, *Religion, Law and Power*, 161–68. Toby Barnard, "The Government and Irish Dissent, 1704–80," in *The Politics of Irish Dissent, 1650–1800*, ed. Kevin Herlihy (Dublin, 1997), 21, 27. See Kilroy for an examination of the doctrinal differences between the Presbyterian Church and the Church of Ireland (*Protestant Dissent*, 171–203).

50. *Conduct of the Dissenters* (Dublin, 1712), cited in John Stevenson, *Two Centuries of Life in Down, 1600–1800* (Belfast, 1920), 139.

51. Reeves Copy Book of Visitations of Armagh, 30 August 1700.

52. Tisdall, *A Sample of True-Blew Presbyterian Loyalty*, 5, 23.

53. *Conduct of the Dissenters*, cited in Stevenson, *Two Centuries of Life in Down*, 135–36.

54. Copy of a Petition from the Bishop of Down to the Lords Justices of Ireland, September 1698, Wodrow Papers, T525, PRONI; Tobias Pullein, *A Defence of the Answer to a Paper Entitled the Case of the Dissenting Protestants of Ireland* (Dublin, 1697), 8.

55. Robert Wodrow to John Williamson, 6 February 1712/13, in *Correspondence of Wodrow*, ed. McCrie, 1:401.

56. John McBride to Wodrow, 4 August 1713, in *Correspondence of Wodrow*, ed. McCrie, 1:484.

57. Stevenson, *Two Centuries of Life in Down*, 163.

58. The Humble Petition of the Presbyterian Ministers and People in the North of Ireland to the Lord Lieutenant, 1708, Wodrow Papers, T 525, PRONI. On the issue of marriages and other discrimination the group faced during this period, see Connolly, *Religion, Law and Power*, 162–64; J. C. Beckett, *Protestant Dissent in Ireland, 1687–1780* (London, 1948), 116–23; McBride, "Presbyterians in the Penal Era," 74.

59. G. Faulkiner, ed., *Letters Written by his Excellency Hugh Boulter, Lord Primate of All Ireland* (Dublin, 1770), 290. Finally, during the abjuration crisis, authorities arrested three Presbyterian ministers for refusing to condemn the Jacob-

ite cause because it meant acknowledging the supremacy of the established church. On this, see Beckett, *Protestant Dissent in Ireland*, 64–69.

60. Wodrow to James Hog, 30 November 1710, in *Correspondence of Wodrow*, ed. McCrie, 1:192.

61. Moody and Vaughan, *A New History of Ireland*, xlviii, 24–25; Kilroy, *Protestant Dissent*, 192. On the formulation of the Test Act, see D. W. Hayton, "Exclusion, Conformity, and Parliamentary Representation: The Impact of the Sacramental Test on Irish Dissenting Politics," in *The Politics of Irish Dissent*, ed. Herlihy, 54; and J. G. Simms, "The Making of a Penal Law (2 Anne, c. 6), 1703–4," *Irish Historical Studies*, 12 (1960–61): 105–18.

62. Rough Draft for a Pamphlet in the Handwriting of Theophilus Bolton, 1730, Massereene Papers, D 207/3/8, PRONI.

63. Hayton, "Exclusion, Conformity and Parliamentary Representation," 54. On the High Tory assault against Ulster Presbyterianism, see Beckett, *Protestant Dissent in Ireland*, 60–61.

64. Connolly, *Religion, Law and Power*, 162–66; Beckett, *Protestant Dissent in Ireland*, 31–38, 48–49, 71–79.

65. William Connolly argued that during the 1715 invasion scare dissenters should be armed to oppose the Pretender. Connolly to Lord Lieutenant, 9 August 1715, T 448/ 90, PRONI.

66. John McBride to Wodrow, 16 May 1715, *Correspondence of Wodrow*, ed. McCrie, 2:47.

67. Sean Connolly argues that the Toleration Act of 1719, which only allowed dissenters to practice their religion openly—something they had been doing for some time—was "introduced to block any attempt at real concessions" (*Religion, Law and Power*, 175).

68. Lease Book of the Manor of Castle Dillon, County Armagh, Observations by William Molyneux, 1696, MIC 80/3/4, PRONI.

69. *A Discourse concerning Ireland*, 26, 36, 37. Cullen, *An Economic History of Ireland*, 29. On the origins and growth of the northeast merchant community, see Jean Agnew, *Belfast Merchant Families in the Seventeenth Century* (Dublin, 1996).

70. Henry Conyngham to Lady Ann Murray, 2 October 1703, Murray of Broughton Papers, D 2860/5/14, PRONI.

71. Thomas Truxes, *Irish-American Trade, 1660–1783* (Cambridge, 1988); L. M. Cullen, "Economic Development, 1691–1750," in *A New History of Ireland*, ed. Moody and Vaughan, 4:133–136.

72. Conyngham to Lady Murray, 2 October 1703, Murray of Broughton Papers, D 2860/5/14, PRONI. Also see Charles O'Hara's memoirs on how his tenants paid rent before money was available in T 2812/19/6, PRONI.

73. Almost all extant session and presbytery records from the period detail the trouble congregants had raising money for ministerial stipends. For a good example of the extent of the problem, how it touched every congrega-

tion within a presbytery's bounds, refer to Minutes of the Monaghan Presbytery, August 1709, PHSB. Quotations are from Aghadowey Session Minutes, 4 February 1707/08 and Minutes of the Route Presbytery, 6 October 1702, PHSB.

74. Precis of orders of the Court of Assistants of the Goldsmiths' Company concerning the Irish estate, 20 March 1694/95, Goldsmiths' Company Records, MIC 9B/12, PRONI. Gillespie, *Settlement and Survival*, xxi–xxii. W. H. Crawford covers these themes more fully in his essay "Landlord-Tenant Relations in Ulster, 1609–1820," *Irish Economic and Social History* 2 (1975): 5–21.

75. W. H. Crawford, *The Handloom Weavers and the Ulster Linen Industry* (Belfast, 1994), 1–4; W. H. Crawford, more than anyone else, is responsible for charting the rise of Ulster's linen industry. Refer to "Economy and Society in Ulster in the Eighteenth Century," Ph.D. diss., Queen's University of Belfast, 1983; *Domestic Industry in Ireland: The Experience of the Linen Industry* (Belfast, 1972); "The Rise of the Linen Industry," in *The Formation of the Irish Economy*, ed. L. M. Cullen, 23–35 (Cork, 1969); "The Significance of Landed Estates in Ulster, 1600–1820," *Irish Economic and Social History* 17 (1990): 44–61; "The Origins of the Linen Industry in North Armagh and the Lagan Valley," *Ulster Folklife* 17 (1971): 42–51; and "Drapers and Bleachers in the Early Ulster Linen Industry," in *Négoce et Industrie en France et en Irlande aux XVIII et XIX siècles*, ed. P. Butel and L. M. Cullen (Paris, 1980), 113–19.

76. Truxes, *Irish-American Trade*, 175–76; Francis James, *Ireland in the Empire, 1688–1700* (Cambridge, MA, 1973), 62–64; Sunderland to Stanhope, 4 June 1715, T 448/51, PRONI, as cited in R. J. Dickson, *Ulster Emigration to Colonial America* (London, 1966), 8.

77. Crawford, *Handloom Weavers*, 3.

78. Charles O'Hara Papers, T 2812/19/6–7, PRONI; Castleward Papers, D 2092/1/2/42, PRONI.

79. Arthur Dobbs, *An Essay upon the Trade of Ireland* (Dublin, 1729), 9.

80. L. M. Cullen, *Anglo-Irish Trade, 1660–1800* (New York, 1968), 59–60; Bristol merchant quoted in Crawford, "Rise of Linen Industry," 25.

81. Hamilton Maxwell, Drum, to Agmondisham Vesey, Dublin, July 21, 1722, T 2524/16, PRONI.

82. T 2942, PRONI, cited in Gillespie, *Settlement and Survival*, xli.

83. *A Topographical and Chronological Survey of the County of Down* (Dublin, 1740), 9.

84. Ibid., 13.

85. Crawford, *Handloom Weavers*, 4–5, 7.

86. Truxes, *Irish-American Trade*, 182, 198; Agnew, *Belfast Merchant Families*, 108, 124–25; Molyneux, "A Journey to the North," 7 August 1708, 4, PHSB.

87. Rosemary Street Church, Belfast, Register of Baptisms and Marriages, 1722–60, T 654/1, 1–70, PRONI.

88. Dobbs, *An Essay upon the Trade of Ireland*, 16.

89. Ibid., 16.

90. Crawford, "Landlord-Tenant Relations," 5–21; Vivienne Pollock, "Contract and Consumption: Labour Agreements and the Use of Money in Eighteenth-Century Rural Ulster," *Agricultural History Review* 43 (1995): 19–34.

91. *A Discourse concerning Ireland*, 34–35.

92. Crawford, *Handloom Weavers*, 24–27; Cullen, *Economic History of Ireland*, 61–64, 81–87; Gillespie, *Settlement and Survival*, xxv, xxxv–xxxvi; Crawford, "Rise of Linen Industry," 24–26; Truxes, *Irish-American Trade*, 172.

93. Graeme Kirkham, introduction to *Ulster Emigration to Colonial America* (Belfast, 1988), by Dickson, viii–ix.

94. Gillespie, *Settlement and Survival*, xxxxix.

95. *A Topographical and Chronological Survey of the County of Down*, as cited in Stevenson, *Two Centuries of Life in Down*, 261.

96. Crawford, "Economy and Society in Ulster," 29–31, 46–47, 88; Crawford, "Landlord-Tenant Relations," 13–15.

97. Hamilton Maxwell to A. Vesey, 13 January 1721/22, T 2524/12, PRONI; Lease Book of the Manor of Castle Dillon, County Armagh, Observations of William Molyneux, MIC 80/3/54, PRONI; Crawford, "Economy and Society in Ulster," 33; Gillespie, *Settlement and Survival*, xx.

98. Gillespie, *Settlement and Survival*, lxii; Kirkham, introduction, ix.

99. The spread of economic change throughout various areas of Ulster is detailed in G. Kirkham, " 'To Pay the Rent and Lay up Riches': The Economic Opportunity in Eighteenth-Century North-West Ulster," in *Economy and Society in Scotland and Ireland, 1500–1939*, ed. R. Mitchison and P. Roebuck (Edinburgh, 1988), 95–104; and W. H. Crawford, "Economy and Society in South Ulster in the Eighteenth-Century," *Clogher Record* 8 (1975): 241–58.

100. Crawford, *Handloom Weavers*, 33.

101. See, for example, Observations of Counties Monaghan, Cavan, and Fermanagh, Lodge MSS, Armagh Public Library.

102. Gillespie, *Settlement and Survival*, lxi–lxii.

103. Crawford, "Economy and Society in Ulster," 15.

104. Stevenson, *Two Centuries of Life in Down*, 276.

105. Minutes of the Presbytery of Down, April 1707, July 1708, 19–20, 94.

106. Ibid., September 1711, 228–29.

107. Minutes of the Presbytery of Strabane, 29 January 1717/18, CR 3/26/2/1, 22, PRONI.

108. Burt Session Minutes, 30 June 1700, 30 August 1709.

109. Stevenson, *Two Centuries of Life in Down*, 183.

110. Minutes of the Presbytery of Down, September 1709, 142.

111. Ibid., 26 July 1709, 135.

112. Ballycarry Session Minutes, 30 October 1718, CR 3/31/2, 25, PRONI. For seating controversies, also refer to the Minutes of the Laggan Meeting,

13 December 1700, 191, PHSB; Minutes of the Presbytery of Strabane, 27 February 1722/23, June 1729.

113. James Orr Sermon delivered at Hollywood and Comber, 1712–1730, MSS 24, 2, Magee Collection.

114. James Duchal Sermon, 2 July 1727, MS 19, Magee College; MS Sermon by James Duchal, 1723, PHSB; MS Sermon by James Duchal, n.d., 7, PHSB.

115. MS Ministerial Notebook of John Kennedy, 1710–60, 4, PHSB.

116. Stevenson, *Two Centuries of Life in Down*, 166.

CHAPTER TWO

1. Peter Brooke in *Ulster Presbyterianism*, contends that this vision defined the group. Although it would be contested, the consolidating ideology would triumph in the church.

2. Ian McBride in *Scripture Politics*, counters that ultimately the New Light agenda defined the group's political ethos. Looking ahead to the 1798 Rising, McBride argues that New Light ideas would animate the Ulster Presbyterian approach to the state.

3. Stevenson, *Two Centuries of Life in Down*, 167.

4. Diary of the Rev. John Kennedy, 8–130, PHSB.

5. Burt Session Minutes, 24 May 1706, Union Theological College.

6. On this theme, see Jane Gray, "Rural Industry and Uneven Development: The Significance of Gender in the Irish Linen Industry," *Journal of Peasant Studies* 20 (1993): 590–611.

7. Templepatrick Session Minutes, 16 October 1727, CR 4/12B/1, PRONI.

8. Carmoney Session Minutes, 18 February 1704/05, MIC/1P/37/4, PRONI.

9. Broadisland or Ballycarry Session Minutes, 27 October 1729, 21 February 1730/31, CR 3/31/1, PRONI; Carmoney Session Minutes, February 1722/23; Burt Session Minutes, 29 October 1710.

10. Connor Session Minutes, 15 January 1705/06, PHSB.

11. Ibid., 17 May 1704.

12. Larne Session Minutes, 16 March 1728, MIC 1B/1A/1B, PRONI.

13. Ibid., 7 August 1723, 31 October 1723.

14. Carmoney Session Minutes, 11 January 1706/07, March 1709.

15. Burt Session Minutes, 9 July 1713.

16. Carmoney Session Minutes, 20 June 1716.

17. Templepatrick Session Minutes, 4 February 1699/00.

18. Larne Session Minutes, 25 July 1725.

19. Ballycarry Session Minutes, 3 July 1715.

20. Burt Session Minutes, 26 June 1712.

21. Minutes of the Presbytery of Down, February 1714/15, 370.

22. Lisburn Session Minutes, 23 January 1717/18, 2 June 1720, MIC/1P/159/8, PRONI.

23. Burt Session Minutes, 22 November 1709.

24. Carmoney Session Minutes, 9 February 1708/09.

25. Minutes of the Laggan Meeting, February 1699/1700, 203.

26. Ballycarry Session Minutes, 18 December 1706.

27. For the Darroch episode, see Minutes of the Monaghan Presbytery, October 1711, February 1711/12, July 1712, 113–44.

28. Letter of Alexander Montgomery re Mr. Darroch, 22 September 1711, T 780/42–43, PRONI.

29. Minutes of the Laggan Meeting, August 1694, 55.

30. Burt Session Minutes, 22 October 1696.

31. Hayton, "Exclusion, Conformity and Parliamentary Representation," in *The Politics of Irish Dissent*, ed. Herlihy, 73. Historians have long debated the ways in which the Test Act affected Ulster Scot political life. Although these effects are admittedly difficult to gauge, some historians claim the test had little impact on Ulster Presbyterian political activity. Few Ulster Scots, the argument goes, had served as MPs before the Revolution, and their purge from municipal corporations had a negligible effect on their voice. The rhetoric of disability in no way reflected the reality of their situation. Ulster Scots used the theme of religious disability to angle for more power in the kingdom. See Beckett, *Protestant Dissent in Ireland*. Other scholars argue that the practical effects of the Test Act were more debilitating than historians have suggested. Presbyterian rhetoric at least underscored the stigma the test represented, and in Belfast and Derry the exclusion from local office permitted fewer Presbyterians to assume positions of authority. Ian McBride takes a more idealist approach, suggesting historians should not be so suspicious of the handicaps Ulster Scots claimed they suffered in "Presbyterians in the Penal Era," 73–86. Finally, some historians claim that the application of the test alternated between ferocity and leniency. Ultimately, as Barnard argues, "a notion of the Protestant Interest" ensured that the full measure of the test was never realized. Barnard, "The Government and Irish Dissent," in *The Politics of Irish Dissent*, ed., Herlihy, 9. Barnard, taking a middle-ground approach, argues that the application of the test alternated between "forbearance and vindictiveness" ("The Government and Irish Dissent," 27). On the political effects of exclusion from municipal corporations, see Hayton, "Exclusion, Conformity, and Parliamentary Representation."

32. Carmoney Session Minutes, 8 June 1712.

33. The jeremiad also became standard by 1710. See, for example, Broadisland Session Minutes, 29 June 1723; Minutes of the Laggan Meeting, February 1714/1715; Carmoney Session Minutes, 8 June 1712. Quotations are from Ministerial Notebook of John Kennedy, 4, PHSB; and Minutes of the Sub-Synod of Derry, 12 May 1724, PHSB.

34. Minutes of the Monaghan Presbytery, 14 February 1708/09, 51.

35. Minutes of the Presbytery of Strabane, November 1728, CR 3/26/2/1, 240.

36. Minutes of the Sub-Synod of Derry, 12 May 1724, 91.

37. P. Kilroy identifies two strands of Presbyterian thought in Scotland as predestinarian and Arminian. See *Protestant Dissent*, 8–9. David Hall discusses the Reformed tradition and its historiography on both sides of the Atlantic in "On Common Ground: The Coherence of American Puritan Studies," *William and Mary Quarterly*, 3rd ser., 44 (1987): 195. Also see Ian Hazlett, "Ebbs and Flows of Theology in Glasgow, 1451–1843," in his *Traditions of Theology in Glasgow, 1450–1990* (Edinburgh, 1993).

38. J. MacKenzie, Sermons written during the Siege of Derry, 1689, PHSB; J. McBride Sermons, 1704, PHSB; J. Magee Sermons, 1721, 94, PHSB.

39. Brooke, *Ulster Presbyterianism*, 74–82; McBride, *Scripture Politics*, 44.

40. Arch-subscriber Duguld quoted in J. Kirkpatrick (originally attributed to V. Ferguson), *A Vindication of the Presbyterian Ministers in the North of Ireland: Subscribers and Non-subscribers* (Belfast, 1721), 9, 11. For a more detailed account of the history of the Confession, see J. S. Reid, *History of the Presbyterian Church in Ireland* (Belfast, 1867), 3:81–83, 110–217; and McBride, *Scripture Politics*, 43–52. Peter Brooke explores the theological issues of the debate in *Ulster Presbyterianism*, 81–92. On theology, also see A.W.G. Brown, "A Theological Interpretation of the First Subscription Controversy," in *Challenge and Conflict: Essays in Irish Presbyterian History and Doctrine*, ed., J.L.M. Haire (Belfast, 1981).

41. The Presbyterian Church of Ireland, *Records of the General Synod of Ulster*, 1:396.

42. Minutes of the Presbytery of Down, 27 October 1708.

43. Stevenson, *Two Centuries of Life in Down*, 146; Gillespie, "Dissenters and Nonconformists," in *The Irish Dissenting Tradition*, ed., Herlihy, 11–28.

44. McCracken to Thomas Linning, 28 June 1710; and McCracken, "The Reasons of the Non-Jurors in Ireland," in *Correspondence of Wodrow*, ed., McCrie, 1:154, 158, 162. For a more in-depth analysis of the abjuration crisis during which McCracken was imprisoned for his staunch views of dissent, see Beckett, *Protestant Dissent in Ireland*, 64–69.

45. Minutes of the Sub-Synod of Derry, 12 May 1724, 90.

46. McBride, *The Overtures Set in a Fair Light*, xii, 24; Minutes of the Sub-Synod of Derry, 3 May 1720.

47. For a theological interpretation of the New Light, see R. Finlay Holmes, "The Reverend John Abernethy: The Challenge of New Light Theology to Traditional Irish Presbyterian Calvinism," in *The Religion of Irish Dissent*, ed., Herlihy; and R. B. Barlow, "The Career of John Abernethy (1680–1740), Father of Nonsubscription in Ireland and Defender of Religious Liberty," *Harvard Theological Review* 78 (1985): 399–419.

48. Brooke, *Ulster Presbyterianism*, 72–81. C. Robbins, *The Eighteenth-Century Commonwealthman: Studies in the Transmission, Development and Circumstance of English Liberal Thought from the Restoration of Charles II until the War with the Thirteen Colonies* (Cambridge, MA, 1959), 169–170; L. Stone, "The Results of the English Revolutions of the Seventeenth Century," in J.G.A. Pocock, ed., *Three British Revolutions*, ed. J.G.A. Pocock (Princeton, 1980), 72–74. Ian McBride charts this influence through the Ulster Scots to the United Irish movement and the Scottish Enlightenment. See "The School of Virtue: Francis Hutcheson, Irish Presbyterians and the Scottish Enlightenment," in *Political Thought in Ireland*, ed. Boyce, Eccleshall and Geoghegan 73–99, and "William Drennan," in *The United Irishmen*, ed. Dickson, Keogh, and Whelan, 49–61. Refer also to A.T.Q. Stewart, *A Deeper Silence: The Hidden Origins of the United Irish Movement* (London, 1993), 72.

49. Stewart, *A Deeper Silence*, 74–77; Kirkpatrick, *Vindication*, 13.

50. William Livingston to Robert Wodrow, n.d., Livingston-Wodrow Correspondence, MS. 30, 26–27, Magee College.

51. J. Abernethy, *Religious Obedience Founded on Personal Persuasion: A Sermon Preach'd at Belfast the 9th of December, 1719* (Belfast, 1720), 10.

52. Ibid., 33, 27, 36.

53. Abernethy, *A Sermon Recommending the Study of Scripture-Prophecie* (Belfast, 1716), 20.

54. Samuel Haliday, *Reasons Against the Imposition of Subscription to the Westminster Confession of Faith* (Belfast, 1724), 39, 24, 7.

55. Kirkpatrick, *A Scripture-Plea against a Fatal Rupture, and Breach of Christian Communion amongst the Presbyterians in the North of Ireland* (Belfast, 1724), 16–17.

56. J. Abernethy, *Seasonable Advice to the Protestant Dissenters in the North of Ireland* (Belfast, 1722), 18; J. Abernethy, *A Letter from the Presbytery of Antrim* (Belfast, 1726), 9.

57. Haliday, *Reasons*, 38, 39. Also see J. Kirkpatrick, *An Essay upon the Important Question, Whether there be a Legislative, Proper Authority in the Church, By Some Non-Subscribing Ministers in the North of Ireland* (Belfast, 1737). New Lights coupled ideas from the Reformed tradition, argues Ian McBride, with secular notions, many of which laid out the proper role of government. Nonsubscribers found that "biblical revelation" complemented "enlightenment rationalism." Refer to " 'When Ulster Joined Ireland': Anti-Popery, Presbyterian Radicalism and Irish Republicanism in the 1790s," *Past and Present* 157 (November 1997): 63–93; and *Scripture Politics*, 7, 43.

58. See Sean Connolly's essay, "Varieties of Britishness: Ireland, Scotland and Wales in the Hanoverian State," in *Uniting the Kingdom?*, ed. Grant and Stringer, 193–207 for a review of this literature. On Ascendancy patriotism, refer to Hayton, "Anglo-Irish Attitudes," 145–57; and Smyth, " 'Like Amphibious Animals," 785–97. The phrase "emulative patriotism" was coined by Colin

Kidd in "North Britishness and the Nature of Eighteenth-Century British Patriotisms," *Historical Journal* 39 (1996): 361–82. T. H. Breen applies this to America's Revolutionary generation in "Ideology and Nationalism on the Eve of the American Revolution: Revisions *Once More* in Need of Revising," *Journal of American History* 84 (1997): 13–39. While H. T. Dickinson argues these ideas were representative of a "country" ideology in *Liberty and Property: Political Ideology in Eighteenth-Century Britain* (London, 1977), J.G.A. Pocock constructs a typology of what he labels "varieties of Whiggism." See *Virtue, Commerce, and History: Essays on Political Thought and History Chiefly in the Eighteenth Century* (London, 1985).

59. Haliday, *Reasons*, 41.

60. Kirkpatrick, *Vindication*, 33.

61. Abernethy, *Personal Persuasion*, 27, 33–34, 5.

62. Kirkpatrick, *Vindication*, 15.

63. Abernethy, *Personal Persuasion*, 10.

64. Haliday, *Reasons*, 114.

65. Livingston-Wodrow Correspondence, MSS 30, 30, 77, 163, Magee College.

66. Presbyterian Church of Ireland, *Records of the General Synod of Ulster*, 1:522, 521. Notable moderate pamphlets included M. Bruce, *The Duty of Christians to Live Together in Religious Communion Recommended in a Sermon Preached at Belfast, January 5th, 1724–25* (Belfast, 1725); and R. Higinbotham, *Reasons against the Overtures* (Belfast, 1726).

67. J. Elder, *Reasons for Moderation in the Present Debates amongst Presbyterians in the North of Ireland* (Belfast, 1725), iii–v; J. Elder, *A Letter to the Reverend Mr. Robert McBride* (Belfast, 1727), 44.

68. Presbyterian Church of Ireland, *Records of the General Synod of Ulster*, 1:536; Westerkamp, *Triumph of the Laity*, 90–91.

69. Presbyterian Church of Ireland, *Records of the General Synod of Ulster*, 2:10; Haliday, *Reasons*, 1.

70. M. Clerk, *A Letter from The Belfast Society to the Rev. Matthew Clerk, with an Answer to the Society's Remarks* (Belfast, 1723), 17, 15–16.

71. Robert Wodrow to James Hog, 30 November 1710, *Correspondence of Wodrow*, ed. McCrie, 1:191–92.

72. Stewart, *A Deeper Silence*, 72.

73. Wodrow to McCracken, 20 October 1709, *Correspondence of Wodrow*, ed. McCrie, 1:70–71.

74. Minutes of the Sub-Synod of Derry, 12 May 1724; Kirkpatrick, *Vindication*, 9, 11.

75. Subscribers, according to Kirkpatrick, were wont to use this term. See *Vindication*.

76. McBride, *The Overtures Set in a Fair Light*, 71.

77. Charles Mastertown, *Christian Liberty Founded in Gospel Truth* (Belfast, 1725), 38.

78. McBride, *The Overtures Set ina Fair Light*, 54.

79. Minutes of the Sub-Synod of Derry, 12 May 1724, 88–91.

80. Ibid., 89.

81. Connor Session Minutes, 2 November 1716.

82. Abernethy, *Seasonable Advice*, 12.

83. Lisburn Session Minutes, 12 June 1723.

84. Kirkpatrick, *Vindication*, 39.

85. Minutes of the Presbytery of Killyleagh, D 1759/1D/10, 170, PRONI.

86. Abernethy, *Seasonable Advice*, vii, 33.

87. Wodrow to Thomas Hog, 1 September 1721, *Correspondence of Wodrow*, ed. McCrie, 2:602.

88. McBride, *Scripture Politics*, 45–47.

89. Abernethy, *Seasonable Advice*, ix, 16.

90. Robert Wodrow, *Analecta: or Materials for a History of Remarkable Providences; Mostly Relating to Scotch Ministers and Christians* (Edinburgh, 1843), 3:468. For problems in Lisburn and other congregations, see Minutes of the Presbytery of Killyleagh, 166–167, October and November 1732.

91. Abernethy, *Seasonable Advice*, 35.

92. Minutes of the Sub-Synod of Derry, 130–31, 147–49, 155; Minutes of the Presbytery of Killyleagh, 162–67, 170.

93. Kirkpatrick, *Vindication*, 17.

94. Wodrow, *Analecta*, 3:466–67.

95. Ibid., 468; McBride, *Scripture Politics*, 47–48.

96. Mastertown to William McKnight, 12 July 1723, 12 November 1723, *Correspondence of Wodrow*, ed. McCrie, 3:73.

97. Wodrow, *Analecta*, 3:468.

98. Connor Session Minutes, 22 November 1710; Aghadowey Session Minutes, May 1728, PHSB; Minutes of the Presbytery of the Killyleagh, 4 December 1728; Lisburn Session Minutes, 14 October 1717.

99. Reid, *History of the Presbyterian Church in Ireland*, 3:115.

100. Livingston to Robert Wodrow, 1 July 1720, Livingston-Wodrow Correspondence, MSS 30, 52.

101. J. S. Reid, *History of the Presbyterian Church in Ireland*, 3:210.

102. Joseph Boyse to Thomas Steward, 1 November 1726, Thomas Steward Correspondence, MSS 46, 21, Magee College.

103. Abernethy, *Seasonable Advice*, 5.

104. J. Abernethy, *The Nature and Consequences of the Sacramental Test Considered, with Reasons humbly offered for the Repeal of It* (Dublin, 1731), 32.

105. Abernethy, *Personal Persuasion*, 34; Haliday, *Reasons*, 28.

106. R. Craighead, *The True Terms of Christian and Ministerial Communion founded on Scripture Alone* (Dublin, 1739), 11.

107. Abernethy, *The People's Choice, the Lord's Anointed: A Thanksgiving Sermon for his Most Excellent Majesty King George* (Belfast, 1714), 9, 5.

108. Abernethy, *Sacramental Test*, 19, 50.

109. Duke of Bolton to ———, 27 June 1719, T 519/147, PRONI.

110. For the campaign, see Presbyterian Church of Ireland, *Records of the General Synod of Ulster*, 2:157, 158, 168, 197; and Beckett, *Protestant Dissent*, 83–96.

111. Beckett, *Protestant Dissent*, 94.

112. Abernethy, *Sacramental Test*, 47, 50.

113. J. Abernethy, *Scarce and Valuable Tracts and Sermons* (Dublin, 1751), 28.

114. Abernethy, *Sacramental Test*, 32, 11.

115. Haliday, *Reasons*, 4.

116. Archbishop Boulter quoted in Reid, *History of the Presbyterian Church in Ireland*, 3:233.

117. Swift, "The Presbyterians Plea of Merit in Order to Take Off the Test Impartially Examined" (1731), in *The Works of the Rev. Jonathan Swift, D. D.*, ed. John Nichols (London, 1801), 5:306, 311.

118. Swift, "The Advantages Proposed by Repealing the Sacramental Test, Impartially Considered" (1732), in *The Works of Swift*, ed. Nichols, 319.

119. Correspondence of William Nicholson, Bishop of Derry, T 1910/3, 135, PRONI; Minutes of the Monaghan Presbytery, 12 January 1708/09.

CHAPTER THREE

1. Lord Carteret to the Lords Justices Arlington, and Stuart, 11 November 1728, T 780/51, PRONI.

2. Instead of constructing the Atlantic as a "salt water curtain," Frank Thistlethwaite believes, migration historians should conceive "the subject *as a whole*," and to "think neither of emigrants or immigrants, but of migrants, and to treat the process of migration as a complete sequence of experience." See "Migration from Europe Overseas in the Nineteenth and Twentieth Centuries," in Comité International des Sciences Historiques, X^{ie} Congres International des Sciences Historiques, *Rapports: V: Histoire Contemporaine* (Stockholm, 1960), 34, 37. On this theme, also refer to Alan Kulikoff's suggestive essay, "Migration and Cultural Diffusion in Early America, 1600–1860: A Review Essay," *Historical Methods* 19 (1986): 167, 168. Gwyn Williams argues that early nineteenth-century Welsh migration to America began, as in the case of Ulster Scots, after immersion in a larger British world. In this context, movement represented "one highly visible symptom of the crisis," which in turn generated a "trans-Atlantic world of dissent." See, "Druids and Democrats: Organic Intellectuals and the First Welsh Nation," in *The Welsh in Their History* (London, 1982), 32, 38, 46. See also "When Was Wales?," in Ibid., 189–201; and *The Search for Beulah Land: The Welsh and the Atlantic Revolution* (London, 1980).

3. The best treatments of eighteenth-century migration are Bailyn's *Peopling of British North America* and *Voyagers to the West*. For reviews of the literature on migration to colonial America, refer to James Horn and I. Altman, eds., *To Make America: European Emigration in the Early Modern Period* (Berkeley, 1991); Canny, *Europeans on the Move*; and James Horn, "British Diaspora: Emigration from Britain, 1680–1815," in *The Oxford History of the British Empire*, vol. 2, *The Eighteenth Century*, ed. P. J. Marshall (Oxford, 1998), 28–52.

R. J. Dickson's *Ulster Emigration to Colonial America* remains the most comprehensive study of Ulster Scot migration to America. Since Dickson, other historians have added to this story. Studies have revised Dickson's estimates of the number of migrants and the volumes of shipping. David Doyle in *Ireland, Irishmen and Revolutionary America, 1760–1820* (Cork, 1981), 70–71, and K. Miller, in *Emigrants and Exiles: Ireland and the Irish Exodus to North America* (New York, 1985), 137–49, argue that Catholics made up nearly a quarter of all Irish migrants to the colonies, and northern Presbyterians 70 percent. Some have recast his rising rents and prices as a "demographic crisis." See L. M. Cullen, "The Irish Diaspora of the Seventeenth and Eighteenth Centuries," in *Europeans on the Move*, ed. Canny, 113–49. Still others have correlated his analyses of the ebb and flow of migration with transatlantic trading trends. Refer to Truxes, *Irish-American Trade*; M. S. Wokeck, *Trade in Strangers: The Beginnings of Mass Migration to North America* (University Park, PA, 1999); Wokeck, "German and Irish Immigration to Colonial Philadelphia," *Proceedings of the American Philosophical Society* 133 (June 1989): 128–43; Wokeck, "Irish Immigration to the Delaware Valley before the American Revolution," *Proceedings of the Royal Irish Academy* ser. C (1996): 103–35; and M. J. Bric, "Ireland, Irishmen, and the Broadening of the Late Eighteenth Century Philadelphia Polity," Ph.D. diss., Johns Hopkins University, 1991. Graeme Kirkham has pointed out some problems with Dickson's economic analysis, arguing Dickson overemphasizes the problems of the economy without focusing on the opportunities, especially the role of the linen trade. See his new introduction to Dickson, *Ulster Emigration* (1988).

4. Graeme Kirkham, "Ulster Emigration to North America, 1680–1720," in *Ulster and North America: Transatlantic Perspectives on the Scotch-Irish*, ed. H. T. Blethen and C. W. Wood (Tuscaloosa, AL, 1997), 84.

5. Boulter to Newcastle, 25 May 1728, *Letters Written by His Excellency Hugh Boulter, D. D., Lord Primate of All Ireland* (Dublin, 1770) vol. 1, 194 (in Dickson, *Ulster Emigration*, 13).

6. Letters dated 24 June 1718, 30 April 1721, 2 June 1721, Correspondence of William Nicolson, Bishop of Derry, T 1910/3, 85, 135, 136.

7. Hamilton Maxwell to Agmondisham Vesey, 21 July 1722, T 2524/16, PRONI.

8. Conrad Gill, *The Rise of the Irish Linen Industry* (Oxford, 1925), 341; Truxes, *Irish-American Trade*, 276.

9. Gill, *Rise of the Irish Linen Industry*, 341.

10. Letter dated 6 December 1720, Correspondence of William Nicolson, 129.

11. Dobbs, *An Essay upon the Trade of Ireland*, 9.

12. Letter dated 2 June 1721, Correspondence of William Nicolson, 136; Cullen, "Economic Development," 145–150.

13. Cullen, *Anglo-Irish Trade*, 157, 178, 195; Kirkham, "Ulster Emigration to North America," 89.

14. Dobbs, *An Essay upon the Trade of Ireland*, 10.

15. Crawford, "Economy and Society in Ulster," 29.

16. Lease book of the manor of Castledillon, Co. Armagh, MIC. 80/3/4, PRONI.

17. Gillespie, *Settlement and Survival*, xxii.

18. Maxwell to A. Vesey, 18 November 1721, T 2524/9, PRONI.

19. Cullen, *Economic History of Ireland*, 44.

20. H. Maxwell to A. Vesey, 15 August 1722, T 2524/17, PRONI.

21. Dickson, *Ulster Emigration*, 11–13.

22. *An Inquiry into some of the Causes of the Ill Situation of the Affairs of Ireland; with Some Reflexions on the Trade, Manufactures, etc. of England* (Dublin, 1732), 1–2.

23. Jonathan Swift, "A Modest Proposal for Preventing the Children of Poor People in Ireland from Being a Burden to the Parents or the Country, and for making Them Beneficial to the Public (1729)," in George Levine, ed., *A Modest Proposal and Other Satires* (Amherst, NY, 1995), 259, 260, 267.

24. Boulter to Lord Carteret, 20 July 1727, in George Faulkiner, ed., *Letters Written by His Excellency Hugh Boulter, Lord Primate of All Ireland* (Oxford, 1769–70) 1:151.

25. Boulter to Archbishop of Canterbury, 24 February 1727/28, Faulkiner, *Letters*, 1:178.

26. Livingston to Robert Wodrow, 29 March 1729, Livingston-Wodrow Correspondence, Magee College.

27. *Pennsylvania Gazette*, 12 April, 25 May, 21 June 1729.

28. Dobbs, *An Essay upon the Trade of Ireland*, 9.

29. Gill, *Rise of the Irish Linen Industry*, 341; Truxes, *Irish-American Trade*, 276.

30. Gill, *Rise of the Irish Linen Industry*, 341.

31. Carteret to Newcastle, 16 June 1729, cited in Cullen, "Economic Development," in *A New History of Ireland*, ed. Moody and Vaughan, 145.

32. Dickson, *Ulster Emigration*, 41.

33. Boulter to the Bishop of London, 13 March 1728/29, Faulkiner, *Letters*, 1:232–33.

34. George Pike cited in Kirkham, "Ulster Emigration to North America," 89.

35. Cullen, "Economic Development," in *A New History of Ireland*, ed. Moody and Vaughan, 4:145–48.

36. William King to the Archbishop of Canterbury, 23 March 1720/21, and Jonathan Swift to Earl of Peterborough, 28 April 1726, in King, *A Great Archbishop of Dublin*, 226.

37. Stevenson, *Two Centuries of Life in Down*, 231.

38. Ibid., 230–31; Cullen, "Economic Development," 145; Kirkham, introduction to Dickson, *Ulster Emigration*, x.

39. Lords Justices (Boulter, Wyndham, Connolly) to Lord Lieutenant, 11 June 1729, T 659/73, PRONI.

40. Thomas Wyndham to Lord [ ], 11 January 1728/29, T 659/64–66, PRONI.

41. Ibid.

42. King to Archbishop of Canterbury, 6 February 1717/18, in King, *A Great Archbishop of Dublin*, 208.

43. Boulter to Duke of Newcastle, 16 July 1728, Faulkiner, *Letters*, 1:202.

44. Letter to the Lords Justices General and General Governor of Ireland, T 659/79, PRONI.

45. Boulter to Lord Carteret, 8 March 1728/29, Faulkiner, *Letters*, 1:229.

46. Boulter to the Bishop of London, 13 March 1728/29, Faulkiner, *Letters*, 1:236.

47. *A Letter from a Gentleman in the North of Ireland* (Dublin, 1729) in E.R.R. Green, "The 'Strange Humours' That Drove the Scotch-Irish to America, 1729," *William and Mary Quarterly*, 3rd ser., 12 (1955): 120.

48. Report of John St. Leger and Michael Ward in a letter from the Lords Justices Boulter, Wyndham, Connolly to the Lord Lieutenant, 11 June 1729, T 659/75, 77, PRONI.

49. Boulter to Duke of Newcastle, 23 November 1728, Faulkiner, *Letters*, 1:209.

50. Boulter to Archbishop of Canterbury, 24 February 1727/28, Faulkiner, *Letters*, 1:178.

51. King to Archbishop of Canterbury, 2 June 1719, in King, *A Great Archbishop of Dublin*, 302–03. Most historians agree that economic factors, not religious issues, and rents in particular, fueled the impetus to leave. As Dickson explained, "Rents, prices and wages formed a mighty triumvirate in determining the extent of north Irish migration" (*Ulster Emigration*, 13).

52. According to Graeme Kirkham, only nine voyages from the northern ports to the colonies carrying passengers have been identified. See "Ulster Emigration to North America," 91.

53. Crawford, "Economy and Society in Ulster," 18, 29, 46–47; Kirkham, introduction to Dickson, *Ulster Emigration*, xi–xiii.

54. George Conyngham to Captain James McCullock, 17 November 1723, Records of Goldsmiths' Company, MIC 9B/12B, PRONI.

55. Account of the Lands and Rent Roll on Vinters' Proportion, D 2094/21, PRONI.

56. An Account of the full Rent of what the proportion of Clothworkers pays Capn. Jackson as they are now Raised, T 656/44, PRONI. For an explanation of the landlords' impetus to offer abatements, see Crawford, "Economy and Society in Ulster," 18.

57. H. Maxwell to A. Vesey, 15 August 1722, T 2524/17, PRONI.

58. Carmoney Session Minutes, February 1722/23, MIC/1P/37/4.

59. Letter to Lord Connolly, 13 November 1718, T 2825/C/27/2, PRONI; Gillespie, *Settlement and Survival,* lii; Kirkham, introduction to Dickson, *Ulster Emigration,* xi, xiii.

60. George Conyngham to Capt. James McCullock, 17 November 1723, Records of the Goldsmiths' Company, MIC 9B/12B, PRONI.

61. Account of the Lands and Rent Roll of the Vinters' Proportion, D 2094/21, PRONI.

62. Emigrants to New England from County Londonderry, Manor of Grocers, William Connolly Estate, 1718, T 2825/C/11/1, PRONI.

63. *Pennsylvania Gazette,* 17 November 1729; Wokeck, *Trade in Strangers,* 189.

64. Charles O'Hara Papers, Report from 1728, T 2812/19/7, PRONI; Gillespie, *Settlement and Survival,* lx–lxii.

65. As Cullen writes, the early part of the century was "a truly exceptional period of serious demographic and economic crisis." The 1720s were marked by "famine and harvest failure" during which settlement opportunities that had earlier enticed Scots to settle Ulster were drying up. Migration, in his opinion, grew from this dynamic ("The Irish Diaspora," 129–30).

66. Steward to Ward, 25 March 1729, D 2092/1/3/141, PRONI.

67. Gillespie, *Settlement and Survival,* lii–lv.

68. To their Excellencies the Lords Justices General and General Governor of Ireland, T 659/79, PRONI. On the selling of lease interests, see *Pennsylvania Gazette,* 17 November 1729, and Dickson, *Ulster Emigration,* 42.

69. Kirkham, "Ulster Emigration to North America," 94–95.

70. Wokeck, *Trade in Strangers,* 176.

71. *Pennsylvania Gazette,* 12 June 1735. Graham Kirkham argues that these regions supplied "most of the emigrants of the period." See his introduction to Dickson, *Ulster Emigration,* ix.

72. Ezekial Steward to Michael Ward, 25 March 1729, D 2092/1/3/141, PRONI.

73. Green, "The 'Strange Humours,' " 116–19.

74. Ibid.

75. Address of Protestant Dissenting Ministers of Dublin and the South of Ireland to the King signed by Francis Iredell, Richard Choppin and Robert Craighead, T 659/20–22, PRONI.

76. Lords Justices to Lord Lieutenant, 11 June 1729, T 659/73, PRONI. On this theme, see Beckett, *Protestant Dissent.*

77. King to Archbishop of Canterbury, 2 June 1719, in King, *A Great Archbishop of Dublin*, 301–02.

78. Boulter to Lord Carteret, 8 March 1728/29, Faulkiner, *Letters*, 1:229.

79. Boulter to Bishop of London, 13 March 1728/29, Faulkiner, *Letters*, 1:235, 236.

80. Steward to Ward, 25 March 1729, D 2092/1/3, PRONI.

81. Robert Wodrow to Benjamin Colman, 30 January 1729/30, in *Correspondence of Wodrow*, ed. McCrie, 3:456.

82. See McBride, "Presbyterians in the Penal Era."

83. Wodrow, *Analecta*, 4:298. Earlier American works found that religious disabilities caused migration. Hagiographers, such as Charles Bolton and H. J. Ford—both of Scotch-Irish stock—argued that a corrupted Ascendancy designed to ruin a fiercely independent Presbyterian people, ironically driving them to a land where their virtues would be made manifest. Examples include C. K. Bolton, *Scotch-Irish Pioneers in Ulster and America* (Boston, 1910); H. J. Ford, *The Scotch-Irish in Colonial Pennsylvania* (Princeton, 1915); and C. Hanna, *The Scotch-Irish* (New York, 1902). For a review of this literature, see Jones, "The Scotch-Irish in British North America," in *Strangers within the Realm*, ed. Bailyn and Morgan.

84. Account of a riot at Armagh, 1717, T 808/14937, Tennison Groves Collection, PRONI.

85. Connor Session Minutes, 17 August 1715, PHSB.

86. Ballycarry Session Minutes, 24 April 1717, CR 3/31/2, PRONI.

87. Minutes of Sub-Synod of Derry, 5 May 1719, 63.

88. Ballycarry Session Minutes, 10 October 1729.

89. Ibid., 9 March 1717/18, 24 November 1719.

90. Wodrow to Cotton Mather, *Correspondence of Wodrow*, ed. McCrie, 2:426.

91. Ballycarry Session Minutes, 29 June 1723, 27 July 1726.

92. Steward to Ward, 25 March 1729, D 2092/1/3/141, PRONI.

93. Minutes of the Presbytery of Strabane, 29 January 1717/18, CR 3/26/2/1, 22, PRONI.

94. Ibid., 5 August 1724, 151, 202.

95. Minutes of the Sub-Synod of Derry, May 1720, May 1721, 68–69, 73.

96. Ibid., 5 May 1719, 62–63.

97. Carmoney Session Minutes, 15 August 1718, 25 March 1719.

98. Ballycarry Session Minutes, 30 October 1718.

99. Ibid., 22 May 1718.

100. Templepatrick Session Minutes, 22 May 1718, 28 June 1722, CR 4/12B/1, PRONI.

101. Minutes of the Presbytery of Strabane, June 1729, 245.

102. Armagh Session Accounts, 1716–1719, 163–95, PHSB.

103. This figure applies to the Brownlow estate. See Crawford, "Landlord-Tenant Relations," 13.

104. Armagh Session Accounts, 1716–19, 163–95.

105. *Pennsylvania Gazette*, 3 February 1728/29.

106. Armagh Session Accounts, 1729, 64.

107. Minutes of the Sub-Synod of Derry, 1730, 135.

108. Minutes of the Presbytery of Strabane, June 1729, 246.

109. Boulter to Sir Robert Walpole, 31 March 1729, Faulkiner, *Letters*, 1:237.

110. Ballycarry Session Minutes, 30 October 1718.

111. James Reid left his congregation of Killinchy for these reasons. See Minutes of the Presbytery of Killyleagh, 6 March 1728/29, D 1759/1D/10, 70, PRONI.

112. Minutes of the Presbytery of Strabane, April 1720, July 1720, August 1722, June 1729, 112, 122, 174, 244.

113. Gillespie, *Settlement and Survival*, xxxii.

114. On the character of these links, see Doyle, *Ireland, Irishmen, and Revolutionary America*, 22, 39–40.

115. Truxes, *Irish-American Trade*, 175–176; James, *Ireland in the Empire*, 62–64.

116. Truxes, *Irish-American Trade*, 276–77, 182, 198.

117. Kirkham, "Ulster Emigration to North America," 76–77; A. C. Myers, *Immigration of the Irish Quakers into Pennsylvania* (Swarthmore, PA, 1902); Landsman, *Scotland and Its First American Colony*, 113–14; Dickson, *Ulster Emigration*, 19–20.

118. Kirkham, "Ulster Emigration to North America," 78–79.

119. Minutes of the Laggan Meeting, July 1691, March 1693, 6, 47.

120. Minutes of the Presbytery of Down, January 1713/14, February 1713/14, May 1714, 335–36, 340, 347–48, PHSB.

121. Bolton, *Scotch-Irish Pioneers*, 68. For the Ulster Scot experience in Massachusetts, see Leyburn, *The Scotch-Irish*, 236–42.

122. Ford, *The Scotch-Irish in America*, 222.

123. Cotton Mather, "Diary of Cotton Mather, 1709–1724," *Massachusetts Historical Society Collections*, 7th ser., 8 (Boston, 1912): 549.

124. Miller, *Emigrants and Exiles*, 158.

125. Minutes of the Sub-Synod of Derry, 5 May 1718, 59.

126. Reid, *A History of the Presbyterian Church in Ireland*, 3:225.

127. Dickson, *Ulster Emigration*, 21–23.

128. Cotton Mather to Robert Wodrow, 6 August 1718, *Correspondence of Wodrow*, ed. McCrie, 2:424.

129. Ford, *The Scotch-Irish in America*, 224; Bolton, *Scotch-Irish Pioneers*, 139.

130. Mather to John Stirling, 5 January 1722/23, in K. Silverman, ed., *Selected Letters of Cotton Mather* (Baton Rouge, LA, 1971), 357.

131. "Diary of Cotton Mather," 718.

132. Dickinson to Ezek. Geremsoll, 2 September 1717, Jonathan Dickinson Copy Book of Letters, 135, Historical Society of Pennsylvania, Philadelphia (hereafter HSP).

133. Dickinson to Edward Hardy, 12 November 1719, Jonathan Dickinson Copy Book of Letters.

134. The number for this period may even have been as high as 7,000. See Kirkham, "Ulster Emigration to North America," 96.

135. Certificate of James Ralston, 30 May 1736, T 1177/1, PRONI.

136. *Pennsylvania Gazette*, 25 December 1728.

137. On this theme, see Truxes, *Irish-American Trade*, 133–37; Wokeck, *Trade in Strangers*, 192–93. In *Trade in Strangers*, Wokeck argues that in this period a "systematic business" of transporting migrants to America arose with the movement of Germans. The Irish migration of 1729, though larger than its German equivalent in the period, did not yet have all the hallmarks of a "trade in strangers," a business venture aimed solely at the transportation of emigrants. The Irish trade would not take on the characteristics of the German business until the time of the American Revolution and would fully come into its own in the nineteenth century. Graeme Kirkham, on the other hand, argues that even before 1717 Irish ships specialized at times in transporting migrants. See "Ulster Emigration to North America."

138. There has been some debate over the numbers of people leaving Ulster at this time. While Dickson argues that 1,000 departed in 1727, 3,000 in 1728, and over 4,000 a year later (*Ulster Emigration*, 32–34), Wokeck believes almost 6,000—the vast majority from the North—left in 1729. See *Trade in Strangers*, 176–77. Graeme Kirkham believes Dickson also underestimates the figures. The volume of migration in the period, he writes, was "substantially greater than was apparent to Dickson" (introduction to Dickson, *Ulster Emigration*, xvi).

139. Truxes, *Irish-American Trade*, 127–29.

140. "Obstructions to Irish Immigration to Pennsylvania, 1736," *Pennsylvania Magazine of History and Biography* 21 (1897): 485.

141. Reports of the Justices of the North East and North West Circuits, 10 May 1729 and 11 June 1729, T 659/1445, PRONI, cited in Truxes, *Irish-American Trade*, 131.

142. Truxes, *Irish-American Trade*, 134.

143. Boulter to Duke of Newcastle, 23 November 1728, *Letters*, Faulkiner, 1:209.

144. Green, "The 'Strange Humours,'" 116–19.

145. Truxes, *Irish-American Trade*, 131.

146. Steward to Ward, 25 March 1729, D 2092/1/3/141, PRONI.

147. Green, "The 'Strange Humours,' " 118.

148. Lancaster County Quarter Sessions, 4 February 1734/35, Lancaster County Historical Society, Lancaster, Pennsylvania (hereafter LCHS).

149. "Education Facsimile 123," *Eighteenth Century Ulster Emigration to North America* (Belfast, 1989). The low percentage of Ulster Scot indentured servants in this period proves an exception to the rule according to Aaron Fogleman. See "From Slaves, Convicts, and Servants to Free Passengers: The Transformation of Immigration in the Era of the American Revolution," *Journal of American History* 85 (June 1998): 43–76.

150. On this theme, see Wokeck, *Trade in Strangers*, 199, 208.

151. *Pennsylvania Gazette*, 1 March 1728/29.

152. *American Weekly Mercury*, 7 August 1729.

153. *Pennsylvania Gazette*, 17 November 1729.

154. Boulter to Duke of Newcastle, 23 November 1728, Faulkiner, *Letters*, 1:210.

155. "Overall," Wokeck argues, "the total number of immigrants from southern Ireland was small and the proportion of servants among them large" in this period (*Trade in Strangers*, 176–77). For the movement of Catholics to the New World, see Audrey Lockhart, *Some Aspects of Emigration from Ireland to the North American Colonies between 1660 and 1775* (New York, 1975).

156. *American Weekly Mercury*, 8 September 1720, 17 August 1721.

157. Charles Browning, ed., "Extracts from the Journal of Charles Clinton, Kept During the Voyage from Ireland to Pennsylvania, 1729," *Pennsylvania Magazine of History and Biography* 26 (1902): 112–14.

158. *Pennsylvania Gazette*, 10 February 1729/30.

159. "Education Facsimile 128," *Eighteenth Century Ulster Emigration to North America*.

160. *Pennsylvania Gazette*, 17 November 1729.

161. Ibid., 30 October 1729.

162. Ibid., 27 May 1736.

163. Lancaster County Quarter Sessions, 3 February 1729/30, LCHS.

164. *Dublin Weekly Journal*, 7 June 1729, cited in Dickson, *Ulster Emigration*, 220.

165. Ezek. Steward to Michael Ward, 25 March 1729, D 2092/1/3, PRONI.

166. Green, "The 'Strange Humours,' " 116–19. For the influence of letters on migration, see Wokeck, *Trade in Strangers*, 194; Doyle, *Ireland, Irishmen, and Revolutionary America*, 52; Miller, *Emigrants and Exiles*, 160; and Kirkham, introduction to Dickson, *Ulster Emigration*, xv.

167. *Pennsylvania Gazette*, 27 October 1737.

168. Green, "The 'Strange Humours,' " 116–19.

169. Autobiography of John Craig, Presbyterian Historical Society, Philadelphia.

170. *Pennsylvania Gazette,* 24 February 1729/30.

CHAPTER FOUR

1. *Pennsylvania Gazette,* 17 November 1729.

2. Browning, "Extracts from the Journal of Charles Clinton," 114.

3. Gottlieb Mittelberger, *Journey to Pennsylvania,* ed. Oscar Handlin and John Clive (Cambridge, MA, 1960), 35–36.

4. *The Itinerarium of Dr. Alexander Hamilton,* in Wendy Martin, ed., *Colonial American Travel Narratives* (New York, 1994), 185, 322.

5. James Lemon has argued that settlers in southeastern Pennsylvania exhibited a middle-class mentality that accepted both the market and its effects. See *The Best Poor Man's Country: A Geographical Study of Early Southeastern Pennsylvania* (Baltimore, 1972); and Lemon, "Comment on James A. Henretta's 'Families and Farms: Mentalite in Pre-Industrial America'," *William and Mary Quarterly,* 3rd. ser. 37 (1980): 695–96. James Henretta, on the other hand, suggested these settlers reveled in a contented pre-commercial existence, setting up farms not for profit but for self-sufficiency. See his "Families and Farms: Mentalite in Pre-Industrial America," *William and Mary Quarterly,* 3rd. ser. 35 (1978): 3–32. Gary Nash offers an extended discussion on what he sees as a case of misunderstanding in "Social Development," in *Colonial British America,* ed. Greene and Pole, 233–61.

6. In examining the Ulster Scot experience in America, some have turned to the role of the American environment to argue that a land abundant and open for settlement melted down distinctive characteristics any group carried to the New World. See Lemon, *The Best Poor Man's Country.* Similarly, by another historian's estimation, William Penn's vision of a tolerant and pluralistic province united the many groups that came over. The environment allowed them to accept, and in some cases to celebrate, difference. Refer to Schwartz, *"A Mixed Multitude."* Alan Tully also argues that a "paradigm of peace," inspired by Quaker ideals and flexibility, made for stable social relations after 1726 in *William Penn's Legacy.* A second group of historians has championed the enduring qualities of Old World customs. The violence of British "borderlands," D. H. Fischer has argued, bred a violent culture in America in *Albion's Seed,* 605–782.

7. For make-up and politics of early Pennsylvania, see Joseph Illick, *Colonial Pennsylvania: A History* (New York, 1976); and Gary Nash, *Quakers and Politics: Pennsylvania, 1681–1726* (Princeton, 1968).

8. *Itinerarium of Dr. Alexander Hamilton,* 191.

9. Jonathan Dickinson to John Askew, 24 October 1717, Jonathan Dickinson Copy Book of Letters, 163–64.

10. Isaac Norris to William Wragg, 13 September 1717, Norris Papers, Isaac Norris Sr. Letterbook, 1716–30, 99, HSP.

11. Logan to Springett Penn, 8 December 1727, Logan Copy Book V, 168, HSP; Logan to John Penn, 6 December 1727, Logan Copy Book, V, 167; Logan to John Penn, 21 July 1729, James Logan Papers, III, 302, HSP. See Schwartz's *"A Mixed Multitude"* for a discussion of the various ethnic groups and elite responses to them (81–119).

12. *Pennsylvania Gazette,* 17 November 1729.

13. Pennsylvania Province, *A Journal of the Votes and Proceedings of the House of Representatives* (Philadelphia, 1728), 8, 12; Logan to —, 22 October 1727, Logan Papers, IV, 145; P. Gordon to Springett and John Penn, 16 May 1729, Penn MSS, Official Correspondence, II, 75, HSP; Thomas Penn to Richard Peters, 17 July 1752, Thomas Penn Papers, Letterbook III, 150, HSP; John Penn to Thomas Penn, 28 January 1732/33, Penn Papers, Letterbook I, 70, HSP.

14. P. Gordon to the Penns, 16 May 1729, Penn MSS, Official Correspondence, II, 75.

15. *Pennsylvania Gazette,* 10 February 1729/30, 3 July 1735, 12 December 1732; *American Weekly Mercury,* 21 August 1729.

16. James Logan to J. Chalmers, 27 September 1727, Logan Copy Book V, 148; Roscommon (pseud.), *To the Author of the Intelligencers* (New York, 1733), 2; *Pennsylvania Gazette,* 10 November 1729. D. W. Hayton covers this Janus-faced English image of the Irish in "From Barbarian to Burlesque: English Images of the Irish c. 1660–1750," *Irish Economic and Social History* 15 (1988): 5–31.

17. *Pennsylvania Gazette,* 16 July 1730.

18. Isaac Norris to Joseph Pike, 28 October 1728, Norris Papers, Isaac Norris Sr. Letterbook, 516.

19. Logan to the Penns, 14 November 1731, Penn MSS, Official Correspondence, II, 213.

20. Logan to James Steel, 18 November 1729, Penn MSS, Official Correspondence, II, 101.

21. Logan to John Wright and Samuel Blunston, 30 August 1727, Logan Papers, III, 111; Isaac Norris to William Wragg, 13 September 1717, Norris Papers, Isaac Norris Sr. Letterbook, 99; Logan to James Anderson and Andrew Galbraith, 2 March 1730/31, Logan Papers, III, 170. Aaron Fogleman has uncovered a similar pattern for German migrants at this time in *Hopeful Journeys),* 76–82.

22. Jonathan Dickinson to Edward Healy, 12 November 1719, Jonathan Dickinson Copy Book of Letters, 289.

23. A. G. Zimmerman, "The Indian Trade of Colonial Pennsylvania," Ph.D. diss., University of Delaware, 1966, 83–86.

24. Francis Jennings, "The Indian Trade of the Susquehanna Valley," *Proceedings of the American Philosophical Society* 110 (1966): 420–22; Jennings, "Mi-

quon's Passing: Indian-European Relations in Colonial Pennsylvania, 1674 to 1755," Ph.D. diss., University of Pennsylvania, 1965, 162.

25. Logan to James Steel, 18 November 1729, Logan Papers, X, 46.

26. Logan to James Steel, 18 November 1729, Penn MSS, Official Correspondence, I, 101; Logan to John Penn, 11 September 1728, Penn MSS, Official Correspondence, II, 21. On these issues, see Tully, *William Penn's Legacy*, 3–11.

27. East Donegal Township Warrant Map, LCHS.

28. See Taylor Papers, XIII, 2020, 2710, 2715, 2717, HSP.

29. For an assessment of Logan's activities in the region, a man intent on "exploitation and domination," see Jennings, "Miquon's Passing," 106–57.

30. Donna Munger, *Pennsylvania Land Records: A History and Guide for Research* (Wilmington, DE, 1991), 68, 8.

31. Samuel Blunston to Thomas Penn, 13 August 1734, Lancaster County MSS, 7, HSP.

32. In 1726, New London township on the lower end contained 47 taxable inhabitants. By 1732, that number had increased to 75. Again, these numbers only take into account those few who sought to have some legitimate basis for their land holdings. See Tax Lists, 1726, 1732, Chester County Archives, West Chester, Pennsylvania (hereafter CCA). West Nottingham, closer to the Maryland border, experienced similar growth (Tax Lists, 1729, 1732, CCA).

33. Logan to the Penns, 25 November 1727, Logan Copy Book, V, 154. As of yet, we have no detailed treatment of Ulster migrant settlement patterns. James Lemon offers a broad picture of the areas migrants settled, as well as a close study of demographic change in the region, in *The Best Poor Man's Country*.

34. Logan to the Penns, 25 November 1727, Logan Copy Book, V, 153–54.

35. Jonathan Dickinson to Joshua Crosby, 17 November 1719, Jonathan Dickinson Copy Book of Letters, 294–95; Steel to John Thomson, 13 February 1731/32, Logan Papers, Letter Book of James Steel, 1730–41, 18, HSP.

36. James Anderson to Thomas Penn, 26 June 1733, Penn Physick Papers, VI, 29, HSP.

37. Samuel Blunston to Thomas Penn, 3 March 1737, Lancaster County MSS, 33; *American Weekly Mercury*, 23 March 1721; *Pennsylvania Archives, Selected and Arranged from Original Documents in the Office of the Secretary of the Commonwealth* (Philadelphia, 1852), vol. 1 (hereafter *Pennsylvania Archives*), 505; Lancaster County Quarter Sessions, 5 August 1729, 15 May 1730.

38. "The Records of the Presbytery of New Castle Upon Delaware," *Journal of the Department of History of the Presbyterian Church in the USA* 15 (1932), 91, 94, 95; *Pennsylvania Gazette*, 28 June 1733, 30 June 1737, 15 September 1737, 24 July 1740.

39. Pennsylvania Province, *The Particulars of an Indian Treaty at Conestogoe* (Philadelphia, 1721), 1.

40. Taylor Papers, XII, 2426.

41. Franklin Ellis and Samuel Evans, *History of Lancaster County, Pennsylvania* (Philadelphia, 1883), 748.

42. "Bishop J.C.F. Camerhoff's Narrative of a Journey to Shamokin, Penna.," *Pennsylvania Magazine of History and Biography* 29 (1905): 163, 167.

43. Tax Assessments, 1722, 1724, CCA.

44. Mittelberger, *Journey to Pennsylvania*, 91.

45. Francis Jennings, " 'Pennsylvania Indians' and the Iroquois," in *Beyond the Covenant Chain: The Iroquois and Their Neighbors in Indian North America*, ed. Daniel Richter and James Merrell (Syracuse, NY, 1987), 76–83.

46. "Camerhoff's Narrative," 165, 167; Jennings, "Miquon's Passing," 157.

47. For this sordid description of fur traders in the region, see James Merrell, *Into the American Woods: Negotiators on the Pennsylvania Frontier* (New York, 1999), 79–83.

48. Pennsylvania Province, *The Particulars of an Indian Treaty at Conestogoe*, 1.

49. *The Itinerarium of Dr. Alexander Hamilton*, 182.

50. Logan to Thomas Penn, 19 December 1730, Penn MSS, Official Correspondence, II, 145.

51. Deposition of Alexander Mitchell, W. H. Egle, ed., *Notes and Queries Historical and Genealogical chiefly relating to Interior Pennsylvania*, 1st and 2nd ser. Vol. II (Baltimore, 1970), 167–69.

52. Mills and Bridges of Lancaster County, Pennsylvania, compiled by R. H. Barton, vol. I, 140, LCHS.

53. See, for example, Susann McCain Inventory, CCA, 387, 1730.

54. Inventories of Middleton, 1732, box 92, folder 2, LCHS; John Robinson, 1721/22, Chester County Probate Records, no. 157; Alexander McConnell, 1729, 348; Joseph Cochran, 1727, 285, CCA.

55. *Itinerarium of Dr. Alexander Hamilton*, 185.

56. Probate Record, 348, CCA.

57. Inventory, box 92, folder 2, LCHS.

58. Inventory, box 146, folder 6, LCHS.

59. Inventory, box 1, folder 1, LCHS.

60. The humble petition of John Galbreath, of Donegal, August 1726, in Ellis and Evans, *History of Lancaster County*, 778.

61. Petition to Patrick Gordon for Erecting a New County, 1728, in H.M.J. Klein, *Lancaster County, Pennsylvania*, vol. 1 (New York, 1924), 17–19.

62. Inventory, box 92, folder 1, LCHS.

63. James Anderson to Thomas Penn, 26 June 1733, Penn Physick Papers, VI, 29.

64. Writs, May 1722, November 1727, CCA. On others who were served with orders to appear before the court of common pleas, see the cases of Collum McCurry, August 1726, and John McDaniel, February 1724/25.

65. Writs and Narrative of the Court of Common Pleas, August 1726, CCA.

66. Quarter Session Indictments, August 1725, CCA.

67. Petition to Patrick Gordon, 1728, in Klein, *Lancaster County, Pennsylvania*, 17–19; Logan to Adam Boyd, 29 February 1731/32, Maria Dickinson Logan Family Papers, Dickinson/Logan Letterbook, Logan Section, 41, HSP.

68. For numerous examples of the drunken character of life in early settlements, see the session minutes from New Londonderry, Presbyterian Historical Society, Philadelphia (hereafter PHSP); and Middle Spring, Cumberland County Historical Society.

69. New Londonderry Session Minutes, 3 January 1743/44.

70. *Pennsylvania Archives*, 1:425.

71. Minutes of the Presbytery of Donegal, vol. 1 (A), 16 October 1734, 62–63, PHSP.

72. *Minutes of the Provincial Council of Pennsylvania* (Philadelphia, 1852), (hereafter *Colonial Records*), 3:266–67.

73. Logan to Adam Boyd, 29 February 1731/32, Maria Dickinson Logan Family Papers, Dickinson/Logan Letterbook, Logan Section, 41.

74. Norris to Joseph Pike, 28 October 1728, Norris Papers, 515–16; Logan to James Steel, 18 November 1729, Penn MSS, Official Correspondence, II, 101.

75. James Merrell presents a colorful and disturbing portrait of Burt in a turd-throwing incident in *Into the American Woods*, 95.

76. Writs for Court of Common Pleas, Jonah Davenport File, November 1724, CCA. See also Criminal Indictments, February 1724/25 and Quarter Session Docket Book, February 1724/25, CCA.

77. Logan to Isaac Taylor, 23 February 1724/25, Taylor Papers, XV.

78. Writs, Jonah Davenport file, November 1724, CCA.

79. Traders' Petitions, 15 February 1724/25, CCA. I am grateful to Jim Merrell for bringing this source to my attention. Ellis and Evans, *History of Lancaster County*, 16.

80. Probate Records, 285, CCA.

81. Lancaster County Wills, 1732, vol. 1, p. 6, LCHS.

82. Will of John Catherwood, 1742, A-1-71, LCHS.

83. Logan to ———, 13 June 1729, Logan Papers, III, 304; *Colonial Records*, 3:599.

84. Merrell, *Into the American Woods*, 115–18, 158–67.

85. *Colonial Records*, 3:514.

86. Logan to Edward Shippen, 3 September 1730, Logan Papers, I, 98.

87. Logan to John Wright and Samuel Blunston, 2 September 1730, Logan Papers, I, 96.

88. "Camerhoff's Narrative," 169.

89. Lancaster County Quarter Sessions, 4 May 1731, LCHS.

90. *American Weekly Mercury*, 21 April 1720.

91. John McAlister to Richard Peters, 28 March 1754, Lamberton Scotch-Irish Collection, I, 15, HSP.

92. David Brainerd Diary, 1745, 32, American Philosophical Society, Philadelphia.

93. Westerkamp, *Triumph of the Laity*, 143.

94. For the life of the early Presbyterian church, refer to Leonard Trinterud, *The Forming of an American Tradition: A Re-examination of Colonial Presbyterianism* (Philadelphia, 1949); and Westerkamp, *Triumph of the Laity*.

95. Richard MacMaster, *Donegal Presbyterians: A Scots-Irish Congregation in Pennsylvania* (Morgantown, PA, 1995), 11–13.

96. "Records of the Presbytery of New Castle Upon Delaware," vol. 14 (1931), 291–93, 304.

97. Autobiography of John Craig, PHSP; Guy Klett, ed., *Minutes of the Presbyterian Church in America, 1706–1788* (Philadelphia, 1976), 35, 89; James Anderson to Thomas Penn, 26 June 1733, Penn Physick Papers, VI, 29.

98. James Anderson to Principal Stirling, 8 August 1717, 29 October 1725, Anderson-Stirling Correspondence, PHSP.

99. Klett, *Minutes of the Presbyterian Church*, 89.

100. Mills and Bridges of Lancaster County, 136.

101. See "Records of the Presbytery of New Castle Upon Delaware," vol. 15, 5 June 1728, 174.

102. Minutes of the Presbytery of Donegal, 5 September 1733, vol. 1(A), 16.

103. Ibid., vol. 1(A), 12, 16, 59.

104. Ibid., vol. 1(A), 15 November 1732, 6.

105. Ibid., Vol. 1(A) 2 April 1734, 16 October 1734, 28, 59.

106. Ibid., Vol. 1(B), 1738, 221.

107. See "Records of the Presbytery of New Castle Upon Delaware" 5 June 1728, Vol. 15, 174.

108. New Londonderry Session Minutes, 5 August 1741.

109. "Records of the Presbytery of New Castle Upon Delaware," vol. 15, 186; Minutes of the Presbytery of Donegal, vol. 1(A), 55–57, 89; Minutes of the Presbytery of Philadelphia, 1733–46, 25, PHSP.

110. "Records of the Presbytery of New Castle Upon Delaware," Vol. 15, 116.

111. Trinterud, *The Forming of an American Tradition*, 45–50; Also see "Records of the Presbytery of New Castle Upon Delaware," Vol. 15, 116, 198, 206–207.

112. Jonathan Dickinson, *The Vanity of Human Institutions in the Worship of God* (New York, 1736), 11; Dickinson, *Some Short Observations made on the Presbyterian Doctrine* (Philadelphia, 1721), 17; Dickinson, *A Sermon Preached at the Opening of the Synod at Philadelphia, 19 September 1722* (Boston, 1723), 2; Dickinson, *Remarks on a Discourse intitled an Overture . . . to the Synod* (New York, 1729), 8.

113. Dickinson, *Remarks on a Discourse intitled an Overture*, 7, 9; Andrews to Benjamin Colman, 7 April 1729, Jedediah Andrews Letters, PHSP.

114. Klett, *Minutes of the Presbyterian Church*, 1720 and 1721, 46–51.

115. J. Thomson, *An Overture Presented to the Reverend Synod* (Philadelphia, 1729), 6, 7.

116. Klett, *Minutes of the Presbyterian Church*, 155; Minutes of the Presbytery of Donegal, Vol. 1(B), 17 November 1737, 210–11.

117. Minutes of the Presbytery of Donegal, 18 September 1735, vol. 1(A), 110; 2 September 1736, 5 April 1739, vol. 1(B), 175, 246; also see vol. 1(A), 32, 97, 112, 128; vol. 1(B), 156, 158, 191, 207, 260, 276.

118. Klett, *Minutes of the Presbyterian Church*, 132; J. Thomson, *The Government of the Church of Christ* (Philadelphia, 1741), 113–14.

119. Benjamin Franklin, *Autobiography and Other Writings*, ed. K. Silverman, (New York, 1986), 108–9. On the Franklin/Hemphill relationship, see M. Christensen, "Franklin on the Hemphill Trial: Deism versus Presbyterian Orthodoxy," *William and Mary Quarterly*, 3rd ser. 10 (1953): 422–40.

120. J. Andrews to ———, 14 June 1735, Jedediah Andrews Letters.

121. *A Vindication of the Rev. Commission . . . against the Rev. Mr. Hemphill* (Philadelphia, 1735), 1; George Gillespie, *A Treatise against the Deists or Free-Thinkers* (Philadelphia, 1735), 1, 58.

122. Benjamin Franklin, *A Defence of the Rev. Mr. Hemphill's Observations* (Philadelphia, 1735), 11; Franklin, *A Letter to a Friend in the Country, Containing the Substance of a Sermon . . . [by] the Rev. Mr. Hemphill* (Philadelphia, 1735), 6.

123. Benjamin Franklin, *Some Observations on the Proceedings against the Rev. Mr. Hemphill* (Philadelphia, 1735), 5; Franklin, *A Letter to a Friend in the Country*, 6, 7; Franklin, *A Defence of the Rev. Mr. Hemphill's Observations*, 4.

124. Elizabeth Nybakken argues that a number of nonsubscribers found subscription palatable in Pennsylvania because, as she contends, the 1729 Adopting Act amounted to an Irish middle-ground solution to subscription, one consistent with a flexible Irish Presbyterian tradition that would define American Presbyterianism for years to come ("New Light on the Old Side," 821). The act, however, was hammered out between Dickinson and the Irish as a compromise between two extreme positions. On this, see Bryan Lebeau, *Jonathan Dickinson and the Formative Years of American Presbyterianism* (Lexington, KY, 1997), chap. 2. Of the ministers she cites to underscore the continuity of Irish doctrinal attitudes, none had arrived by 1729. The two Irish nonsubscribers who arrived in time to cast their votes for the 1736 measure were Robert Jamison and James Martin. Later arrivals, who also lent their support to unqualified subscription in subsequent votes, were Francis Alison, Samuel Cavin, John Craig, Francis McHenry, and Samuel Thomson. Only one Ulster nonsubscriber cannot be accounted for. In 1736, John McDowell presented himself before the Donegal Presbytery, but was not heard from again. For positions of these ministers in Ireland and America, refer to Presbyterian

Church of Ireland, *Records of the General Synod of Ulster,* 2:160, 189, 203, 213; and Klett, *Minutes of the Presbyterian Church,* 121, 137, 146, 168, 175.

125. J. Andrews to ———, 14 June 1735, Jedediah Andrews Letters.

126. Klett, *Minutes of the Presbyterian Church,* 121, 131, 137, 146, 168, 175; S. G. McConnell, *Fasti of the American Presbyterian Church* (Belfast, 1936), 3, 6, 7, 16, 17, and unpaginated section titled "Corrigenda and Addenda."

127. Klett, *Minutes of the Presbyterian Church,* 141, 189; "Records of the Presbytery of New Castle Upon Delaware," vol. 15, 2 September 1730, 206–207; *A Protestation Presented to the Synod of Philadelphia, June 1, 1741* (Philadelphia, 1741), 7; Thomson, *An Overture Presented,* 12. Marilyn Westerkamp argues that the laity determined the outcome in the Irish debate over subscription, pushing nonsubscribers out of the church. "Tensions between the clergy and laity," she writes, "would never cease." For the American debate, however, she asks, "Why did the laity not become involved in the colonial controversy?" Westerkamp contends that the "dogmatic Scots-Irish" ministers foisted subscription upon the American church, thus positing that little change in their heavy handed ways and doctrinaire views occurred after crossing the ocean. See Westerkamp, *Triumph of the Laity,* 137, 156, 163.

128. Anderson to Stirling, 3 December 1717, 25 October 1725, Anderson-Stirling Correspondence. Some of the best studies that recognize the influence of old traditions in a new context, and a people's ability to derive meaning from both, do not deal with migrants, but instead explore the experience of Indians and slaves. For prominent examples, see Richard White, *The Middle Ground: Indians, Empires, and Republics in the Great Lakes Region* (Cambridge, 1991), 52, 93; and Ira Berlin, "From Creole to African: Atlantic Creoles and the Origins of African-American Society in Mainland North America," *William and Mary Quarterly,* 3rd Ser., 53 (1996): 253.

129. Thomson, *An Overture Presented,* 7, 8.

130. Ibid., 23, 28.

131. Ibid., 7, 8, 21.

CHAPTER FIVE

1. Gilbert Tennent, *The Danger of Forgetting God* (New York, 1735), 8, 28. On Tennent's life and career and a solid narrative of the experience of Presbyterians during the Great Awakening, see Trinterud, *The Forming of an American Tradition,* chap. 3; and M. Coalter, *Gilbert Tennent, Son of Thunder: A Case Study of Continental Pietism's Impact on the First Great Awakening in the Middle Colonies* (Westport, CT, 1986).

2. Trinterud, *The Forming of an American Tradition,* 57; Gilbert Tennent, *The Necessity of Religious Violence* (New York, 1735), 16, 42, 43. Trinterud (*The Forming of an American Tradition*) has argued that revival in the colonial Presbyterian church set the laity against the clergy. Deference to authority withered

as ministers tried to foist a high clerical model of church government on the people. Marilyn Westerkamp (*Triumph of the Laity*) similarly contends that the Awakening represented a "triumph of the laity," which had for generations hungered for a vital religion. The plea for vital religion set them against the ministry who understood that a church inspired by the concerns of the laity did not bode well for their privileged position in Scots-Irish society.

The "Great Awakening" throughout the colonies has received much attention from historians. For a good overview of the spread of vital religion throughout the American colonies, see Patricia Bonomi, *Under the Cope of Heaven: Religion, Society and Politics in Colonial America* (New York, 1986). Jon Butler has led a revisionist reaction against the notion that any organized "awakening" ever occurred in "Enthusiasm Described and Decried: The Great Awakening as Interpretive Fiction," *Journal of American History* 69 (1982–83): 305–25; and *Awash in a Sea of Faith: Christianizing the American People* (Cambridge, MA, 1990).

3. Samuel Blair, *The Great Glory of God . . . in the Gospel of Christ* (Boston, 1739), 101.

4. *A Protestation Presented to the Synod of Philadelphia*, 12; Klett, *Minutes of the Presbyterian Church*, 213, 189.

5. By one account, Ulster's migrants—the laity, that is—united around a vital piety similar to that which had flourished in Ireland a century earlier. In these cases, the Irish contested and overpowered other traditions that clashed with theirs. On these themes, see Westerkamp, *Triumph of the Laity.* Another interpretation argues that Ulster's migrants embraced Scottishness in the New World. The revival spirit and the Confession arose from Scottish, not Irish, ecclesiastical traditions. Although most on the frontier who supported Scottish church practices migrated from Ireland, their attraction to Scottish revival traditions united them. See Landsman, *Scotland and Its First American Colony*, 4, 165, 174–76, 184–85, 250; and Schmidt, *Holy Fairs.*

6. *Pennsylvania Gazette*, 9 April 1741, 8 January 1740/41, 19 February 1740/41.

7. *Colonial Record*, 3:343; *Pennsylvania Archives*, 1:252; Lemon, *The Best Poor Man's Country*, 131–32; Jerome Wood, *Conestoga Crossroads: Lancaster, Pennsylvania, 1730–1790* (Harrisburg, PA, 1979), 96–97. For the economic changes in Pennsylvania during this period, see John McCusker and Russell Menard, *The Economy of British America, 1607–1789* (Chapel Hill, 1985), 189–208; and Arthur Jensen, *The Maritime Commerce of Colonial Philadelphia* (Madison, 1963).

8. Lancaster County Quarter Sessions, 7 November 1732, 7 August 1733, 5 February 1733/34, 4 May 1735; Wood, *Conestoga Crossroads*, 15–16.

9. Lancaster County Quarter Sessions, 7 May 1734, 1 November 1737, 7 November 1738.

10. Records of Donegal Presbyterian Church, vol. 3, Rev. John Roan's Subscription Account Book, LCHS.

11. Lancaster County Quarter Sessions, 5 August 1729. The eight jurors were James Mitchell, George Stewart, James Patterson, Andrew Galbraith, Patrick Campbell, John Galbraith, Matthew Atkinson, and Epraim Moore.

12. Common Pleas Appearance Dockets, 3 August 1731, 1 February 1731/32, LCHS.

13. Klett, *Minutes of the Presbyterian Church*, 1729, 105.

14. Minutes of the Presbytery of Donegal, vol. 1 (A), 28 August 1734, 55–57.

15. Ibid., vol. 1(A), 5 September 1733, 16.

16. Common Pleas Appearance Dockets, 5 February 1733/34, 6 August 1734.

17. See especially the session of 4 February 1734/35, LCHS.

18. Minutes of the Presbytery of Donegal, vol. 1(A), 5 June 1734.

19. Middle Spring United Presbyterian Church Session Minutes, 22 June 1744, MIC 5, Cumberland County Historical Society, Carlisle, Pennsylvania.

20. New Londonderry Session Minutes (Fagg's Manor), 2 March 1741/42, PHSP.

21. Ibid., 5 January 1741/42.

22. Ibid., 5 August 1741.

23. Middle Spring Session, 2 May 1743, 7 August 1745.

24. Ibid., 16 January 1744/45.

25. The Orr affair took up much attention both in the Presbytery of Donegal and the synod during these years. For the dispute, see the Minutes of the Presbytery of Donegal, vol. 1(A), 20–27, 32, 93, 100–103, 121, Vol. 1(B) 154; Klett, *Minutes of the Presbyterian Church*, 126–27, 136. Marilyn Westerkamp also covers the controversy surrounding Orr in *Triumph of the Laity*. She finds, however, in support of her argument that the principal dynamic evident in Scotch-Irish congregations at this time was a clerical/laity power struggle, that the Orr controversy can only be understood in reference to the revivals that were just beginning in Scotch-Irish communities.

26. Minutes of the Presbytery of Donegal, vol. 1(A) 7 June 1734, 47–48, 50.

27. Donegal and Paxton Tax Valuations, 1750, LCHS.

28. Wills, A-1–188; A-1–48, LCHS; Inventory, box 123, folder 3; Inventory, box 1, folder 1, LCHS.

29. Inventory, box 1, folder 1, LCHS.

30. Probate Record 387, CCA.

31. Inventory, box 123, folder 3, LCHS.

32. Inventory, box 146, folder 2, LCHS.

33. Inventory, box 146, folder 6, LCHS.

34. Inventory, box 93, folder 33, LCHS.

35. John Sterrat and Elizabeth Allison Inventories, box 124, folder 21, and box 1, folder 1, LCHS. On the commercial revolution in the colonies, see T. H. Breen, " 'Baubles of Britain': The American Consumer Revolutions of the Eighteenth Century," *Past and Present* 119 (1988): 73–104; and "An Empire of Goods: The Anglicization of Colonial America, 1690–1776," *Journal of British Studies* 25 (1986): 467–99.

36. Thomas Penn to James Logan, 23 January 1732/33, cited in Ellis and Evans, *History of Lancaster County*, 770. Also see Tully, *William Penn's Legacy*, 11–15.

37. Patrick Gordon to Governor Calvert, 13 September 1731, *Pennsylvania Archives*, 1:291; Logan to John, Thomas, and Richard Penn, 14 November 1731, Penn MSS, Official Correspondence, II, 213. Minutes of the Presbytery of Donegal, vol. 1, p. A.

38. *Pennsylvania Archives*, 1:271, 364.

39. *Colonial Records*, 4:570–71; *Pennsylvania Archives*, 1:239. Peter Mancall has found a similar dynamic at work in the Upper Susquehanna Valley later in the period. He emphasizes, however, the ecological impact of European farming practices and the ways in which they undermined the trade for furs. "Ultimately," he writes, "colonists promoting new settlements replaced traders in the valley economy . . . The successful development of trade hastened its own collapse by altering the regional environment, destabilizing the Indian populations along the river, and providing colonists with increased knowledge of and interest in settling the area." See *Valley of Opportunity: Economic Culture along the Upper Susquehanna* (Ithaca, NY, 1991), 69–70.

40. Jennings, "Miquon's Passing, 276–77.

41. *Pennsylvania Archives*, 1:291.

42. Ibid., 1:295, 349, 451, 465.

43. *Colonial Records*, 4:69, 63; *Pennsylvania Archives*, 1:334, 509, 505, 514; *Pennsylvania Gazette*, 27 January 1736/37.

44. *Pennsylvania Archives*, 1:336, 505. Tully, *William Penn's Legacy*, 8–11.

45. Ellis and Evans, *History of Lancaster County*, 750.

46. James Steel to John Taylor, 14 June 1733, Taylor Papers, XV.

47. Mills and Bridges of Lancaster County, 131.

48. Requests for Surveys by Jacob Hoover, 17 May 1734; Christian Bumberrier, 1 May 1734; John Kinrigh, 1 May 1734, Taylor Papers, IV.

49. Requests for Surveys, Michael Beksley, 15 April 1735, John Hare, 21 May 1735; Woolrich Soak, 25 November 1735, Taylor Papers, V.

50. J. S. Futhey and Gilbert Cope, *History of Chester County, Pennsylvania* (Philadelphia, 1881), 174. For surveys on the lower end, particularly in New London Township, see Taylor Papers, 9 February 1733.

51. James Steel to John Taylor, 20 February 1737/38, Taylor Papers, XV.

52. Donegal Tax List, 1750; Rapho Tax List, 1751, LCHS.

53. *Pennsylvania Archives*, 1:625, 635.

54. Logan to John Wright, 30 August 1727, Logan Papers, III, Letter Book of James Logan, 111, HSP; Logan to James Anderson and Andrew Galbraith, 2 March 1730/31, Logan Papers, III, Letter Book of James Logan, 170.

55. Logan to James Anderson and Andrew Galbraith, 2 March 1730/31, Logan Papers, III, Letter Book of James Logan, 170.

56. Field Notes, 1736, Taylor Papers, XVII.

57. Lemon, *The Best Poor Man's County*, 23, 65–67, 69. For an examination of similar trends in Chester County, see Lucy Simler, "Tenancy in Colonial Pennsylvania: The Case of Chester County," *William and Mary Quarterly*, 3rd ser. 43 (1986): 542–69; Simler, "The Landless Worker: An Index of Economic and Social Change in Chester County, Pennsylvania," *Pennsylvania Magazine of History and Biography* 114 (1990): 163–99; James Lemon and Gary Nash, "The Distribution of Wealth in Eighteenth-Century America: A Century of Change in Chester County, Pennsylvania," *Journal of Social History* 11 (1968):1–24; Duane Ball, "Dynamics of Population and Wealth in Eighteenth-Century Chester County, Pennsylvania," *Journal of Interdisciplinary History* 6 (1976): 621–44; Ball and G. M. Walton, "Agricultural Productivity Change in Eighteenth-Century Pennsylvania," *Journal of Economic History* 36 (1976): 102–17.

58. Donegal Tax List, 1750, LCHS.

59. Will, A-1–112, 1746, LCHS.

60. Will, A-1–101, 27 August 1745, LCHS.

61. Will, A-1–46, 1740, LCHS. For similar settlements, see Donegal wills of Thomas Mitchell, 1734, A-1–17, and Mary Dunning, 1735, A-1–20, LCHS.

62. Will, A-1–24, 12 August 1736, LCHS.

63. Will, A-1–109, 2 September 1745, LCHS.

64. Will, A-1–117, 15 September 1740, LCHS.

65. Officials only recorded the practice when a dispute arose. Otherwise they did not record such transactions. See Taylor Papers, XVI, 3371.

66. Samuel Blunston to Thomas Penn, 3 March 1737, Lancaster County MSS, 33.

67. Deed Book, A 96, LCHS. Some have concluded that the "high geographic mobility" had its roots in the "mobile individualism" that animated the lives of Ulster migrants. For this approach, see Jackson Turner Main, *Social Structure of Revolutionary America* (Princeton, 1965); and Lemon, *The Best Poor Man's Country*.

68. Paxton Township Tax Valuation, 1750, LCHS.

69. Egle, *Notes and Queries*, vol. II 3.

70. James Steel to John Taylor, 20 May 1734, Taylor Papers, XV.

71. Request for Surveys, 6 February 1739/40, Taylor Papers, V.

72. See the warrant map for East Donegal Township, LCHS.

73. Samuel Blunston to Thomas Penn, 3 January 1736/37, Lancaster County MSS, 23.

74. James Steel to Proprietors, 25 February 1730/31, Logan Papers, Letter Book of James Steel, 18–19, HSP.

75. Logan to Proprietors, 17 February 1730/31, Penn MSS, Official Correspondence, II, 65.

76. Inventory, box 146, folder 6, LCHS.

77. Field Notes, 1736–1741, Taylor Papers, XVII.

78. Common Pleas Appearance Dockets, 1 November 1743, 1 May 1744, LCHS.

79. New Londonderry Session Minutes, 22 March 1743/44.

80. Will, A-1-139, LCHS.

81. See Craig Horle, and Joseph Foster, and Jeffrey Scheib, eds., *Lawmaking and Legislators in Pennsylvania: A Biographical Dictionary*, vol. II (Philadelphia, 1997), 374–76.

82. Trinterud, *The Forming of an American Tradition*, 61.

83. Minutes of the Presbytery of Philadelphia, 1733–46, 1 September 1734, 11–12, PHSP; New Londonderry Session Minutes, 8 December 1740.

84. Minutes of the Presbytery of Philadelphia, 29 June 1736, 27.

85. Thomson as quoted in Gilbert Tennent's *Remarks on a Protestation Presented to the Synod of Philadelphia, June 1, 1741* (Philadelphia, 1741), 22; Alison to Ezra Stiles, 10 July 1761, Selected Papers and Documents of Francis Alison, PHSP; Minutes of the Presbytery of Donegal, vol. 1 (B), 301; Autobiography of John Craig, PHSP.

86. Minutes of the Presbytery of Donegal, 4 May 1736, Vol. 1 (B), 165–66.

87. Minutes of the Presbytery of Philadelphia, 26 October 1738, 12 July 1739, 97–98.

88. Trinterud, *Forming of an American Tradition*, 63–82.

89. Autobiography and Journal of the Reverend John McMillan, 2, HSP; George Whitefield, *A Continuation of the Rev. Mr. Whitefield's Journal* (Philadelphia, 1740), 32; Richard Hofstadter, *America at 1750: A Social Portrait* (New York, 1971), 251.

90. Klett, *Minutes of the Presbyterian Church*, 162.

91. Minutes of the Presbytery of Philadelphia, 19 September 1738, 18 September, 1739, 76, 100.

92. New England's revivalists also downplayed the importance of creedal orthodoxy. A number of historians have argued that qualms over creeds signaled a deeper misgiving over the transition to modernity. New Lights, or so the argument goes, tried to contest the spread of rationalist religion, of which creeds and formal learning formed but one aspect. The theme of reaction to change is a strong current in Great Awakening historiography. Gary Nash and Richard Bushman believe awakeners embraced the New Light to escape the troubling transformations that gripped eighteenth-century America. Patricia Bonomi similarly argues that revivalists responded to the rising tide of rationalism with a renewed emphasis on piety. Change meant declension in their

eyes. See Nash, *The Urban Crucible: Social Change, Political Consciousness, and the Origins of the American Revolution* (Cambridge, MA, 1979); Bushman, *From Puritan to Yankee: Character and the Social Order in Connecticut, 1690–1765* (Cambridge, MA, 1967); and Bonomi, *Under the Cope of Heaven*.

93. Gilbert Tennent, *The Espousals* (New York, 1735), 50.

94. Tennent, *The Espousals*, 14, 50; Gilbert Tennent, *A Solemn Warning to a Secure World* (Boston, 1735), 32.

95. Tennent, *Remarks on a Protestation*, 27.

96. Hofstadter, *America at 1750*, 252.

97. Samuel Blair, *A Particular Consideration of a Piece Entitled the Querists* (Philadelphia, 1741), 46; Tennent, *Remarks on a Protestation*, 27.

98. Blair, *A Particular Consideration*, 7, 9.

99. Tennent, *Remarks on a Protestation*, 24. For the meaning of itinerancy and the ways in which it epitomized the new world of possibilities open to colonial Americans in the mid-eighteenth century, see Timothy Hall's *Contested Boundaries: Itinerancy and the Reshaping of the Colonial American Religious World* (Durham, NC, 1994).

100. There was one exception, one that proves the rule. Alexander Craighead advocated unqualified subscription to the Confession. But he also joined the New Side and even traveled with Whitefield throughout the Pennsylvania region. He found himself in a no-man's land. Craighead left the Synod of Philadelphia with the rest of the New Side in 1741. Two years later his New Side presbytery ousted him for his insistence on applying the Confession to the letter. Unable to find a home in either camp, he attached himself to a Covenanter congregation. For his many travails, refer to "Craighead against Confessional Revision," *Journal of Presbyterian History* 45 (1967): 125–42.

101. Both Trinterud (*The Forming of an American Tradition*) and Nybakken ("New Light on the Old Side") argue that a "Scotch-Irish party" had formed within the synod, and that this group consisted of ministers who formed the core of the "subscriptionist" party. Westerkamp (*Triumph of the Laity*), however, believes no distinction can be made between Tennent and his followers and the Old Lights of the synod. Both groups, she argues, had migrated from Ireland and were informed by its traditions. Indeed, the New Side Scotch-Irish, as she would call them, remained truer to their Irish Presbyterian roots by advocating a revival spirit that drew from Ulster and tried to steer away from a Scottish-like high clerical system of church government. But she does not see that age, experience, and region set them apart from their older, Scottish-trained colleagues who had worked as ministers in Ireland.

102. George Gillespie, *A Sermon Against Divisions in Christs Churches* (Philadelphia, 1740), i–ii, 7, 12, appendix ix–x.

103. Klett, *Minutes of the Presbyterian Church*, 153.

104. Gilbert Tennent, *The Danger of an Unconverted Ministry* (Philadelphia, 1740), 3, 4. Richard Hofstadter sees this sermon as a turning point in Pennsyl-

vania's Great Awakening. Tennent, by taking the message to Nottingham and assailing the ministry, transformed the terms and tenor of the debate. What before had been a disagreement became a struggle between two world views (*America at 1750*).

105. Tennent, *The Danger of an Unconverted Ministry,* 14, 4, 13, 12.

106. Ibid., 9, 28, 31, 18, 22, 20, 21.

107. Gilbert Tennent, *Three Letters to the Rev. Mr. George Whitefield* (Philadelphia, 1739), 8.

108. Whitefield, *A Continuation of the Rev. Mr. Whitefield's Journal,* 71–72. Trinterud argues that Whitefield's arrival signaled a turning point in the fortunes of the New Side. His preaching turned the tide. See *The Forming of an American Tradition.* On Whitefield's role in the Awakening, refer to Frank Lambert, *"Pedlar in Divinity": George Whitefield and the Transatlantic Revivals, 1734–1770* (Princeton, 1994); Lambert, " 'Pedlar in Divinity': George Whitefield and the Great Awakening, 1737–1745," *Journal of American History* 77 (1990–91), 812–37; and Harry Stout, *The Divine Dramatist: George Whitefield and the Rise of Modern Evangelicalism* (Grand Rapids, MI, 1991).

109. Whitefield, *A Continuation of the Rev. Mr. Whitefield's Journal,* 71–72.

110. *A Protestation Presented to the Synod of Philadelphia,* 5.

111. Autobiography of John Craig, PHSP.

112. Klett, *Minutes of the Presbyterian Church,* 1745, 201–2.

113. Minutes of the Presbytery of Donegal, 9 December 1740, vol. 1(B), 307.

114. Ibid., September through November 1740, 282–94.

115. Autobiography of John Craig.

116. *A Protestation Presented to the Synod of Philadelphia,* 6, 15, 9–10.

117. Minutes of the Presbytery of Donegal, Vol. 1(B), 26 October 1736, 184–85.

118. Tennent, *Remarks on a Protestation,* 9.

119. Thomson, *The Government of the Church of Christ),* vii.

120. Tennent, *Remarks on a Protestation,* 11, 22.

121. *A Protestation Presented to the Synod of Philadelphia,* 8.

122. See Schmidt, *Holy Fairs;* and Westerkamp, *Triumph of the Laity.* David Miller counters that Ulster's Presbyterians had not experienced a revival for many years, nor would they again for quite some time. Revivals flourished in the mid-seventeenth century when Ulster, as Miller argues, was a "frontier," and during the process of nineteenth-century industrialization. See "Presbyterianism and 'Modernization' in Ulster," *Past and Present* 80 (1978): 66–90.

123. *Pennsylvania Gazette,* 22 May 1740. Westerkamp argues that the Scots-Irish men and women in frontier regions embraced the Awakening, although much of her evidence comes from the lower end (*Triumph of the Laity,* 182–83, 198, 200).

124. Paxtang and Derry's Call to Mr. Jno. John Elder, 26 September 1754, John Elder Papers, Dauphin County Historical Society; Tax Assessment for

Paxton, 1750, LCHS. For divisions over revival on the upper end, see MacMaster, *Donegal Presbyterians*, 34–39.

125. Notes for Sermons and Prayers of the Rev. Mr. John Elder, Elder Papers.

126. Tennent, *The Danger of an Unconverted Ministry*, 17; Tenent, *Remarks on a Protestation*, 27.

127. Account Book of the Reverend John Roan, LCHS; Paxton Tax Assessment, 1750, LCHS.

128. On similar themes in New England, see Peter Onuf, "New Lights in New London: A Group Portrait of the Separatists," *William and Mary Quarterly*, 3rd ser. 37 (1980): 627–43; and Rosalind Remer, "Old Lights and New Money: A Note on Religion, Economics, and the Social Order in 1740 Boston," *William and Mary Quarterly*, 3rd ser. 47 (1990): 566–73. T. H. Breen and Timothy Hall write that debates about the economy and religious revival in New England during this period "reveal creative concern about the nature of boundaries, social and spatial, about the fluidity of social relations, about the problematic character of foundational values, and, finally about the possibility of a recognizably 'liberal' or 'modern' self, one defined primarily by the exercise of individual choice in an expanding marketplace of ideas and goods." While no causal link bound together economic and religious controversies, they represented "parallel efforts to gain interpretive control over a larger social and economic reality." See "Structuring Provincial Imagination: The Rhetoric and Experience of Social Change in Eighteenth-Century New England," *American Historical Review* 103 (1998): 1412–13, 1414.

129. Alison to Ezra Stiles, 10 July 1761, Francis Alison Papers, PHSP.

CHAPTER SIX

1. Cullen, "Economic Development," in *A New History of Ireland*, ed. Moody and Vaughan, 146–48; Dickson, *Ulster Emigration*, 49–52; Wokeck, *Trade in Strangers*, 177, 192.

2. *Pennsylvania Gazette*, 25 September 1740, 14 May 1741, 27 January 1741/42, 14 August 1740.

3. See the *Pennsylvania Gazette* for the years 1740 and 1741, especially the May, August, and September issues.

4. Cases of Margaret Moran and Charles McCordy, Lancaster County Quarter Sessions, 1751, 1753.

5. Lancaster County Quarter Sessions, 1756.

6. Case of David McClure and Patrick Connor, Lancaster County Quarter Session, 1747.

7. General Quarter Session Docket, 1752, York County Historical Society, York, Pennsylvania.

8. Ibid., 1753.

9. Lancaster County Quarter Session, 1753.

10. *Pennsylvania Gazette*, 29 July 1742.

11. The first group of migrants can usefully be called a "charter group." They set the standards of acculturation. They constructed institutions and established practices to which new arrivals would have to assimilate. For this concept see, T. H. Breen, "Creative Adaptations: Peoples and Cultures," in *Colonial British America*, ed. Greene and Pole, 215–21.

12. The Seceders, Burghers and Antiburghers Being Extracts from the Original Minutes of both Synods, 1736, 1742, D1759/1F/3, PRONI.

13. Brooke, *Ulster Presbyterianism*, 106–9.

14. A. S. Aiken and J. M. Adair, A Biographical Sketch of the Rev. John Cuthbertson, File 12517, York County Historical Society, 32–34.

15. Middle Spring United Presbyterian Church Session Minutes, 7 June 1745, 15 August 1748, Cumberland County Historical Society.

16. Thomas Penn to Richard Peters, 17 July 1752, Thomas Penn Papers, Letterbook III, 150.

17. Leyburn, *The Scotch-Irish*, 200–205; Warren Hofstra, "Land, Ethnicity, and Community at the Opequon Settlement, Virginia, 1730–1800," in *Ulster and North America: Transatlantic Perspectives on the Scotch-Irish*, ed., H. T. Blethen and C. W. Wood (Tuscaloosa, 1997), 171–75.

18. R. C. Beatty and W. J. Mulloy, eds., *William Byrd's Natural History of Virginia* (Richmond, VA, 1940), xxi–xxii.

19. Richard Hooker, *The Carolina Backcountry on the Eve of the Revolution: The Journal and Other Writings of Charles Woodmason, Anglican Itinerant* (Chapel Hill, 1953), 60, 52.

20. Richard Beeman, *The Evolution of the Southern Backcountry: A Case Study of Lunenburg County, Virginia, 1746–1832* (Philadelphia, 1984), 61.

21. Klett, *Minutes of the Presbyterian Church*, 221, 264.

22. Although the New Light circuit included the Shenandoah Valley, their efforts largely centered east of the Blue Ridge Mountains in Hanover County where preachers had encountered Anglicans caught up in the revival spirit sweeping the colonies. On Old and New Lights in Virginia, see Wesley Gewehr, *The Great Awakening in Virginia, 1740–1790* (Durham, NC, 1930), 43–52.

23. Klett, *Minutes of the Presbyterian Church*, 249.

24. Ibid., 400–401.

25. Rhys Isaac, *The Transformation of Virginia, 1740–1790* (Chapel Hill, 1982); Butler, *Awash in a Sea of Faith*, 179.

26. According to Richard Beeman, those caught up in Baptist revivals were in all likelihood more recent arrivals, less prominent settlers, and those less likely to remain (*The Evolution of the Southern Backcountry*, 115).

27. On the initial movement of settlers from Virginia to Kentucky, see Eric Hinderaker, *Elusive Empires: Constructing Colonialism in the Ohio Valley, 1673–1800* (Cambridge, 1997), 195–99. Nathan Hatch covers the "Second Great

Awakening" in this region in *The Democratization of American Christianity* (New Haven, 1989).

28. Klett, *Minutes of the Presbyterian Church,* 307, 315, 349, 356, 366, 385, 396.

29. Richard Peters to Proprietors, 20 July 1750, 12 July 1750, Penn MSS, Official Correspondence, V, 39, 29.

30. Cumberland County Indictments, 21 July 1751, 1753, Cumberland County Historical Society; Cumberland County Quarter Session Dockets, 1753, Cumberland County Courthouse.

31. Richard Peters to Proprietors, 5 May 1750, Penn MSS, Official Correspondence, V, 3.

32. See ibid.

33. Hinderaker, *Elusive Empires,* 28–32, 152–53; Gregory Dowd, *A Spirited Resistance: The North American Indian Struggle for Unity* (Baltimore, 1992).

34. Hinderaker, *Elusive Empires,* 138–41. For the most comprehensive account of the Seven Years' War, see Fred Anderson, *Crucible of War: The Seven Years' War and the Fate of Empire in British North America* (New York, 2000), 108–10, 162.

35. George Franz, *Paxton: A Study of Community Structure and Mobility in the Colonial Pennsylvania Backcountry* (New York, 1989), 50.

36. Petitions of 30 October and 3 November 1755, Lamberton Scotch-Irish Collection, 23, 25, HSP.

37. John Dunbar, ed., *The Paxton Papers* (The Hague, Netherlands, 1957), 4.

38. Anderson, *Crucible of War,* 160–63; Hinderaker, *Elusive Empires,* 140–41.

39. On Pontiac's War, see Anderson, *Crucible of War,* 535–46, 617–37.

40. *Pennsylvania Gazette,* 5 July 1763.

41. Joseph Shippen, Jr., to John Elder, 12 July 1763, Elder Papers.

42. Elder to Governor Penn, 24 August 1763, Elder Papers; Franz, *Paxton,* 62–63.

43. Anderson, *Crucible of War,* 373–76. On colonists and British nationalism in these years, see Breen, "Ideology and Nationalism on the Eve of the American Revolution," 13–39; Fred Anderson, *A People's Army: Massachusetts Soldiers and Society in the Seven Years' War* (Chapel Hill, 1984); and Nathan Hatch, *The Sacred Cause of Liberty: Republican Thought and the Millennium in Revolutionary New England* (New Haven, 1977). On the ways in which Britishness tied together the margins of the empire, see Patrick Griffin, "America's Changing Image in Ireland's Looking-Glass: Provincial Construction of an Eighteenth-Century British Atlantic World," *Journal of Imperial and Commonwealth History* 26 (1998): 28–49.

44. *A Declaration and Remonstrance of the distressed and bleeding Frontier Inhabitants* (Philadelphia, 1764) in Dunbar, *The Paxton Papers,* 101, 105.

45. *Colonial Records,* 9:89–90.

46. Dunbar, *The Paxton Papers,* 29, 31. For a detailed account of the Paxton Boys' raids at Conestoga and Lancaster and the subsequent march on Phila-

delphia, see Brooke Hindle, "The March of the Paxton Boys," *William and Mary Quarterly* 3rd ser. 4 (1946): 461–86; James Crowley, "The Paxton Disturbance and Ideas of Order in Pennsylvania Politics," *Pennsylvania History* 37 (1970): 317–39; Alden Vaughan, "Frontier Banditti and the Indians: The Paxton Boys' Legacy, 1763–1775," *Pennsylvania History* 51 (1984): 1–29.

47. Dunbar, *The Paxton Papers*, 44–45.

48. Ibid., 45.

49. *A Serious Address to . . . the Inhabitants of Pennsylvania* (Philadelphia, 1764), in Dunbar, *The Paxton Papers*, 97.

50. Dunbar, *The Paxton Papers*, 156, 168, 225. The Paxton affair witnessed an unprecedented number of pamphlets published, many of which are compiled in Dunbar, *The Paxton Papers*. On the battle over style, see Alison Olson, "The Pamphlet War over the Paxton Boys," *Pennsylvania Magazine of History and Biography* 123 (1999): 31–55.

51. Elder to Governor Penn, 16 December 1763; Elder to Colonel Shippen, 1 February 1764, Elder Papers. Thomas Slaughter argues that the violent response of discontented frontier folk like the Paxton Boys stemmed from their "territorial liminality" in society. In other words, they lived on society's margins. See "Crowds in Eighteenth-Century America: Reflections and New Directions," *Pennsylvania Magazine of History and Biography* 115 (1991): 3–34.

52. Benjamin Franklin, *A Narrative of the Late Massacre in Lancaster County* (Philadelphia, 1764), in Dunbar, *The Paxton Papers*, 63, 69, 71, 73.

53. *The Conduct of the Paxton-Men Impartially represented* (Philadelphia, 1764), in Dunbar, *The Paxton Papers*, 272, 293, 297. There is some debate over the authorship of this pamphlet. See James Myers, "The Rev. Thomas Barton's Authorship of the Conduct of the Paxton Men," *Pennsylvania Magazine of History and Biography* 61 (1994): 155–84. On the significance of "Cato's Letters" in the rhetoric of the American Revolution, see Bernard Bailyn, *The Ideological Origins of the American Revolution* (Cambridge, MA, 1967).

54. Elder to Governor Penn, 16 December 1763, Elder Papers.

55. Elder to Colonel Shippen, 1 February 1764, Elder Papers. Elder originally wrote that frontier inhabitants were incensed with "the Quakers." Keeping propriety in mind, however, he crossed out the phrase, inserting instead "a particular set of men."

56. *A Declaration and Remonstrance of the distressed and bleeding Frontier Inhabitants* (Philadelphia, 1764), in Dunbar, *The Paxton Papers*, 101–8.

57. William McClenachan, *A Letter from a Clergyman in Town* (Philadelphia, 1764), 3–8.

58. It could be argued that far from "becoming American," settlers on the Pennsylvania frontier were resurrecting Britishness in an American backcountry context, a variation of a common imperial theme. This interpretation runs counter to the argument that colonists through modernization were distanc-

ing themselves from Britain. See Jon Butler, *Becoming America: The Revolution before 1776* (Cambridge, MA, 2000).

59. The language of liberty could also justify the perpetuation of slavery and de-peopling of Indian lands, rally indebted tobacco planters to contest the British, unite the lower classes to confront their betters, and of course, galvanize principled resistance to government corruption. When viewed as a dynamic discourse that could be appropriated for many often contradictory reasons, the "rhetoric" of the Revolution addressed any number of "realities." Separating the two creates a false dichotomy. Gordon Wood pointed to the growing gulf between idealist and behavioralist interpretations of the Revolution in the aptly titled "Rhetoric and Reality in the American Revolution," *William and Mary Quarterly*, 3rd ser., 23 (1966): 3–32. For just a handful of examples of the many faces of the language of liberty, see Edmund Morgan, *American Slavery, American Freedom: The Ordeal of Colonial Virginia* (New York, 1975); Hinderaker, *Elusive Empires*; T. H. Breen, *Tobacco Culture: The Mentality of the Great Tidewater Planters on the Eve of Revolution* (Princeton, 1985); Isaac, *The Transformation of Virginia*; Alfred Young, *The Shoemaker and the Tea Party: Memory and the American Revolution* (Boston, 2000); Woody Holton, *Forced Founders: Indians, Debtors, Slaves, and the Making of the American Revolution in Virginia* (Chapel Hill, 1999); Edmund Morgan and Helen Morgan, *The Stamp Act Crisis: Prologue to Revolution* (New York, 1963); Pauline Maier, *From Resistance to Revolution: Colonial Radicals and the Development of American Opposition to Britain* (New York, 1972); Bailyn, *Ideological Origins of the American Revolution*.

✤ *Bibliography* ✤

MANUSCRIPT COLLECTIONS

Armagh Public Library, Armagh

    Lodge MSS
    Reeves Copy Books of Visitations

Magee College, Derry

    James Duchal Sermons
    Livingston-Wodrow Correspondence
    James Orr Sermons
    Thomas Steward Correspondence

Presbyterian Historical Society, Belfast

    Aghadowey Session Minutes
    Armagh Session Accounts
    Connor Session Minutes
    Sermons by James Duchal
    Diary of the Rev. John Kennedy
    Ministerial Notebook of John Kennedy
    J. Magee Sermons, 1721
    J. McBride Sermons, 1704
    Sermons by Rev. John McKenzie written during the Siege of Derry
    Minutes of the Antrim Meeting
    Minutes of the Sub-Synod of Derry
    Minutes of the Presbytery of Down
    Minutes of the Laggan Meeting
    Minutes of the Monaghan Presbytery
    Minutes of the Route Presbytery

Public Record Office of Northern Ireland, Belfast

    Broadisland or Ballycarry Session Minutes
    Carmoney Session Minutes
    Castleward Papers
    Larne Session Minutes
    Lisburn Session Minutes

London Company Records
Massereene Papers
Minutes of the Presbytery of Killyleagh
Minutes of the Presbytery of Strabane
Murray of Broughton Papers
Correspondence of William Nicholson, Bishop of Derry
Charles O'Hara Papers
Tennison Groves Collection
Templepatrick Session Minutes
Transcripts of State Papers Relating to Ireland
Wodrow Papers

Union Theological College, Belfast

Burt Session Minutes

American Philosophical Society, Philadelphia

David Brainerd Diary

Chester County Archives, West Chester, Pennsylvania

Probate Records
Quarter Session Indictments and Docket Book
Tax Lists and Assessments
Traders' Petitions
Writs and Narrative of the Court of Common Pleas

Cumberland County Courthouse, Carlisle, Pennsylvania

Cumberland County Quarter Session Dockets

Cumberland County Historical Society, Carlisle, Pennsylvania

Cumberland County Indictments
Middle Spring United Presbyterian Church Session Minutes

Dauphin County Historical Society, Harrisburg, Pennsylvania

John Elder Papers

Historical Society of Pennsylvania, Philadelphia

Jonathan Dickinson Copy Book of Letters

Lamberton Scotch-Irish Collection
Lancaster County MSS
James Logan Papers, I, III, IV, V, X
Maria Dickinson Logan Family Papers, Dickinson/Logan Letterbook
Isaac Norris Sr. Letterbook
Norris Papers
Penn MSS, Official Correspondence, I, II, V
Penn Physick Papers, VI
Thomas Penn Papers, Letterbook III
Taylor Papers, IV, V, XII, XIII, XV, XVI, XVII

Lancaster County Historical Society, Lancaster, Pennsylvania

Court of Common Pleas Appearance Dockets
Lancaster County Quarter Session Records
Lancaster County Wills and Inventories
Mills and Bridges of Lancaster County, Pennsylvania, compiled by R.H. Barton
Records of Donegal Presbyterian Church
Tax Valuations
Township Warrant Maps

Presbyterian Historical Society, Philadelphia

Anderson-Stirling Correspondence
Jedediah Andrews Letters
Autobiography of John Craig
Minutes of the Presbytery of Donegal
Minutes of the Presbytery of Philadelphia
New Londonderry Session Minutes
Selected Papers and Documents of Francis Alison

York County Historical Society, York, Pennsylvania

General Quarter Session Docket

PRINTED PRIMARY SOURCES

Abernethy, John, *A Letter from the Presbytery of Antrim.* Belfast, 1726.
———. *The Nature and Consequences of the Sacramental Test Considered, with Reasons humbly offered for the Repeal of It.* Dublin, 1731.
———. *The People's Choice, the Lord's Anointed: A Thanksgiving Sermon for his Most Excellent Majesty King George.* Belfast, 1714.

Abernethy, John. *Religious Obedience Founded on Personal Persuasion: A Sermon Preach'd at Belfast the 9th of December, 1719*. Belfast, 1720.

———. *Scarce and Valuable Tracts and Sermons*. Dublin, 1751.

———. *Seasonable Advice to the Protestant Dissenters in the North of Ireland*. Belfast, 1722.

———. *A Sermon Recommending the Study of Scripture-Prophecie*. Belfast, 1716.

Blair, Samuel. *The Great Glory of God . . . in the Gospel of Christ*. Boston, 1739.

———. *A Particular Consideration of a Piece Entitled the Querists*. Philadelphia, 1741.

Boyse, Joseph. *Remarks on a Pamphlet publish'd by William Tisdal, D.D.*. Dublin, 1716.

Bruce, Michael. *The Duty of Christians to Live Together in Religious Communion Recommended in a Sermon Preached at Belfast, January 5th, 1724–25*. Belfast, 1725.

Clerk, Matthew. *A Letter from The Belfast Society to the Rev. Matthew Clerk, with an Answer to the Society's Remarks*. Belfast, 1723.

Craighead, Robert. *The True Terms of Christian and Ministerial Communion founded on Scripture Alone*. Dublin, 1739.

Dickinson, Jonathan. *Remarks on a Discourse intitled an Overture . . . to the Synod*. New York, 1729.

———. *A Sermon Preached at the Opening of the Synod at Philadelphia, 19 September 1722*. Boston, 1723.

———. *Some Short Observations made on the Presbyterian Doctrine*. Philadelphia, 1721.

———. *The Vanity of Human Institutions in the Worship of God*. New York, 1736.

A Discourse concerning Ireland and the Different Interests thereof. Dublin, 1697/98.

Dobbs, Arthur. *An Essay upon the Trade of Ireland*. Dublin, 1729.

Elder, John. *A Letter to the Reverend Mr. Robert McBride*. Belfast, 1727.

———. *Reasons for Moderation in the Present Debates amongst Presbyterians in the North of Ireland*. Belfast, 1725.

Franklin, Benjamin. *A Defence of the Rev. Mr. Hemphill's Observations*. Philadelphia, 1735.

———. *A Letter to a Friend in the Country, Containing the Substance of a Sermon . . . [by] the Rev. Mr. Hemphill*. Philadelphia, 1735.

———. *Some Observations on the Proceedings against the Rev. Mr. Hemphill*. Philadelphia, 1735.

Gillespie, George. *A Sermon Against Divisions in Christs Churches*. Philadelphia, 1740.

———. *A Treatise against the Deists or Free-Thinkers*. Philadelphia, 1735.

Haliday, Samuel. *Reasons Against the Imposition of Subscription to the Westminster Confession of Faith*. Belfast, 1724.

Higinbotham, Robert. *Reasons against the Overtures*. Belfast, 1726.

An Inquiry into some of the Causes of the Ill Situation of the Affairs of Ireland; with Some Reflexions on the Trade, Manufactures, etc. of England. Dublin, 1732.

Kirkpatrick, James. *An Essay upon the Important Question, Whether there be a Legislative, Proper Authority in the Church, By Some Non-Subscribing Ministers in the North of Ireland.* Belfast, 1737.

———. *An Historical Essay upon the Loyalty of Presbyterians in Great Britain and Ireland from the Reformation to the Present Year, 1713.* Belfast, 1713.

———. *A Scripture-Plea against a Fatal Rupture, and Breach of Christian Communion amongst the Presbyterians in the North of Ireland.* Belfast, 1724.

———. (originally attributed to V. Ferguson). *A Vindication of the Presbyterian Ministers in the North of Ireland: Subscribers and Non-subscribers.* Belfast, 1721.

Mackenzie, John. *A Narrative of the Siege of London-derry.* London, 1690.

Mastertown, Charles. *Christian Liberty Founded in Gospel Truth.* Belfast, 1725.

McBride, Robert. *The Overtures Set in a Fair Light.* Belfast, 1726.

McClenachan, William. *A Letter from a Clergyman in Town.* Philadelphia, 1764.

Molyneux, William. *The Case of Ireland's being bound by Acts of Parliament in England, stated.* Dublin, 1698.

Pennsylvania Province. *A Journal of the Votes and Proceedings of the House of Representatives.* Philadelphia, 1728.

———. *The Particulars of an Indian Treaty at Conestogoe.* Philadelphia, 1721.

A Protestation Presented to the Synod of Philadelphia, June 1, 1741. Philadelphia, 1741.

Pullein, Tobias. *A Defence of the Answer to a Paper Entitled the Case of the Dissenting Protestants of Ireland.* Dublin, 1697.

Roscommon (pseud.). *To the Author of the Intelligencers.* New York, 1733.

Tennent, Gilbert. *The Danger of Forgetting God.* New York, 1735.

———. *The Danger of an Unconverted Ministry.* Philadelphia, 1740.

———. *The Espousals.* New York, 1735.

———. *The Necessity of Religious Violence.* New York, 1735.

———. *Remarks on a Protestation Presented to the Synod of Philadelphia, June 1, 1741.* Philadelphia, 1741.

———. *A Solemn Warning to a Secure World.* Boston, 1735.

Thomson, John. *The Government of the Church of Christ.* Philadelphia, 1741.

———. *An Overture Presented to the Reverend Synod.* Philadelphia, 1729.

Tisdal, William. *A Sample of True-Blew Presbyterian Loyalty in all Changes and Turns of Government.* Dublin, 1709.

A Topographical and Chronological Survey of the County of Down. Dublin, 1740.

A Vindication of the Rev. Commission . . . against the Rev. Mr. Hemphill. Philadelphia, 1735.

Walker, George. *A True Account of the Present State of Ireland.* London, 1689.

———. *A True Account of the Siege of London-derry.* London, 1689.

Whitefield, George. *A Continuation of the Rev. Mr. Whitefield's Journal.* Philadelphia, 1740.

NEWSPAPERS

American Weekly Mercury
Pennsylvania Gazette

EDITED PRIMARY COLLECTIONS

Beatty, R. C., and W. J. Mulloy, eds. *William Byrd's Natural History of Virginia.* Richmond, VA, 1940.

Browning, Charles, ed. "Extracts from the Journal of Charles Clinton, Kept During the Voyage from Ireland to Pennsylvania, 1729." *Pennsylvania Magazine of History and Biography* 26 (1902): 112–14

"Bishop J.C.F. Camerhoff's Narrative of a Journey to Shamokin, Penna." *Pennsylvania Magazine of History and Biography* 29 (1905): 160–79

Crevecoeur, Hector. *Letters from an American Farmer and Sketches of Eighteenth-Century America.* Ed. A. E. Stone. New York, 1986.

Davis, Herbert, ed. *The Drapier's Letters and Other Works.* Oxford, 1941.

Dunbar, John, ed. *The Paxton Papers.* The Hague, Netherlands, 1957.

Egle, W. H., ed. *Notes and Queries Historical and Genealogical chiefly relating to Interior Pennsylvania.* 1st and 2nd ser. Baltimore, 1970.

Faulkiner, George, ed. *Letters Written by his Excellency Hugh Boulter, Lord Primate of All Ireland.* 2 vols. (Oxford, 1769–70).

Franklin, Benjamin. *Autobiography and Other Writings.* Ed. K. Silverman. New York, 1986.

Hooker, Richard, ed. *The Carolina Backcountry on the Eve of the Revolution: The Journal and Other Writings of Charles Woodmason, Anglican Itinerant.* Chapel Hill, 1953.

———. *The Itinerarium of Dr. Alexander Hamilton.* In *Colonial American Travel Narratives.* Ed. Wendy Martin, 178–327. New York, 1994.

King, C. S., ed. *A Great Archbishop of Dublin, William King, 1650–1729.* London, 1906.

Klett, Guy, ed. *Minutes of the Presbyterian Church in America, 1706–1788.* Philadelphia, 1976.

Levine, George, ed. *A Modest Proposal and Other Satires.* Amherst, NY, 1995.

Mather, Cotton. *Diary of Cotton Mather, 1709–1724.* Massachusetts Historical Society Collections, 7th ser., vol 8. Boston, 1912. Pp. 435–509, 514–95

McCrie, Thomas, ed. *The Correspondence of the Reverend Robert Wodrow.* 3 vols. Edinburgh, 1842.

Minutes of the Provincial Council of Pennsylvania. 10 vols. Philadelphia, 1852.

Mittelberger, Gottlieb. *Journey to Pennsylvania.* Ed. Oscar Handlin and John Clive. Cambridge, MA, 1960.

Nichols, John, ed. *The Works of the Rev. Jonathan Swift, D.D.* 24 vols. London, 1801.

"Obstructions to Irish Immigration to Pennsylvania, 1736," *Pennsylvania Magazine of History and Biography* 21 (1897): 485–87.

Pennsylvania Archives, Selected and Arranged from Original Documents in the Office of the Secretary of the Commonwealth. 138 vols. Philadelphia, 1852–1949.

The Presbyterian Church of Ireland. *Records of the General Synod of Ulster, from 1691 to 1820.* 3 vols. Belfast, 1890.

"The Records of the Presbytery of New Castle Upon Delaware." *Journal of the Department of History of the Presbyterian Church in the USA* 14 (1931): 289–308, 377–84, 15 (1932): 73–120, 174–207.

Silverman, Kenneth, ed. *Selected Letters of Cotton Mather.* Baton Rouge, LA, 1971.

Stevenson, John. *Two Centuries of Life in Down, 1600–1800.* Belfast, 1920.

Wodrow, Robert. *Analecta: or Materials for a History of Remarkable Providences; Mostly Relating to Scotch Ministers and Christians.* 4 vols. Edinburgh, 1843.

SECONDARY SOURCES

Agnew, Jean. *Belfast Merchant Families in the Seventeenth Century.* Dublin, 1996.

Anderson, Fred. *Crucible of War: The Seven Years' War and the Fate of Empire in British North America.* New York, 2000.

Asch, Ronald, ed. *Three Nations—A Common History? England, Scotland, Ireland and British History c. 1600–1920.* Bochum, Germany, 1994.

Bailyn, Bernard. "The Idea of Atlantic History." *Itinerario* 20 (1996): 19–44.

———. *The Peopling of British North America: An Introduction.* New York, 1986.

———. *Voyagers to the West: A Passage in the Peopling of America on the Eve of the Revolution.* New York, 1986.

Bailyn, Bernard, and Philip Morgan, eds. *Strangers within the Realm: Cultural Margins of the First British Empire.* Chapel Hill, 1991.

Ball, Duane. "Dynamics of Population and Wealth in Eighteenth-Century Chester County, Pennsylvania." *Journal of Interdisciplinary History* 6 (1976): 621–44.

Ball, Duane, and G. M. Walton. "Agricultural Productivity Change in Eighteenth-Century Pennsylvania." *Journal of Economic History* 36 (1976): 102–17

Barlow, R. B. "The Career of John Abernethy (1680–1740), Father of Nonsubscription in Ireland and Defender of Religious Liberty." *Harvard Theological Review* 78 (1985): 399–419.

Barnard, Toby. "The Government and Irish Dissent, 1704–80." In *The Politics of Irish Dissent, 1650–1800,* ed. Kevin Herlihy, 9–27. Dublin, 1997.

———. "Identities, Ethnicity and Tradition among Irish Dissenters c. 1650–1750." In *The Irish Dissenting Tradition, 1650–1750,* ed. Kevin Herlihy, 29–48. Dublin, 1995.

Beckett, J. C. *Protestant Dissent in Ireland, 1687–1780.* London, 1948.

Beeman, Richard. *The Evolution of the Southern Backcountry: A Case Study of Lunenburg County, Virginia, 1746–1832.* Philadelphia, 1984.

Bolton, C. K. *Scotch-Irish Pioneers in Ulster and America.* Boston, 1910.

Bonomi, Patricia. *Under the Cope of Heaven: Religion, Society and Politics in Colonial America.* New York, 1986.

Boyce, D. George, Robert Eccleshall, and V. Geoghegan, eds. *Political Thought in Ireland since the Seventeenth Century.* London, 1994.

Bradshaw, Brendan, and John Morrill, eds. *The British Problem, c. 1524–1707.* London, 1996.

Bradshaw, Brendan, and Peter Roberts, eds. *British Consciousness and Identity: The Making of Britain, 1533–1707.* Cambridge, 1998.

Breen, T. H. " 'Baubles of Britain': The American Consumer Revolutions of the Eighteenth Century." *Past and Present* 119 (1988): 73–104

———. "Creative Adaptations: Peoples and Cultures." In *Colonial British America: Essays in the New History of the Early Modern Era* ed. Jack Greene and J. R. Pole, 195–232. Baltimore, 1984.

———. "An Empire of Goods: The Anglicization of Colonial America, 1690–1776." *Journal of British Studies* 25 (1986): 467–99.

———. "Ideology and Nationalism on the Eve of the American Revolutoin: Revisions *Once More* in Need of Revising." *Journal of American History* 84 (1997): 13–39.

Breen, T. H. and Timothy Hall. "Structuring Provincial Imagination: The Rhetoric and Experience of Social Change in Eighteenth-Century New England." *American Historical Review* 103 (1998): 1411–39.

Bridenbaugh, Carl. *Myths and Realities: Societies of the Colonial South.* New York, 1966.

Brooke, Peter. *Ulster Presbyterianism: The Historical Perspective, 1610–1970.* New York, 1987.

Brown, A.W.G. "A Theological Interpretation of the First Subscription Controversy." In *Challenge and Conflict: Essays in Irish Presbyterian History and Doctrine,* ed. J.L.M. Haire (Belfast, 1981).

Brown, Richard. *Church and State in Modern Britain, 1700–1715.* London, 1991.

Butler, Jon. *Awash in a Sea of Faith: Christianizing the American People.* Cambridge, MA, 1990.

———. *Becoming America: The Revolution before 1776.* Cambridge, MA, 2000.

———. "Enthusiasm Described and Decried: The Great Awakening as Interpretive Fiction." *Journal of American History* 69 (1982–83): 305–25.

———. *The Huguenots in America: A Refugee People in New World Society.* Cambridge, MA, 1983.

Canny, Nicholas. *Kingdom and Colony: Ireland in the Atlantic World, 1560–1800.* Baltimore, 1988.

———. ed. *Europeans on the Move: Studies in European Migration, 1500–1800.* Oxford, 1994.

——— "Writing Atlantic History, or, Reconfiguring the History of Colonial British America." *Journal of American History* 86 (1999): 1093–1114.

Canny, Nicholas, and Anthony Pagden, eds. *Colonial Identity in the Atlantic World, 1500–1800.* Princeton, 1987.

Christensen, Merton. "Franklin on the Hemphill Trial: Deism versus Presbyterian Orthodoxy." *William and Mary Quarterly,* 3rd ser., 10 (1953): 422–40.

Colley, Linda. *Britons: Forging the Nation, 1707–1837.* New Haven, 1992.

Connolly, Sean J., *Religion, Law and Power: The Making of Protestant Ireland.* Oxford, 1992.

———. "Varieties of Britishness: Ireland, Scotland and Wales in the Hanoverian State." In *Uniting the Kingdom?: The Making of British History* ed. Alexander Grant and keith J. Stringer, 193–207. London, 1996.

Cornell, Stephen. "The Variable Ties That Bind: Content and Circumstance in Ethnic Processes." *Ethnic and Racial Studies* 19 (1996): 265–89.

Crawford, W. H., *Domestic Industry in Ireland: The Experience of the Linen Industry.* Belfast, 1972.

———. "Drapers and Bleachers in the Early Ulster Linen Industry." In *Négoce et Industrie en France et en Irlande aux XVIII et XIX siècles,* ed. P. Butel and L. M. Cullen, 113–19. Paris, 1980.

———. "Economy and Society in South Ulster in the Eighteenth-Century." *Clogher Record* 8 (1975): 241–58.

———. "Economy and Society in Ulster in the Eighteenth Century." Ph.D. diss., Queen's University of Belfast, 1983.

———. *The Handloom Weavers and the Ulster Linen Industry.* Belfast, 1994.

———. "Landlord-Tenant Relations in Ulster, 1609–1820." *Irish Economic and Social History* 2 (1975): 5–21.

———. "The Origins of the Linen Industry in North Armagh and the Lagan Valley." *Ulster Folklife* 17 (1971): 42–51.

———. "The Rise of the Linen Industry." In *The Formation of the Irish Economy,* ed. L. M. Cullen, 23–35. Cork, 1969.

———. "The Significance of Landed Estates in Ulster, 1600–1820." *Irish Economic and Social History* 17 (1990): 44–61.

Crowley, James. "The Paxton Disturbance and Ideas of Order in Pennsylvania Politics." *Pennsylvania History* 37 (1970): 317–39.

Cullen, L. M., *Anglo-Irish Trade, 1660–1800.* New York, 1968.

———. *An Economic History of Ireland since 1660.* New York, 1972.

———. "The Irish Diaspora of the Seventeenth and Eighteenth Centuries." In *Europeans on the Move: Studies in European Migration, 1500–1800,* ed. Nicholas Canny, 113–49. Oxford, 1994.

———. "Population Trends in Seventeenth-Century Ireland." *Economic and Social Review* 6 (1974–75): 149–66.

Dickson, David, Dáire Keogh, and Kevin Whelan, eds. *The United Irishmen: Republicanism, Radicalism, and Rebellion.* London, 1993.

Dickson, R. J. *Ulster Emigration to Colonial America.* London, 1966.

Dowd, Gregory. *A Spirited Resistance: The North American Indian Struggle for Unity.* Baltimore, 1992.

Doyle, David. *Ireland, Irishmen and Revolutionary America, 1760–1820.* Cork, 1981.

Eccleshall, Robert. "Angelican Political Thought in the Century after the Revolution of 1688." In *Political Thought in Ireland since the Seventeenth Century,* ed. D. George Boyce, Robert Eccleshall, and Vincent Geoghegan, 36–72. London, 1993.

Ellis, Franklin, and Samuel Evans. *History of Lancaster County, Pennsylvania.* Philadelphia, 1883.

Ellis, Steven, and Sarah Barber, eds. *Conquest and Union: Fashioning a British State 1485–1725.* London, 1996.

Ferguson, William. *Scotland, 1689 to the Present,* vol. 1. Edinburgh, 1968.

Fischer, David Hackett. *Albion's Seed: Four British Folkways in America.* New York, 1989.

Fogleman, Aaron. "From Slaves, Convicts, and Servants to Free Passengers: The Transformation of Immigration in the Era of the American Revolution." *Journal of American History* 85 (June 1998): 43–76.

———. *Hopeful Journeys: German Immigration, Settlement, and Political Culture in Colonial America, 1717–1775.* Philadelphia, 1996.

Ford, H. J. *The Scotch-Irish in America.* Princeton, 1915.

Ford, Alan, James McGuire, and Kenneth Milne, eds. *As by Law Established: The Church of Ireland since the Reformation.* Dublin, 1995.

Franz, George. *Paxton: A Study of Community Structure and Mobility in the Colonial Pennsylvania Backcountry.* New York, 1989.

Futhey, J. S., and Gilbert Cope. *History of Chester County, Pennsylvania.* Philadelphia, 1881.

Games, Alison. *Migration and the Origins of the English Atlantic World.* Cambridge, MA, 1999.

Gewehr, Wesley. *The Great Awakening in Virginia, 1740–1790.* Durham, NC, 1930.

Giddens, Anthony. *The Constitution of Society: Outline of the Theory of Structuration.* Berkeley, 1984.

———. *Modernity and Self-Identity: Self and Society in the Late Modern Age.* Cambridge, 1991.

Gill, Conrad. *The Rise of the Irish Linen Industry.* Oxford, 1925.

Gillespie, Raymond. "Dissenters and Nonconformists, 1661–1700." In *The Irish Dissenting Tradition, 1650–1750,* ed. Kevin Herlihy, 11–28. Dublin, 1995.

———. "The Presbyterian Revolution in Ulster, 1660–1690." In *The Churches, Ireland and the Irish: Papers Read at the 1987 Summer Meeting and the 1988 Winter Meeting of the Ecclesiastical History Society,* ed. W. J. Sheil and D. Wood, 159–70. (Oxford, 1989).

————. *Settlement and Survival on an Ulster Estate: The Brownlow Leasebook, 1667–1711*. Belfast, 1988.

Gleason, Philip. "Identifying Identity: A Semantic History." *Journal of American History* 69 (1983): 910–31.

Grant, Alexander, and Keith J. Stringer, eds. *Uniting the Kingdom?: The Making of British History*. London, 1996.

Gray, Jane. "Rural Industry and Uneven Development: The Significance of Gender in the Irish Linen Industry." *Journal of Peasant Studies* 20 (1993): 590–611

Greaves, R. L. *God's Other Children: Protestant Nonconformists and the Emergence of Denominational Churches in Ireland, 1660–1700*. Stanford, CA, 1997.

————. "'That's no good religion that disturbs government': The Church of Ireland and the Nonconformist Challenge, 1660–1688." In *As by Law Established: The Church of Ireland since the Reformation*, ed. Alan Ford, James McGuire, and Kenneth Milne, 210–35. Dublin, 1995.

Green, E.R.R. "The 'Strange Humours' That Drove the Scotch-Irish to America, 1729." *William and Mary Quarterly*, 3rd ser., 12 (1955): 113–23.

Greene, Jack. "Interpretive Frameworks: The Quest for Intellectual Order in Early American History." *William and Mary Quarterly* 3rd ser., 48 (1991): 515–30.

Greene, Jack, and J. R. Pole, eds. *Colonial British America: Essays in the New History of the Early Modern Era*. Baltimore, 1984.

Hall, Timothy. *Contested Boundaries: Itinerancy and the Reshaping of the Colonial American Religious World*. Durham, NC, 1994.

Hanna, Charles. *The Scotch-Irish*. New York, 1902.

Hatch, Nathan. *The Democratization of American Christianity*. New Haven, 1989.

Hayton, David. "Anglo-Irish Attitudes: Changing Perceptions of National Identity among the Protestant Ascendancy in Ireland, ca. 1690–1750." *Studies in Eighteenth-Century Culture* 17 (1987): 145–57.

————. "From Barbarian to Burlesque: English Images of the Irish c. 1660–1750." *Irish Economic and Social History* 15 (1988): 5–31.

————. *Ireland after the Glorious Revolution*. Belfast, 1976.

————. "The Williamite Revolution in Ireland, 1688–91." In *The Anglo-Dutch Moment: Essays on the Glorious Revolution and Its World Impact*, ed. Jonathan Israel, 185–214. Cambridge, 1991.

Henretta, James. "Families and Farms: Mentalité in Pre-Industrial America." *William and Mary Quarterly*, 3rd ser., 35 (1978): 3–32.

Herlihy, Kevin, ed. *The Irish Dissenting Tradition, 1650–1750*. Dublin, 1995.

————. *The Politics of Irish Dissent, 1650–1800*. Dublin, 1997.

————. *The Religion of Irish Dissent, 1650–1800*. Dublin, 1996.

Hinderaker, Eric. *Elusive Empires: Constructing Colonialism in the Ohio Valley, 1673–1800*. Cambridge, 1997.

Hindle Brooke. "The March of the Paxton Boys." *William and Mary Quarterly,* 3rd ser., 4 (1946): 461–86.

Hofstadter, Richard. *America at 1750: A Social Portrait.* New York, 1971.

Hofstra, Warren. "Land, Ethnicity, and Community at the Opequon Settlement, Virginia, 1730–1800." In *Ulster and North America: Transatlantic Perspectives on the Scotch-Irish,* ed. H. T. Blethen and C. W. Wood, 167–88. Tuscaloosa, AL, 1997.

Horle, Craig, Joseph Foster, and Jeffrey Scheib, eds. *Lawmaking and Legislators in Pennsylvania: A Biographical Dictionary,* vol. 2. Philadelphia, 1997.

Horn, James. "British Diaspora: Emigration from Britain, 1680–1815." In *The Oxford History of the British Empire: vol. 2, The Eighteenth Century,* ed. P. J. Marshall, 28–52. Oxford, 1998.

Horn, James, and Ida Altman, eds. *"To Make America: European Emigration in the Early Modern Period.* Berkeley, 1991.

Illick, Joseph. *Colonial Pennsylvania: A History.* New York, 1976.

Isaac, Rhys. *The Transformation of Virginia, 1740–1790.* Chapel Hill, 1982.

Israel, Jonathan, ed. *The Anglo-Dutch Moment: Essays on the Glorious Revolution and Its World Impact.* Cambridge, 1991.

James, Francis. *Ireland in the Empire, 1688–1700.* Cambridge, MA, 1973.

Jennings, Francis. "The Indian Trade of the Susquehanna Valley." *Proceedings of the American Philosophical Society* 110 (1966): 406–24.

———. "Miquon's Passing: Indian-European Relations in Colonial Pennsylvania, 1674 to 1755." Ph.D. diss., University of Pennsylvania, 1965.

———. " 'Pennsylvania Indians' and the Iroquois." In *Beyond the Covenant Chain: The Iroquois and Their Neighbors in Indian North America,* ed. Daniel Richter and James Merrell, 75–92. Syracuse, NY, 1987.

Jones, Maldwyn. "The Scotch-Irish in British North America." In *Strangers within the Realm: Cutural Margins of the First British Empire,* ed. Bernard Bailyn and Phillip Morgan, 284–313. Chapel Hill, 1991.

Kidd, Colin. *British Identities before Nationalism: Ethnicity and Nationhood in the Atlantic World, 1600–1800.* Cambridge, 1999.

———. "North Britishness and the Nature of Eighteenth-Century British Patriotisms." *Historical Journal* 39 (1996): 361–82.

Kilroy, Phil. *Protestant Dissent and Controversy in Ireland, 1660–1714.* Cork, 1994.

Kirkham, Graeme. Introduction to *Ulster Emigration to Colonial America,* by R. J. Dickson. Belfast, 1988.

———. " 'To Pay the Rent and Lay up Riches': The Economic Opportunity in Eighteenth-Century North-West Ulster." In *Economy and Society in Scotland and Ireland, 1500–1939,* ed. R. Mitchison and P. Roebuck, 95–104. Edinburgh, 1988.

———. "Ulster Emigration to North America, 1680–1720." In *Ulster and North America: Transatlantic Perspectives on the Scotch-Irish,* ed. H. T. Blethen and C. W. Wood, 76–117. Tuscaloosa, AL, 1997.

Klein, H.M.J. *Lancaster County, Pennsylvania*, vol. 1. New York, 1924.

Kulikoff, Alan. "Migration and Cultural Diffusion in Early America, 1600–1860: A Review Essay." *Historical Methods* 19 (1986): 153–69.

Lambert, Frank. *"Pedlar in Divinity": George Whitefield and the Transatlantic Revivals, 1734–1770*. Princeton, 1994.

Landsman, Ned. "Ethnicity and National Origin among British Settlers in the Philadelphia Region: Pennsylvania Immigration in the Wake of *Voyagers to the West*." *Proceedings of the American Philosophical Society* 133 (1989): 170–74.

———. *Scotland and Its First American Colony, 1683–1765*. Princeton, 1985.

Lebeau, Bryan. *Jonathan Dickinson and the Formative Years of American Presbyterianism*. Lexington, KY, 1997.

Lemon, James. *The Best Poor Man's Country: A Geographical Study of Early Southeastern Pennsylvania*. Baltimore, 1972.

———. "Comment on James A. Henretta's 'Families and Farms: Mentalité in Pre-Industrial America.' " *William and Mary Quarterly*, 3rd ser., 37 (1980): 688–96.

Lemon, James, and Gary Nash. "The Distribution of Wealth in Eighteenth-Century America: A Century of Change in Chester County, Pennsylvania." *Journal of Social History* 11 (1968): 1–24.

Leyburn, James. *The Scotch-Irish: A Social History*. Chapel Hill, 1962.

Lockhart, Audrey. *Some Aspects of Emigration from Ireland to the North American Colonies between 1660 and 1775*. New York, 1975.

Macafee, William, and V. Morgan. "Population in Ulster, 1660–1760." In *Plantation to Partition: Essays in Ulster History in Honour of J. L. McCracken*, ed. P. Roebuck, 46–63. Belfast, 1981.

MacMaster, Richard. *Donegal Presbyterians: A Scots-Irish Congregation in Pennsylvania*. Morgantown, PA, 1995.

Mancall, Peter. *Valley of Opportunity: Economic Culture along the Upper Susquehanna*. Ithaca, NY, 1991.

McBride, Ian. "Presbyterians in the Penal Era." *Bullan* 1 (1994), 73–86.

———. "The School of Virtue: Francis Hutcheson, Irish Presbyterians and the Scottish Enlightenment." In *Political Thought in Ireland since the Seventeenth Century*, ed. D. George Boyce, Robert Eccleshall, and Vincent Geoghegan, 73–99. London, 1994.

———. *Scripture Politics: Ulster Presbyterians and Irish Radicalism in the Late Eighteenth Century*. Cambridge, 1998.

———. " 'When Ulster Joined Ireland': Anti-Popery, Presbyterian Radicalism and Irish Republicanism in the 1790s." *Past and Present* 157 (November 1997): 63–93.

McConnell, S. G. *Fasti of the American Presbyterian Church*. Belfast, 1936.

McCusker, John, and Russell Menard. *The Economy of British America, 1607–1789*. Chapel Hill, 1985.

McGuire, J. I. "The Church of Ireland and the 'Glorious Revolution' of 1688." In *Studies in Irish History Presented to R. Dudley Edwards*, ed. Art Cosgrove and D. Macartney, 137–49. Dublin, 1979.

Merrell, James. *Into the American Woods: Negotiators on the Pennsylvania Frontier.* New York, 1999.

Miller, David. "Presbyterianism and 'Modernization' in Ulster." *Past and Present* 80 (1978): 66–90.

Miller, Kerby. *Emigrants and Exiles: Ireland and the Irish Exodus to North America.* New York, 1985.

Moody, T. W., and W. E. Vaughan. *A New History of Ireland.* Vol. 4, *Eighteenth-Century Ireland, 1691–1800.* Oxford, 1986.

Moody, T. W., F. X. Martin, and F. J. Byrne, eds. *A New History of Ireland.* Vol. 3, *Early Modern Ireland, 1534–1691.* Oxford, 1976.

Morill, John. "The British Problem." In *The British Problem, c. 1524–1707*, ed. Brendan Bradshaw and John Morrill, 1–38. London, 1996.

Munger, Donna. *Pennsylvania Land Records: A History and Guide for Research.* Wilmington, DE, 1991.

Murtagh, Harman. "The War in Ireland, 1689–91." In *Kings in Conflict: The Revolutionary War in Ireland and Its Aftermath, 1689–1750*, ed. W. A. Maguire, 61–91. Belfast, 1990.

Nash, Gary. *Quakers and Politics: Pennsylvania, 1681–1726.* Princeton, 1968.

Nybakken, Elizabeth. "New Light on the Old Side: Irish Influences on Colonial Presbyterianism." *Journal of American History* 68 (1982): 813–32.

Onuf, Peter. "New Lights in New London: A Group Portrait of the Separatists." *William and Mary Quarterly,* 3rd ser., 37 (1980): 627–43.

Perceval-Maxwell, M. *The Scottish Migration to Ulster in the Reign of James I.* London, 1973.

Pocock, J.G.A. "British History: A Plea for a New Subject." *Journal of Modern History* 47 (1975): 601–21.

———. "The Limits and Divisions of British History: In Search of the Unknown Subject." *American Historical Review* 87 (1982): 311–36.

———. "The New British History in Atlantic Perspective: An Antipodean Commentary." *American Historical Review* 104 (1999): 497.

Pollock, Vivienne. "Contract and Consumption: Labour Agreements and the Use of Money in Eighteenth-Century Rural Ulster." *Agricultural History Review* 43 (1995): 19–34.

Reid, J. S. *A History of the Presbyterian Church in Ireland.* 3 vols. Belfast, 1867.

Remer, Rosalind. "Old Lights and New Money: A Note on Religion, Economics, and the Social Order in 1740 Boston." *William and Mary Quarterly,* 3rd ser., 47 (1990): 566–73.

Roeber, A. G. *Palatines, Liberty, and Property: German Lutherans in Colonial British America.* Baltimore, 1993.

Schmidt, Leigh Eric. *Holy Fairs: Scottish Communion and American Revivals in the Early Modern Period.* Princeton, 1989.

Schwartz, Sally. *"A Mixed Multitude": The Struggle for Toleration in Colonial Pennsylvania.* New York, 1987.

Simler, Lucy. "The Landless Worker: An Index of Economic and Social Change in Chester County, Pennsylvania." *Pennsylvania Magazine of History and Biography* 114 (1990): 163–99.

———. "Tenancy in Colonial Pennsylvania: The Case of Chester County." *William and Mary Quarterly,* 3rd ser., 43 (1986): 542–69.

Simms, J. G. "The Making of a Penal Law (2 Anne, c. 6), 1703–4." *Irish Historical Studies* 12 (1960–61): 105–18..

Slaughter, Thomas. "Crowds in Eighteenth-Century America: Reflections and New Directions." *Pennsylvania Magazine of History and Biography* 115 (1991): 3–34.

Smyth, Jim. "The Communities of Ireland and the Bristish State, 1660–1707." In *The British Problem, c. 1524–1707,* ed. Brendan Bradshaw and John Morrill, 246–61. Londoin, 1996.

———. " 'Like Amphibious Animals': Irish Protestants, Ancient Britons." *Historical Journal* 36 (1993): 785–97.

Speck, W. A. *Reluctant Revolutionaries: Englishmen and the Revolution of 1688.* Oxford, 1988.

Spurr, John. "The Church of England, Comprehension and the Toleration Act of 1689." *English Historical Review* 104 (1989): 927–46.

Stewart, A.T.Q. *A Deeper Silence: The Hidden Origins of the United Irish Movement.* London, 1993.

Stone, Lawrence. "The Results of the English Revolutions of the Seventeenth Century." In *Three British Revolutions,* ed. J.G.A. Pocock, 23–108. Princeton, 1980.

Stout, Harry. *The Divine Dramatist: George Whitefield and the Rise of Modern Evangelicalism.* Grand Rapids, MI, 1991.

Thistlehwaite, Frank. "Migration from Europe Overseas in the Nineteenth and Twentieth Centuries." In Comité International des Sciences Historiques, X^{ie} Congrès International des Sciences Historiques, *Rapports: V: Histoire Contemporaine,* 32–60. Stockholm, 1960.

Trinterud, Leonard. *The Forming of an American Tradition: A Re-examination of Colonial Presbyterianism.* Philadelphia, 1949.

Truxes, Thomas. *Irish-American Trade, 1660–1783.* Cambridge, 1988.

Tully, Alan. "Ethnicity, Religion and Politics in Early Pennsylvania." *Pennsylvania Magazine of History and Biography* 107 (1983): 491–536.

———. *William Penn's Legacy: Politics and Social Structure in Provincial Pennsylvania, 1726–1755.* Baltimore, 1977.

Vaughan, Alden. "Frontier Banditti and the Indians: The Paxton Boys' Legacy, 1763–1775." *Pennsylvania History* 51 (1984): 1–29.

Westerkamp, Marilyn. *Triumph of the Laity: Scots-Irish Piety and the Great Awakening, 1625–1760.* New York, 1988.

Williams, Gwyn. *The Search for Beulah Land: The Welsh and the Atlantic Revolution.* London, 1980.

———. *The Welsh in Their History.* London, 1982.

Wokeck, M. S. "German and Irish Immigration to Colonial Philadelphia." *Proceedings of the American Philosophical Society* 133 (June 1989): 128–43.

———. "Irish Immigration to the Delaware Valley before the American Revolution." *Proceedings of the Royal Irish Academy,* ser. C (1996): 103–35.

———. *Trade in Strangers: The Beginnings of Mass Migration to North America.* University Park, PA, 1999.

Wood, Jerome. *Conestoga Crossroads: Lancaster, Pennsylvania, 1730–1790.* Harrisburg, PA, 1979.

Zimmerman, A.G. "The Indian Trade of Colonial Pennsylvania." Ph.D. diss., University of Delaware, 1966.

Zuckerman, Michael. "Farewell to the 'New England Paradigm' of Colonial Development." *Pennsylvania History* 57 (1990): 66–73.

———. "Introduction: Puritans, Cavaliers, and the Motley Middle." In *Friends and Neighbors: Group Life in America's First Plural Society,* ed. Zuckerman, 3–25. Philadelphia, 1982.

❖ *Index* ❖